BLACK RELIGIOUS LEADERSHIP
FROM THE SLAVE COMMUNITY
TO THE MILLION MAN MARCH

BLACK RELIGIOUS LEADERSHIP FROM THE SLAVE COMMUNITY TO THE MILLION MAN MARCH

Flames of Fire

Edited by

Felton O. Best

Black Studies
Volume 3

The Edwin Mellen Press
Lewiston•Queenston•Lampeter

Library of Congress Cataloging-in-Publication Data

Black religious leadership from the slave community to the Million Man
   March : flames of fire / edited by Felton O. Best.
        p.   cm.-- (Black Studies ; v. 3)
      Includes bibliographical references and index.
      ISBN 0-7734-8345-4
      1. Afro-Americans--Religion.   2. Afro-American clergy--History.
3. Afro-Americans--Social conditions.   4. Church and social
problems--United States--History.   I. Best, Felton O. (Felton
O'Neal) II. Series.
BR563.N4B574   1998
277.3'08'08996073--dc21   98-7594
                                                                           CIP

This is volume 3 in the continuing series
Black Studies
Volume 3 ISBN 0-7734-8345-4
BIS Series ISBN 0-88946-220-8

A CIP catalog record for this book is available from the British Library.

Copyright © 1998   The Edwin Mellen Press

The Edwin Mellen Press   The Edwin Mellen Press
        Box 450   Box 67
   Lewiston, New York   Queenston, Ontario
   USA 14092-0450   CANADA L0S 1L0

                      The Edwin Mellen Press, Ltd.
                      Lampeter, Ceredigion, Wales
                      UNITED KINGDOM SA48 8LT

Printed in the United States of America

TABLE OF CONTENTS

INTRODUCTION

Felton O. Best, Central Connecticut State University, and

Charles Frazier, St. Joseph's College

CHAPTER I

Harold E. Massey, Boston University

CHAPTER II

Nannetta Durnell, Florida Atlantic University

CHAPTER III

Stacey K. Close, Eastern Connecticut State University

CHAPTER IV

Benjamin Sevitch, Central Connecticut State University

CHAPTER V

Benjamin Sevitch, Central Connecticut State University

CHAPTER VI

Larry Little, Villanova University

CHAPTER VII

Larry Little, Villanova University

INTRODUCTION

FELTON O. BEST AND CHARLES FRAZIER

Scholars of African-American Studies have argued that Black communities in urban and rural sectors of America have deteriorated since the 1970's. The plight of black children and the elderly suggests that the once vulnerable and protected after the modern Civil Rights Movement are the new victims of hideous crimes in urban cities. As a result, our society is looking to leadership from Black religious institutions for direction, support and answers. Historically the Black church has been viewed as a social institution whose primary focus was to provide spiritual insight and economic relief to its congregates. In the 1960's the Black church expanded its focus to embrace the social gospel, education and politics. However, as historian Manning Marable argues in his *How Capitalism Underdeveloped Black America* it appears that the church's role was diminished to a Sunday event after the Modern Civil Rights Movement. As the social service profession became more sophisticated the Black church was viewed as an element that was not welcome in "the helping profession." This trend is changing in that social experts are looking to local Black church to become involved in program development and community based intervention. The federal and state governments has recognized its failure in attempting to effectively address the social problems of African-American communities. Despite the billions of dollars spent on prevention and intervention programs as well as the thousands of programs developed to address teenage pregnancy, homelessness, and substance abuse the situation has retrogressed. Social service agencies are turning to the black church not because they believe they have the answers, instead they perceive that no other options are available. In recent years Black churches have been viewed as viable candidates to receive grants and administer federal programs. In contrast, Black churches because of their long history of social services were prepared to manage these programs in a responsible manner.

Upon examining the state of African-American families and communities in the inner city one may conclude that social service systems have failed—thus validating the role of the Black church as a social service agency. Historically during the past fifty years African-American churches and their counterpart religious institutions have been excluded from receiving federal funds thus limiting its ability to collaborate with other systems in addressing Black family needs. Prior to World War II the Black church and its leadership was viewed as a critical partner in servicing the community. According to sociologist Aldon Morris in his *The Origins of the Civil Rights Movement: Black Communities Organizing for Change* the Black Church historically has been the most stable institution in serving African-American communities from slavery to freedom. It provided avenues whereas cultural retention could occur, Black leadership could emerge during Reconstruction, made possible the establishment of Black educational institutions, financed and supported protest movements, developed economic relief and social service agencies, and financed the Modern Civil Rights Movement.

Social welfare scholar Stanley Battle and social work practitioner Charles Frazier (1993) in *The State of Black Hartford* indicated that the leadership from the Black church is the only viable answer to the 20th century problems of teenage pregnancy, drugs, crime, and violence. Battle and Frazier cited that each year there are over one million teenage pregnancies in the U.S. As a result numerous programs were developed to reduce the incidence of teenage pregnancy. As prevention dollars increased the effects were marginal in terms of reducing teenage pregnancy. Another major social problem in African-American communities is that one of five children live in single parented families. In 1989, three out of ten babies were born to single mothers with almost a third of such babies born to teenagers. In 1991, The Center for Population Options conducted a study which found that nationally the public cost for all families started by a teen birth was $25 billion dollars including AFDC, Food Stamps, and Medicaid. By delaying parenthood until early adulthood, the government could save eight billion dollars per year.

In 1991 Battle and Frazier estimated that there were 1.8 million cocaine addicts and 700,000 heroin addicts in the U.S., the highest addiction rates ever. It is estimated that between five and six million Americans are in need of serious drug treatment with a substantial percentage of them being African-Americans. In the 1980's crack cocaine became very affordable resulting in small-local crack dealers sprouting up on many corners of America's urban and minority cities. As the drug infiltration increased in Black communities since the 1970's the prison population escalated proportionately by 150%. What is most alarming is that in the United States twenty five percent of African American men are on parole, in prison or awaiting sentencing. Many scholars have determined that these alarming statistics reveal that the Black church and their counterpart religious institutions have historically been socially rather that economically and politically driven, thus accelerating the decay of Black urban communities. For example, it has been argued that Black pastors have been perceived as money driven womanizers whose personal interests superseded the well being of the parishioners. However this study *Flames of Fire: Black Religious Leadership from the Slave Community to the Million Man March* argues against this conventional thesis.

The focus of *Flames of Fire* is to examine the multifaceted means by which Black religious leaders have embarked upon campaigns to eradicate social injustice. The assumption is not that a leadership group needs to be birthed—in contrast the argument is that such leadership emerged out of the slave community as a necessary entity to combat Euro-centric theology, and physical incarceration and has continued to exist until the present as an endeavor to eradicate poverty and promote economic development within African-American communities in an autonomous manner.

Black religious leadership was clearly recognized as early as the development of the slave community in America. An African-American Christian population of significant size and in some places of surprising independence developed. Initially the majority of African-American Christians belonged to mixed congregations. However, there were some cases in which independent African-American preachers emerged. For example, Rev. Andrew Bryan of the First African Church of Savannah, established in 1788, organized numerous Baptist congregations until a petrified white South curbed the religious freedom of African-Americans in the wake of the Denmark Vessey insurrection of 1822 as well as that led by Nat Turner in 1831. The religious outlook of enslaved Africans was a complex and highly creative adaptive acculturation process of European Christianity and the retention of African traditional religion. Some African-Americans rejected Christianity and retained Islam or their African religion, or became perpetual skeptics. Other enslaved African religious leaders were know as "conjurers" however after a period of religious instruction—they were convinced that conjuration was the "work of the devil."

Black religious leadership also emerged in the North during the Antebellum period. There were individual African-American Christians of note such as Lemuel Haynes, the first African-American officially ordained to the Christian ministry and who served as the pastor of white congregations in New England. Although few in number until the beginning of the nineteenth century-independent black churches were organized in the North. During the late eighteenth and early nineteenth centuries African-American Christians organized into denominations. In many cases the struggle for denominational independence was dramatic as in the case of Richard Allen the founder of the African Methodist Episcopal Church. By the Civil War the (A.M.E.) African Methodist Episcopal Church had approximately twenty thousand member and had established missions as far as California. Urged on by the leadership efforts of Bishop Daniel Alexander Payne the AME church established Wilberforce University one of the first African-American institutions of higher education. In 1805 Thomas Paul became the first pastor of First African Baptist Church of Boston and in 1808 he assisted in the organization of the famous Abyssianian Baptist Church in New York City.

One of the most important issues concerned the role that women should play in male-dominated institutions such as the church, where the pulpit had been traditionally defined as "men's space" and the pew as "women's place." The AME Zion church authorized the ordination of women in the 1890's, the AME church in 1948, and the CME church in 1954. Appealing to the principle of congregational autonomy, the major black Baptist conventions had not legislated policy regarding the ordination of women. Conservative attitudes at the congregational level, has proved to be an obstacle to many women who have sought ordination. Likewise the Church of God In Christ, the largest black Pentecostal body, prohibited the ordination of women as ministers in the same era.

Historically, women have been in the majority in the mainline black denominations, yet men have dominated the leadership. Women serve as "mothers of the church" are active in missionary societies, educational efforts, and a wide variety of charitable causes; and serve local congregations in numerous capacities, such as teachers, stewardesses, and deaconess's. Yet men hold denominational offices and monopolize the clergy rosters to a greater degree than in the more liberal white Protestant churches. Women who wish to exercise the gift of the

Spirit had to operate as independent evangelists, such as Jarena Lee did after an originally futile appeal to Richard Allen and the African Methodists in the early 1800s. Sojourner Truth, Harriet Tubman, and Rebecca Cox Jackson, who eventually joined the Shakers, possessed spiritual gifts which the established black denominations did not formerly recognize. Amanda Berry Smith left the AME Church in order to exercise her ministry more freely, joined the holiness movement, and thereby served as a precursor for the many women who found the freedom to develop their own ministries within the orbit of the burgeoning Pentecostal and Holiness movement, which flourished in the "sanctified" storefronts of the urban North. For example, Elder Lucy Smith (1874-1952) founded All Nations Pentecostal Church in Chicago and conducted a multidimensional ministry that dealt with the material as well as the spiritual need of her members. What was and continues to be most notorious about African-American female religious leadership is that they formed "unofficial" social service agencies. Sociologist Cheryl Townshend-Gilkes has argued that such black "church mothers" developed economic relief agencies, soup kitchens, elderly housing centers, educational programs, and educational institutions.

Closed out of male-dominated ecclesiastical centers of power, African-American women developed auxiliary organizations. The Women's Parent Mite Missionary Society, a social service organization of the AME Church, founded in 1874, supported new churches in western United States and in South Africa. Baptist women led by Nanny Helen Burroughs formed the Women's Convention of the National Baptist Convention in 1900 and operated the National School for Girls in Washington. Many of these church women were also active in the club movement, which stressed self-help, charitable, civic work, and served as a focal point for women's independent identity. Beset by racism in the larger society and confronted by patriarchal attitudes within their denominations, African-American church women had to confront multiple challenges. They played an especially important role in bridging the gap between church work as traditionally defined and secular reform activity.

The centrality of Black female leadership in the local congregation became all the more apparent because of external social forces in the flight from field to factory once the call for labor went out from the North. After 1910, in the early years of the Great Migration, males, particularly young males, went north lured by the promise of better jobs. Women and the young were left to carry on congregational life. Urbanization proved to be no panacea. Indeed, in poor urban areas, church adherence was increasingly the sphere of women and children. This is especially true of the independent churches, known as "storefronts." In an extensive study done in the 1980s, researchers found that in 2,150 black churches, of various denominations, women outnumbered men by a factor of 2.5 to 1. Some observers have spoken of the "feminization of the black church" because of the relative absence of males, especially young males, in urban congregations. Whether or not the disproportionate representation of females in contemporary black churches is principally a result of the urbanization of African Americans is yet to be determined. It is clear, however, that the gender questions is one that black Christians, regardless of denominational affiliation, have yet to fully and adequately addressed.

The urbanization of African-American religion precipitated an institutional crisis in the existing black churches. In 1910 nearly 90 percent of the nation's black population lived in the South, mostly in rural regions and small towns. Since the end of the Civil War, the church had assumed a dominant position in the life of southern blacks, whose institutional development in other areas was restricted by racial apartheid. By default, then, the churches served multiple purposes-worship, education, recreation, and socialization. Northern black leaders, as well as some Southern leaders (e.g., Booker T. Washington) pointed to such problems as overchurching, undereducated ministers, pastors with multiple charges, congregations too small to adequately maintain programs and property, and too little emphasis on the social and political problems of the day. Carter G. Woodson, the noted historian of the Black church, referred to rural churches as "mystic shrines" while writing approvingly of northern urban churches as progressive centers of "social uplift." This debate over the mission of the black church was heightened by the Great Migration because it placed new demands upon existing denominational and local church resources and social programs.

The population shift put severe strains upon existing denominational structures. Home missionary social service boards lacked adequate resources to cope with the need in the North and congregations in the South were left depleted and deserted. Competition among the three major black Methodist bodies prevented a cooperative effort in addressing the needs of the migrants. The

National Baptist Convention, U.S.A., Inc., underwent a contentious division in 1915, which resulted in the formation of a rival body, the National Baptist Convention of America Unicorporated, later named National Baptist Convention of America in 1916. The internecine war continued for years, draining away critically needed resources. The secretary of the Home Mission Board of the National Baptist Convention, U.S.A., Inc., reported in 1921: "We have quite a number of destitute fields both North and South and in many cases no opportunity for religious worship."

The regional shift in America's black population portended difficulties because as World War I began the black denominations were heavily weighted to the South. In 1916 the U.S. Census of Religious Bodies credited the National Baptists with 2,939,579 members, 89 percent of whom were in the South. The AME Church had 548,355 members and was 81.2 percent southern. The AMEZ Church was 84.6 percent southern with a total membership of 257,169. The CME Church, composed principally of the descendants of ex-slaves, was 95.5 percent southern and 245,749 strong. None of the Pentecostal or Holiness bodies, which became so important in the urban North after the Great Migration, received recognition in the 1916 religious census.

In addition to placing strains upon ecclesiastical structures inherited from the nineteenth century and oriented primarily toward the small town and rural church, urbanization offered African Americans new religious options. Baptist and Methodist preachers now had to compete with the agents of the Pentecostal and Holiness churches. These churches played against great emphasis on an intense personal experience of the Holy Spirit. The Church of God in Christ, led by Charles Harrison Mason, held its first Pentecostal general assembly in 1907. Having started as a rural church in Mississippi, the denomination grew to become a fixture in the northern city. Ill at ease in the more formal worship services of the established northern churches, many migrants organized prayer bands, started house churches, or moved into the storefronts where speaking in tongues (sometimes refereed to as the practice of glossolalia) received the blessing of the Pentecostals. The Church of Christ (Holiness), U.S.A., under the leadership of Elder C.P.Jones, likewise expanded as a result of the burgeoning black populations of urban industrial America. Other Holiness and Pentecostal churches were founded by denominationally-independent religious entrepreneurs who recognized that the migrants from the South desired something that the northern black middle-class churches did not offer.

Many of the migrants wanted religious environments that reminded them of their churches back home, where they were known by name and part of an extended family. The ecstatic worship services and musical styles favored by the Pentecostal and Holiness preachers caught the attention of these ex-Southerners. When hard times befell them in the North, the migrants sought out spiritual havens in the urban churches and simultaneously looked to them for the economic assistance that they provided. Holiness and Pentecostal churches multiplied everywhere, and existing Baptist and Methodist churches split or sponsored daughter congregations as the migration population swelled. On occasion, northern black Christians criticized their "brothers and sisters" from the South for falling short of northern cultural expectations and the existing class norms. In turn, migrants shunned some northern black churches, where the elaborate and elegant services made them feel out of place. Some fell away from organized religion all together. Others responded to their crisis of faith in the city by transplanting churches from the South led by the pastors who had followed them northward.

The tension between the two cultural streams that came together after the beginning of World War I is illustrated by the reluctance of the older African-American congregations in Chicago to readily accept gospel music. Gospel music was popularized by Thomas Dorsey, the "father of gospel music," who joined Pilgrim Baptist Church in Chicago in 1921. Unlike the purveyors of contemporary gospel today, early gospel music was church centered. Yet as Mahalia Jackson, the best-known singer of gospel, learned while growing up in New Orleans, the musical distance between the honky-tonk and a Holiness revival with its beating and tambourine shaking was not that great. Dorsey, building on the work of predecessors such as Charles Albert Tindley, was the principal force behind the introduction of blues-like gospel songs into the northern black churches. About 1930, observers of the Chicago scene reported that "Negro churches, particularly the storefront congregations, the Sanctified groups and the shouting Baptists, were swaying and jumping as never before. Mighty rhythms rocked the churches. A wave of worldwide acclamation for her solo renditions of gospel classics, and the pioneering touring groups such as the Dixie Hummingbirds and the Five Blind

Boys of Mississippi helped make gospel so popular that today it is rare to find a black church, of whatever denomination or class composition, that closes its doors to gospel music.

Black religious leadership in America also experienced activity from non-Christian leaders and organizations. After examining data from the 1926 Federal Census of Religious Bodies, Miles Mark Fisher exclaimed: "Almost in every center, particularly urban, is some unorthodox religious group which makes a definite appeal to Negroes." The Jamaican-born black nationalist Marcus Garvey discouraged talk of establishing a new church, but he and his Universal Negro Improvement Association (1918-1927) had many followers who sought collective redemption in the back-to-Africa ideology. There were also some supporters, such as George Alexander McGuire, the founder of the African Orthodox Church, who did initiate Garveyite inspired demonstrations. The UNIA collapsed after the deportation of its "Black Moses" in 1927, but other charismatic personalities came forward offering often exotic visions of heaven on earth. Father Divine set up a series of Peace Missions during the Great depression, offering his devotees the unusual mix of "God" in the flesh and a refuge from society's problems. Scores of religious entrepreneurs established businesses in the black ghettos, where they competed with the mainline denominations. Frequently referred to as cults and sects, the groups led by these new messiahs often died when their founders did, but some managed to survive under different leadership, as, for example, the one led by Daddy Grace known as the United House of Prayer for All People. Representatives of the mainline churches frequently decried the proliferation of these alternative groups, arguing, as the Baptist Miles Mark Fisher did, that the principle message of the cults and sects was "Let us prey," not "Let us pray."

The appearance on urban street corners of black adherents of Islam and Judaism added to the perception that African-American religion was undergoing a radical reorientation in the interwar period at the expense of the historic black denominations. The first black Jewish group recognized by the federal religious census was founded in 1896 by William S. Crowdy, a Santa Fe Railroad cook, in Lawrence, Kansas African Americans wearing the yarmulke and speaking Yiddish came to the attention of a wider public in the 1920s. Located primarily in the boroughs of New York City, these teachers of black Hebraism appropriated and adapted the rituals and teachings of Orthodox Judaism. Though never large in number, the followers of Rabbi Arnold Ford and other proponents of Black Judaism generated a great deal of interest among the curious and the skeptical.

Islam was not entirely unheard of among African Americans before the mysterious figure of W.D. Fard appeared in the "Paradise Valley" of Detroit in 1930 to wake up the sleeping "Lost-Found Nation of Islam." There is increasing evidence that a small but not insignificant number of slaves brought knowledge of the Koran and Islamic law to North America. But modern Islam among African Americans begins with the career of Noble Drew Ali, a native of North Carolina and founder of Moorish Science in Newark, N.J. , about 1913. However, the man who most popularized Islam for African Americans, was the one-time disciple of Wallace Fard, Elijah Muhammad, who capitalized on the interest of urbanized blacks in the religiously exotic. Muhammed, formerly Elijah Poole assumed leadership of the Nation of Islam after Fard's disappearance in 1934 and moved its headquarters to Chicago. The Nation's version of Islam did not fare well under the scrutiny of orthodox scholars of the Koran, and eventually the sect broke into rival factions. Nevertheless, it has had a significant impact upon many African Americans, chiefly the young and angry Malcolm X who believed that traditional black Christianity was a "pie-in-the-sky" religion.

Attention to the new religious options that appeared in black urban American during the period between World War I and World War II should not be at the expense of the story of the mainline black churches. Stimulated by the crisis brought about by the influx of thousands from the South, the established churches struggled with a redefinition of mission during these decades. Some religious leaders had moved their churches into campaigns to address urban poverty by the early 20th Century. Richard R. Wright, Jr., examined the record of black church involvement within the public sphere in 1907 and concluded that several Black religious leaders "attacked the problems of real city Negroes." His own work in Chicago's Institutional Church and Social Settlement, founded by Revered Ransom, and later at Chicago's Trinity Mission and Culture Center, which Wright organized in 1905, convinced him that black churches needed a more compelling definition of urban mission than presently at hand prior to World War I, when outreach of black churches primarily involved mission and charity work with the intent of recruiting new members. As Wright and Ransom discovered for themselves, pastors who addressed contemporary social problems born of urban and industrial growth were deemed too radical by denominational officials. Yet despite such perceptions the social gospel was not purged.

Beginning with the era of the Great Migration, many black churches incorporated programs into their understanding of "church work" that went beyond the traditional emphasis on praying and preaching. They assisted with needs in housing, employment, education, recreation, and health care. The instrumentalist use of the church to better the community is today so widely accepted that black clergy or congregations that show no interest in everyday problems have little appeal or credibility among African Americans.

Although black denominations were spared the bitter battles that erupted in the 1920s between the white fundamentalists and modernists over such issues as the interpretation of the Creation story in Genesis, their efforts to merge have failed. Concerned about institutional inefficiency and lost opportunities to influence the larger society and motivated by the ideal that Christ's church be one, representatives of the three principal branches of black Methodism began meetings in 1915 to discuss the possibility of merger. But Black leaders of the CME church, balked at union because of fears of being dominated by the two larger northern black Methodist bodies: the AME and the AMEZ churches. Division among black Methodists was widened by the segregation of 315,000 in the Central Jurisdiction, a United Methodist Church in 1939 after the merger of the northern and southern branches of Methodism, the segregated structure was abolished in the 1960s. Black Baptists likewise have been unable to heal the divisions within their ranks. The National Baptist Convention, U.S.A., Inc., remains the largest of all members and 30,000 local churches in the late 1980s. On the other hand, the Full Gospel Baptist Fellowship led by Bishop Paul Morton is perceived by many black clergy to be the fastest growing Baptist convention.

The contemporary black Baptist story is still best told in terms of the local congregation. Ministerial alliances at the local level have fostered interdenominational cooperation where there has been sufficient need for common action. In many congregations, the minister is still the dominant personality. Critics have argued that the domineering role played by the pastor in black congregations has retarded the development of lay leadership. However in reality research has demonstrated the opposite. Most ministers have sparked congregational leadership. The preeminence of the black minister in African-

American religious culture has historical roots. Because of the class and caste attitudes of whites in the South, the ministry remained one of the few professions accessible—thus meaning that younger congregants perceived it as an able career option especially in the Civil Rights era. Even in the North, where political boundaries were defined by patterns of residential segregation and black political participation was restricted, black ministers were called upon to speak for their community before local authorities. Participation in electoral and protest politics has engaged the energies of many contemporary black clergy.

The political and economic power of the Black Church and its leaders was best seen during the Civil Rights Movement when Rev. Martin Luther King, Jr., began to catch the eye and ear of the news media. Rooted deep in the black Baptist tradition of the black church of the South while doing advanced theological training in the North, he became proficient in the major currents of thought among liberal socially aware protestants. This made it possible for him to appeal to the conscience of white America during the civil rights struggle and to enlist the aid of allies from the more liberal white denominations. Yet the grassroots participation of thousands of black church goers who marched and sang and prayed transformed King's protest of racial segregation in Montgomery, Ala., into a mass movement. From the vantage point of these people of faith, a civil rights march was as much an economic and political crusade as a social and religious movement. While the cause of civil rights united black religious leaders across denominational lines and cemented alliances with progressive forces in the predominantly white Protestant, Catholic, and Jewish communities, there were disharmonious chords. The Rev. Joseph L. Jackson, who served as president of the National Baptist Convention from 1953 to 1982, resisted the attempt of King and others to move the largest Protestant denomination in the world into activist or protest politics. As a result, King, with the Rev. Ralph David Abernathy, Gardner C. Taylor, and others, formed the Progressive National Baptist Convention in 1961 under the motto: "Unity, service, fellowship, peace." The civil rights movement, of course, was not confined to institutional church circles. Nor are its religious dimensions fully measured by focusing, for example on the Southern Christian Leadership Conference (SCLC) led by King. And of course, organizations with a more secular orientation, such as the Student Nonviolent Coordinating Committee also had crucial roles to play. But even the members of

SNCC were animated by a vision of the day when truth and justice would prevail in the United States. Indeed the bulwark of the civil rights movement, especially in the South, was the grassroots black church, which propelled the crusade that eventually broke down the barriers of legalized segregation. While a form of religious sectarianism among many African Americans has led to withdrawal and isolation from the public sphere, orthodox or mainline black churches have for the most part been instrumental in bringing America closer to Dr. King's dream of the "beloved community."

During the 1960's the "Black Power" movement developed a theological campaign of "Black Liberation Theology" led throughout by the religious leadership of James Cone. Originating among young radicals, many of whom were estranged from the traditional black church, the largely secular Black Power movement quickly drew a theological response. It came first from individuals such as James Cone, who were situated in academic environments, but it eventually engaged the thinking of denominational representatives. Their statements revealed both agreement with the diagnosis of the wrongs of American society as portrayed by advocates of Black Power but also some uneasiness regarding the means necessary to achieve a just society. King had taught that nonviolence was ethically essential given the witness of the New Testament. During the civil rights crusade, local churches served as training grounds in nonviolent resistance. In contrast, the more strident advocates of Black Power carried weapons and, rhetorically at least, endorsed their use in conflicts with the police and others in authority. Steeped in the traditional Christian doctrine that the use of violence is a betrayal of the ethics of Jesus, most black Christians remained skeptical of the means the militants justified. Nevertheless, the Black Power advocates made a lasting impact on black churches.

By raising cultural awareness as black nationalists like Garvey had done in the 1920s and earlier, and as back-to-Africa proponents such as the Methodist leader Bishop Henry M. Turner of the AME church did in the 1880s—interest and debate was stimulated over the essential question of "how black is black religion?" African-American clergy in the predominantly white Protestant groups organized caucuses in which they examined their historic and contemporary relationship with their host denominations. This analysis led to demands for representation in the higher echelons of institutional life, for more black clergy, and for the incorporation of distinctively African-American religious styles in worship. Black Roman Catholics also experienced a renaissance of pride in "blackness," variously defined. Representations of a Black Jesus appeared in Roman Catholic sanctuaries, and the refrains of gospel music could be heard during Mass sung in English following the reforms of Vatican II (1963-1965). In other religious traditions such as the Presbyterians, Episcopals, and Lutherans, African Americans also pressed for a greater appreciation of the rich African and African-American religious heritage.

At the core of the complex religious pilgrimage of peoples of African descent in America is the importance of the local congregation of believers who celebrate together the rites of passage of its members from baptism to Christian burial. Most black churches, however, emphasize preaching over the sacraments, in contrast to the liturgical traditions such as Roman Catholicism and Lutheranism. The spoken word, whether in sermon or song, is at the core of black worship. The roster of celebrated black preachers is long. The Rev. C.L.Franklin of Detroit is but one example who Jesse Jackson referred to as "the most imitated soul preacher in history". Rev. C.L. Franklin carried the sermon to an art form which was heard on the radio by a large audiences, and sold millions of records.

Black churches historically have served as the centers of African-American life and identity. Benjamin Mays, the distinguished educator in Atlanta and mentor of Martin Luther King, Jr., wrote of the church of his youth in rural South Carolina. "In my community Negroes had nowhere to go but to choir sing, to listen to the preacher, and to hear and see people shout. The young people went to Mount Zion to socialize, or simply to stand around and talk. It was a place of worship and a social center as well. There was no other place to go." As the twentieth century draws to a close some scholars of African-American religion have raised concern as to whether or not black churches will be equipped to meet the challenges of the next millennium. Already there are some who argue that the major black denominations have succumbed to the lure of middle-class America and left the poorest of the poor behind. The Nation of Islam is often credited with being able to reach into the ranks of the youthful street gangs and has had success in making converts among African Americans in this country's prisons. Often overlooked in the media, the attention that has been given to Black religious organizations include the economic programs of the Nation of Islam, the various street ministries sponsored by black churches or independent evangelical preachers, and the extensive community services such as "meals on wheels" programs, Head Start schools, and recreational facilities, found in most places where black churches are active.

Black religious leaders have been "flames of fire" in the communities that they served. This study demonstrates that they have not only been concerned with social issues but they have embarked upon economic and political issues as well. In fact prior to the development of the social welfare system of the New Deal era African-American religious organizations were providing economic relief to distressed families, taking care of orphans, sheltering fugitive slaves from the South, creating and securing jobs, educating their masses prior to the establishment of public schools, founded and supported black colleagues, and simultaneously agitated for civil rights. These charismatic religious leaders and organizations studied in this book reveal that their religious activity has provided economic salvation for African-Americans from slavery to freedom. While African-Americans for the most part prior to the Modern Civil Rights Movement were individually poor collectively their economic dollars within black churches and their counterpart religious organizations stabilized their communities. Thus the myth that most black religious leaders have been self serving is erroneous. They have been for the most part been self-sacrificing. Several such as Rev. Dr. Martin Luther King Jr. and Malcolm X have been matyred as a result of the campaigns to deteriorate capitalistic exploitation of Black Americans. Others such as Jesse Jackson called for economic and social equality of African-Americans through his vision of the rainbow coalition and Operation Push at the expense of political isolation by his own Democratic party. And yet today these "flames of fire" through the agency of their religious institutions have managed to sustain black private colleges with their economic resources, provide low income housing within their communities, and establish multiple types of business, as well as additional economic benefits. In short, Black religious institutions continue to be the most economical and politically stable agencies owned by African-Americans. This fact speaks to the benefit instead of the detriment of Black religious leaders.

CHAPTER I

THE PARADOX OF EMBEDDED LEADERSHIP: BLACK RELIGIOUS LEADERS AS
FOLLOWERS, PASTORS, AND PROPHETS

HAROLD E. MASSEY,

BOSTON UNIVERSITY[1]

*"Patterns of leadership are changing, and will continue to change in an attempt
to keep up with mass demands. Gandhi's oft-quoted statement is so applicable
today, 'There go my people, I must catch them, for I am their leader.'"* [2]

While Mahatma Gandhi and Martin Luther King, Jr. are viewed by many
as the consummate religious leaders, it is revealing that even they found it
important to stress deference to the attitudes and behaviors of those whom they
sought to serve with their leadership. This is intriguing because leaders are, by
definition, decision-makers, successful, wielders of authority, achievers
distinguished in their fields and important to their constituents in both symbolic
and substantive aspects.[3] Religious leaders may assume and intend postures of
humility, but their community roles traditionally have found them giving guidance
rather than receiving it.

Religion has been defined concomitantly as "the search for God" and "the
opiate of the masses." Religious leadership, therefore, may carry distinctions that
are at once divine (in keeping with the former definition) and dubious (in keeping
with the latter). Leaders who are critically conscious of their place on this axis and
its affect upon their constituents have attained international stature. By modelling
their religious convictions in challenging the dominant social order, some leaders
have been able to speak directly to the highest qualities and aspirations of their

[1] The author wishes to thank Dr. Felton Best of Central Connecticut State University, Gaye
Massey, Guillermo Chavez, Harvey Pannell, Lynroy Grant, Ella Bell, Lou Chesimard, Joyce King,
Bishop John Hurst Adams, and Rev. Nicholas Tweed for their direct or vicarious insights. I also
wish to acknowledge Professors William Kahn, Marion McCollom, Gerry Leader of Boston
University and Mavis Campbell and Asa Davis of Amherst College.
[2] King, Martin Luther, Jr., "Foreword" to Daniel C. Thompson's *The Negro Leadership Class*
(Prentice-Hall: 1963).
[3] Mays, Benjamin, *The Negro's God as Reflected in his Literature* (NY: Athaneum, 1938/1996), p.
28.

followers in ways which have transcended both the limitations of their identities as victims and the broader, oppressive social dynamics in which their groups are embedded.

Both Gandhi and King, for instance, were leaders of groups that were characteristically distinct as well as diverse in terms of race, culture, and social power in the national context. Gandhi was leading his peoples toward self-determination rooted in faith in the context of British colonial violence and exploitation. King was the leader of an ethnic minority group seeking recognition of its human dignity in the face of racial violence, cultural alienation and economic exploitation on these bases in the United States. In this sense, both were leaders of peoples embedded within a broader, institutionalized status quo. The strategic interests and cultural values of these subordinate groups were, at best, secondary considerations to the concerns and values of those with institutionalized power. That is, these leaders could not proceed without acknowledging the existence of strategic interests at the national level to which they were captive, beyond any immediate and distinct interests or objectives of their particular groups. For Gandhi, it meant recognizing the economic impact of decolonization upon British society. For King, it meant that the struggle for African American civil rights had to be understood in the context of the Cold War, the arms race, and the Vietnam War. If America's perceived interests at home and abroad were in jeopardy, the then-called Negro's survival was contingent upon the nation's success. In contrast, U.S. history shows that it has been perfectly plausible that the national interest could be framed to exclude the humanity of African Americans. King's status as the leader of a minority group held implications for the socio-cultural embeddedness of Black Americans that were qualitatively different than those faced by Gandhi and Indian nationalists.

We use the terms "group" and "embeddedness" here, in the senses that they are utilized within the interdisciplinary field of organizational behavior. In this field, human groups are defined by significant interdependent relations, self-perception and cohesion distinguishing members from non-members, identification as a group by non-members, significant individual and collective interdependencies with other groups, and roles pursuant to expectations of other members, of non-members and of themselves.[4] The concept of embeddedness comes from role theory where it is understood that one's personal disposition and role are interdependent with the broader needs of the social context and groups in which they are enacted. That is, where our society is inclined to attribute most behavior to individual, intrapersonal choice, the social context is a major force that can often supercede any degree of personal volition or choice.[5] What is important for our investigation of Black religious leaders, moreover, is that the individual (intrapersonal) aspect of group members is understood as a microcosm of the group-as-a-whole. Individual members of groups are believed to carry with them the dynamics, attitudes and assumptions—in a word, culture—of the broader group even while they are isolated from direct association with it. In fact, the very etymology of the word "individual" derives from the sense of collective wholeness found in its relation to the word "indivisible."[6] This reality is particularly poignant in the context of religious leadership in the African American experience.

It is possible, therefore, to delineate the levels at which the basic struggle for human development is embedded. Each aspect of the intrapersonal (individual personality and ego), interpersonal (member-to-member), group (suprapersonal—group-as-a-whole), intergroup (identity, task and subgroup), and interorganizational contexts of human relations involves dynamics which can occur simultaneously on any (or possibly all) of the other contexts.[7] For this reason, embeddedness and paradox are mutually reinforcing qualities which all leaders must consider. African American religious leaders are particularly well-served by attention to paradoxes unique to their socio-cultural embeddedness within an American experience where the very concept of leadership, itself, has been mired largely in a cultural and political hegemony. U.S. dominance in this

---

[4] Alderfer, C.P., in Gillette, J. and McCollom, M., *Groups In Context: A New Perspective on Group Dynamics* (Reading, MA.: Addison-Wesley, 1990), p. 5.

[5] Wells, L., "The Group as a Whole: A Systemic Socioanalytic Perspective on Interpersonal and Group Relations", in Gillette, J. and McCollom, M., *Groups In Context: A New Perspective on Group Dynamic* (Reading, MA.: Addison-Wesley, 1990), pp.68-70.

[6] Williams, Raymond, *Keywords, A Vocabulary of Culture and Society.* (New York. Oxford Press, 1976), p. 86.

[7] Wells, L., "The Group as a Whole: A Systemic Socioanalytic Perspective on Interpersonal and Group Relations" in Gillette, J. and McCollom, M., *Groups In Context: A New Perspective on Group Dynamic* (Reading, MA.: Addison-Wesley, 1990) p.54.

sense has dulled the appreciation of alternate (yet, no less effective) models of leadership across cultures, continents and social classes.[8]

By characterizing African American historicity in terms of paradox, we mean it beyond the sense of the Latin etymology of the word denoting "apparent contradiction."[9] Rather than contradiction or irony, however, we use the term, as do physicists, to convey a sense of mutually contradictory realities occurring simultaneously, yet accepted as definitional aspects of a state or phenomenon. The critical variable in appreciating paradox is the shifting of perspectives in order to ascertain the countervailing reality. In much the same way that scientists regarded light as a particle for decades before recognizing that assessing it with different instruments showed that it also behaves as a wave phenomenon, paradox in social phenomenon requires the application of different priorities and values in order to be recognized.

In terms of Black religious leadership, the paradox of its role in both limiting and inspiring African Americans on their paths toward empowerment must be accepted simultaneously. In its pastoral dimension, Black religious leadership is defined by its attention to alleviating the immediate suffering and ministering to the basic human needs of an historically oppressed people. In its prophetic dimension, Black religious leadership is defined by its denunciation of the existing order of oppression, dehumanization and betrayal of divined mandates for social justice while simultaneously announcing a new order predicated upon those mandates. Traditionally, a focus on either the pastoral or the prophetic dimensions of religious leadership has been perceived as incompatible with the other where a Cartesian dualism has been in effect. In reality, however, an appreciation of paradox allows the recognition of both dimensions as something of a yin/yang antinomy where the integrated whole is comprised by pursuing them in complementary fashion. Historically, however, one can see how the pastoral focus has matured into more prophetic voices in Black religious leadership.

---

[8] Hofstede, Geert, "Do American Theories Apply Abroad?" in *Culture's Consequences: International Differences in Work-Related Values*, (Beverly Hills, Calif.: Sage Publications, 1980), p. 411.

[9] Slaatte, H.A., *The Pertinence of Paradox*. (New York: Humanities Press, 1968), p. 13.

Even the most prophetic examples of Black religious leaders may be understood as followers and pastors when assessed from different perspectives. Several contextual and historical factors help explain this definitive reality for Black religious leadership.

Leadership of American oppressed groups, especially Black and religious in nature, seldom has received its proper respect in research concerned with models and methods. This is true, despite the fact that the African American leadership experience and Black scholars assessing it have been anything but marginal to the American experience.[10] In fact, we argue here that the social maturity and materialistic progress of United States, to date, can be assessed by using the struggles and achievements of African Americans as the quintessential benchmark for measuring its moral, ethical and economic development. As an enslaved identity group regarded as a source of labor for the "land of opportunity" or "land of the free", African American social, economic and spiritual development offers a unique guage of the degree to which the most noble ideals of the United States are, indeed, relevant to all citizens.

Ostensibly positive, this reality can be perceived also as a severe limitation when considering Black religious leadership as the standardbearer of African American empowerment and liberation. While appearing to be a contradiction, it is actually a paradox that is unique to the circumstances of African Americans and their leaders throughout history. The African American community is a culturally ensconced ethnic and racial enclave within a predominant European cultural context. The religious community, understood as a distinct dialogue with God, is further embedded within this secular enclave, which has its own socioeconomic diversity and a medley of African, Caribbean, Native American and Latino cultural influences tempering the eurocentric social superstructure. Constrained by a broader social context within which it historically has suffered from an unequal, yet mutual, dependency the African American experience is wedged uniquely between providing its talent without adequate recompense, and achieving its own development in spite of (rather than because of) U.S. global preeminence.

---

[10] Harding, V., *There is a River, The Black Struggle for Freedom in America.* (New York. Harcourt Brace, 1981). See also Aptheker, H. *Afro-American History, The Modern Era: A Pioneering Chronicle of the Black People in Twentieth Century America.* (New York. Citadel Press, 1971).

Until we recognize the effects of social embeddedness in defining and validating rudimentary realities such as the very concept of leadership, consciousness of the paradox of embedded leaders will remain, at best, an intellectual exercise without the practical impact necessary for social influence. As slaves within the hold of the U.S. ship of state, African Americans have ridden the waves of world history under the orders of captains of industry or politics who usually were not of their own choosing. Within their experience, however, have been brief moments of liberation which may be likened to the Amistad incident where an African slave, Cinque, led his companions in the breaking their bondage and liberated a slave ship only to find themselves put to trial in New England. Where Cinque and the Amistad mutineers eventually were freed to return home to Sierra Leone, the question for African American leaders today is whether or not they might be supported by the general nation in steering the ship of state in directions that would maximize the development and well-being of African Americans. In many ways, it is a question of whether or not national leadership can be defined in terms that address the historical benefits of dominant identity groups from the suffering of others within the American experience. This very volume speaks directly to this question by investigating the qualities of leaders for one such group, African Americans, and their most salient institution.

Embeddedness, dependency, and spirituality are compelling dynamics for any identity group. Cultural, racial and socioeconomic minority groups embedded within larger, social superstructures must devise unique means of self-perception and socialization to maintain their unique worldviews. This is true whether the minority group is privileged or oppressed. If oppressed and victimized by discrimination, however, the effects of dependency become a direct affront to the natural impetus for self-determination as a definitive aspect of freedom.[11] In a society where progress has been defined in terms of material acquisition, abstract technological development, and global hegemony, spiritually-focused groups are distinct. Freedom in this context has no greater manifestation than the ability to develop to one's potential and practice a chosen discipline for spiritual development.

---

[11] Memmi, Albert, *Dependence: A Sketch for a Portrait of the Dependent* (Boston: Beacon Press, 1984), p. 93.

As an embedded, ethnic minority group with generally lower socioeconomic achievement, African Americans wrestle daily with what may be called a "psychology of oppression." This psychology manifests itself in paradoxical ways. Assimilationist social behaviors may be found in the midst of social movements for cultural distinction. Racial pride may be cherished in demonstrably self-destructive attitudes. Material accumulation may be showcased in religious events highlighting the primacy of spiritual development. Black religious leaders have struggled with this paradoxical dynamic in both their personal lives and their leadership roles. Yet, even as we seek to characterize contemporary Black religious leadership, broad social changes are afoot which, for better or for worse, will profoundly influence the future effectiveness of such leaders.

LEADERS IN A NEW AGE

Researchers and pundits postulate certain requirements for considering leadership in "the postindustrial age" of more empowered workers, and new organizational designs.[12] Yet, there remains an unexamined, implicit bias to view leadership in terms that are wholly consistent with the "American Century" of global hegemony and cultural dominance. In this chapter, we describe some nuances and consistent findings of research on leadership manifestations within the United States. We argue that it may not be until theoretical perspectives on human nature transcend their embeddedness within the predominant North American cultural and historical ethos that leadership research and practice can be appreciated fully in its global complexity. Moreover, Black leadership (religious or secular) neither can be appreciated fully in theory, nor liberated practically, until it can see itself and its mission beyond the confines of its North American historicity. The very essence of freedom and empowerment for African Americans, their leaders, and their religious institutions is contingent upon developing and maintaining this transcendent vision. Defined by several qualities, Black liberation is determined keenly by the extent to which it can be envisioned and exercised, regardless of social context, beyond the politics of minority status, and above any concomitant psychology of oppression/victimization. If this chapter

---

[12] Such as Hirschhorn, Larry, *The Workplace Within: Psychodynamics of Organizational Life.* (Cambridge, Mass: MIT Press, 1988).

and this book are about anything, they are about soul, the very soul of freedom for African Americans. Freedom comes first and foremost from the spirit, and spiritual development has been the central mission of the Black religious experience and its authentic leaders.

We assess the traditional model of leadership, citing historical epochs germane to our notion of socio-historically ensconced leadership theory. We then outline some of the psychological theories of motivation and human need, normed on the dominant caste of male Caucasians, and serving as the empirical roots of even the most recent research from the North American perspective. It is our intention to highlight the paradigmatic and cultural embeddedness of leadership, as both a theoretical construct and a social dynamic, in order to elucidate new perspectives on leadership, particularly Black religious leadership. To do so, we look at some contemporary writings of African scholars distinguishing contemporary African leaders in the most culturally stressful context of organization and management from superimposed colonial vestiges or neocolonial innovations. They describe the Africentric worldview in terms that are immediately relevant to African American leaders and their similarly superimposed social reality.

Ultimately, we look at some of the effects of this socio-historical embeddedness upon Black religious leadership. Our goal here is to raise serious questions about the essence of freedom in the Black religious movement. First, how are the very models of leadership in African American communities limited by their embeddedness within a social history that is, itself, unique to the human experience? Secondly, how will the people know when they have, indeed, "reached the mountaintop" of social liberation? It must be remembered, however, that leadership, embeddedness and paradox are dynamic realities. As such, they represent something of a moveable feast for researchers and practitioners. Therefore, as social conditions and awareness transform, the effects and validity of certain beliefs about leadership, liberation, and identity must be revisited. That is the overriding purpose of this chapter, beginning with the broadest traditional beliefs about leadership and concluding with a prognosis of future considerations for the narrow caste of Black religious leaders.

NORTH AMERICAN PERSPECTIVES OF LEADERSHIP

Leadership as a construct in organizational and social research has been viewed traditionally in terms of individualistic, hierarchical, rational, linear(cause to effect), control/authority, dualistic or Cartesian, masculine, and materialistic phenomena. This, of course, is a direct reflection of the predominant cultural norms and ideological worldview of a North American society yet to experience the social movements which surfaced the unique interests of humanism, women, ecology, civil rights, global interdependence or the effects of open systems theory.[13] This, however, is changing, albeit with great resistance since it reflects a dominant worldview. ("Power," Frederick Douglass once advised, "concedes nothing without a struggle.")

Leadership has been viewed largely as an individualized phenomenon of social influence because North American and western European societies have valued individualism[14]. Because the leadership phenomenon has been perceived through this naturally biased cultural lens, much of the research on leadership has spent inordinate attention on leaders' "traits" and behaviors [15], on individualized roles[16] and on contingency variables affecting individual leaders.[17]

Rational, linear and control characterizations of leadership follow from the very earliest works on management, motivation and organization after the industrial revolution and found in the works of Henri Fayol, Frederick W. Taylor, Max Weber and Elton Mayo.[18] These pioneering writers on organization and

---

[13] Tannenbaum, R. and Schmidt, W.H. "How To Choose A Leadership Pattern" *Harvard Business Review*; 1973, Vol.51, Issue 3, pp. 162-180; Hofstede, Geert, *Cultures and Organizations; Software of the Mind: Intercultural Cooperation and its Importance for Survival,* (NY: McGraw Hill, 1991).

[14] Hofstede, Geert, "Do American Theories Apply Abroad?" in *Culture's Consequences: International Differences in Work-Related Values* (Beverly Hills, Calif.: Sage Publications, 1980).

[15] Stogdill and Coons, *Leader Behavior: Its Description and Measurement* (Columbus, Ohio: Ohio State University; 1957); Vroom, Victor H. *A Multi-Dimensional Measure of Leadership Behavior.* (New Haven: Yale Univ. Press, 1973).

[16] Fiedler, David and Hunter, Bruce H. (eds.) *UNIX Systems IV: Adminstration.* (Hasbrouck Heights, N.J. : Hayden Book Co., 1986).

[17] Heller, Agnes, *The Theory of Need in Marx.* (London: Allison and Bushby, 1976); and Vroom, H. R., No Other Gods: *Christian Belief in Dialog with Buddhism, Hinduism, and Islam.* (Grand Rapids: Erdsman Publishing Co., 1996).

[18] Fayol, Henri, *General and Industrial Management.* (London: Pitman, 1949); Taylor, Frederick Winslow, *The Principles of Scientific Management* (New York: Harper & Brothers, 1916); Weber, *The Protestant Ethic and the Spirit of Capitalism* (Chicago, University of Chicago Press, 1947).

management emerged from social contexts in which the application of engineering techniques for more "scientific management" were prized. Theirs was a general mistrust of "charismatic leaders" in favor of the "efficient discharge" of scientifically-determined tasks. This seminal mistrust extended well beyond the personalities of leaders. It was found also in their generally low expectations of workers *cum followers*. Leaders had their objectives and followers needed cajoling or coercion to fulfill them. A direct line of cause and effect were understood to exist between leader commanding or persuading and workers "soldiering".[19] Rational "men" and trade union "workmen" were the topics of the day and the formality of bureacracy and science were expected to add new measures of control as people pursued their work "*'Sine ira et studio,'* without hatred or passion, hence without affection or enthusiasm".[20]

Each of these qualities had been prized, in some fashion or another, by the dominant caste in North American society under conditions of racial segregation and formal sexism. Thus, these can be said to carry the implicit assumption that leaders were presumed to be Caucasian and masculine. The results of effective leadership, therefore, were believed to be most visible in the material success of white males and the "offices" (bureaus) or organizations under their control.[21] Power and authority, wielded primarily by white males, were paramount in this first generation of "scientific management" theorists. This focus on power and individual authority was perfectly compatible with the mistrust of human nature underlying all other (more innovative) ideas. Lines of authority, methods of political (as opposed to statistical or quality) control, and both the literal and figural trappings of scientific dualism, are issues discernable even today in traditionally-designed organization charts, binary code technologies, and the breakdown of traditional bureacratic and hierarchical dynamics.[22] The difficulty in appreciating leadership more broadly, however, may be attributable directly to the fact that we seem to be struggling to see and understand clearly new socio-

---

[19] A. Taylor (ed.), *Educational and Occupational Selection in West Africa.* (London: Oxford Univ. Press, 1962).

[20] Weber, Max, *The Protestant Ethic and the Spirit of Capitalism* (Chicago, University of Chicago Press, 1947).

[21] Henri Fayol, *General and Industrial Management* (London: Pitman, 1969); Taylor, 1916, op. cit; Weber, 1947, op. cit.

[22] ibid, p. 184.

historical realities through a monocular cultural lens. These lenses have required both eyes and more facets as different identity groups have come into public focus and as the world community has grown and developed. Only a compound eye is appropriate to accurately perceive the new dimensions of effective leadership.

It is revealing to compare this obsolete, individualistic, masculine focus to the role of the United States as a newly-emerged military power in the global community. Following the Depression of the 1930's, the American self-concept was left groping for answers, the questions to which evolved from the crises of the stock market, of international credibility and of domestic gangwars. With General Douglas MacArthur still withdrawing troops from Europe behind World War I and the nation facing the expenses of war debt and reparations under conservative President Herbert Hoover, the United States was experiencing a national gestalt of insecurity and social change guided by forceful Caucasian men at home and abroad. Hitler was beginning construction of concentration camps in Nazi Germany and Roosevelt replaced Hoover with his "New Deal" programs. Trotsky, Mussolini, Chiang Kai-shek and Huey Long were amongst leaders in the news. As American interests were increasingly threatened by fascist aggression, scientific management was needed for an improved effort in World War II. The improved effort involved rationing foodstuffs while watching the former League of Nations become the United Nations as John D. Rockefeller donated $8.5 milllion for a permanent headquarters for world leaders in New York.

Ultimately, America's national self-concept of leadership would be depicted as a more or less parochial form of international individualism by the words and deeds of intellectual and political leaders. According to Henry R. Luce, it was time "to accept wholeheartedly our opportunity as the most powerful and vital nation in the world and in consequence to exert upon the world the full impact of our influence, for such purposes as we see fit and by such means as we see fit.", and Secretary of State Dean Acheson offered the benevolent, yet paternalistic view that, "We are willing to help people who believe the way we do to continue to live the way they want to live."[23] (Considering the fact that a major aspect of America's belief system was segregation to safeguard a presumed racial superiority amongst Caucasians, it is easy to understand the national and global

---

[23] Williams, W. A., *History as a Way of Learning: Articles, Excerpts, and Essays* (NY: New Viewpoints Press, 1973).

implications of such a statement.) These leaders articulated a sort of imprimatur from a *nouveau riche* child having its way in the global community of nation-states and, undoubtedly, exercised a proselytizing influence and missionary zeal usually associated with religious enterprise seeking to "civilize non-believers." It could not have been lost on religious leaders that their own stock and trade was being parallelled by the state.

Thus, from a social context in which American power was attributed largely to individual, Caucasian male industrial magnates, politicians and military leaders, a behavioral focus on their individualized personalities, characters, behaviors (habits) and contexts was quite logical. Such a focus, combined with a Cartesian dualism, has led naturally to definitions of "leaders vs. followers", "autocrats vs. democrats" in authority, and of "strong vs. permissive" leadership styles in research and practice.[24] These dualistic and linear inquiries into "cause and effect" dynamics around leaders mirrored a growing quagmire of trait theories and factor analyses of individual leaders that was only as specific as human differences of personality.[25] The weight of this ambiguity, diffusion and fragmentation threatened to sink the ship of investigators in new waters where minority groups and women brought into public focus new styles and contingencies of leadership and broader social dynamics than had been entertained, heretofore.

In fact, the emergence of these new actors on the stage of leadership even threatened to betray the validity of research predicated upon a "rational man" thesis as leaders from ethnic minority communities engaged techniques such as non-violent, passive resistance that were manifestly "irrational."[26] Concurrently, the global community began to shrink as newly-independent, Third World nations sent new and indigenous leaders to the United Nations and before television cameras. Otherwise remote, guerrilla movements and their different social values became living room conversation in North American homes through the new technology of telecasting pictures live from locations around the world. Defining

---

[24] Tannenbaum, R. and Schmidt, W.H., "How To Choose A Leadership Pattern". *Harvard Business Review*; 1973, Vol. 51, No. 3, pp. 162-180.

[25] Pfeffer, J. *et al.* "The Effect of Uncertainty on the Use of Social Influence in Organizational Decision-Making", *Administrative Science Quarterly*; 1976, 21: 2, pp. 227-245.

[26] Joanne Grant, *Black Protest: History, Documents, and Analysis, 1619 to the Present* (NY: St. Martin's Press, 1970).

and controlling the world's view of leadership became as untenable as fighting a war on both domestic and international fronts. Satellite technology brought new ways of thinking and behavior from the political "satellite nations" of superpowers. New realities emerged and newer realities became possible.

The very construct of leadership required revamping. Notions of hoarding a relative scarcity of power[27], organizational structures rewarding autocracy[28] and superhuman or android-like depictions of heroic leaders with little human emotion and even less sympathy were no longer viable.[29] A fragmentation inherent in the North American research paradigm used to define leadership met its counterpart in social dynamics now deemed inadequate as workers insisted upon a consistency of democratic principles and personal empowerment at home, at work and in their representation abroad. These were *de facto* challenges to notions of universal truth, hierarchical decision-making and strictly materialistic assessments of leader effectiveness. More importantly, the very basis of human motivation was questioned and the role of industrial and social psychology was highlighted as the very foundation of culturally-biased leadership theory.

THE PSYCHOLOGY OF TRADITIONAL LEADERSHIP

Not unlike the leadership theory which sprang from it, traditional psychology views patients much like leaders are said to regard followers. There is an objectification of the patient in western psychology and there is, likewise, a belief in universal truths for treatment and/or recovery. As one writer puts it, "The dominant psychology is founded and imbued with the outlook that ... the Euro-American worldview...and the experiencs of white, middle class males are the only or the most valid experiences in the world."[30] In a parallel manner, leadership theory has sought a singular set of traits to define leadership and held an almost monolithic view of the follower's non-role. New understandings in psychology from clinical endeavors such as social therapy are bringing new challenges to that

---

[27] Conger, J. A., "Leadership: The Art of Empowering Others", *Academy of Management Executive*, 1989. Vol. 3, Issue 1, pp. 17-24.

[28] Ackoff, R., "The Circular Organization: An Update", *Academy of Management Executive*, 1989, Vol. 3, Issue 1.

[29] ibid, p. 681

[30] Hussein Abdilahi Bulhan, in *Franz Fanon and the Psychology of Oppression* (NY: Plenum Press, 1985).

field. And similar challenges are coming to leadership theory from new organizational designs such as circular organizations and new trends toward group motivation and performance appraisal in increasingly diverse teams. Moreover, computer-mediated communication and organization, where identity may be obscured by the medium, has yet to make its full impact upon leadership theory.

Evidence of the lack of explanatory power afforded researchers of leadership can be found in the very titles of literature on the subject. Increased numbers of reports on the "ambiguity of leadership", "the ways women lead", "feminine leadership or how to succeed without being one of the boys", and "the uncertain future of the leadership concept" may be cited as any of what Arthur Jago described as "multiple interpretations...but each remaining an incomplete and wholly inadequate explanation of complex relationships."[31]

Social trends for deeper appreciation of group dynamics have resulted in closer looks at the empirical psychology understanding leadership theory. Psychological theories of power and the need to achieve in individualistic terms[32], self-actualization[33] and expectancy/drive satisfactions by individual leaders[34] are now at issue as comprehensive explanations of the most complex phenomena of social influence. Virtually all of the psychology serving as a foundation for leadership theory is itself embedded in a European cultural and historical context of male dominance. Works by Freud, Maslow, Herzberg, McClelland and Vroom ought not be discounted for external validity across the boundaries of identity groups simply because of their embeddedness in the Caucasian male ethos. However, the fact of their embeddedness does raise issues for investigations of phenomena such as leadership when even these theoretical foundations of such research may not have been tested rigorously for such validity. There are, moreover, cultural values implicit within the psychological theory and without their explication little effective cross-cultural analysis can be done. Ultimately, there is more than adequate evidence that precious little of the research predicated

---

[31] Jago, Arthur, *Uncertain Futures: Challenges for Decision Makers* (NY: Wiley, 1979).

[32] Vroom, Victor H., *A Multi-Dimensional Measure of Leadership Behavior* (New Haven: Yale Univ. Press, 1987).

[33] Maslow, Abraham. *The Farther Reaches of Human Nature* (NY: Viking Press, 1971)

[34] Vroom, Victor H., *A Multi-Dimensional Measure of Leadership Behavior* (New Haven: Yale Univ. Press, 1987).

upon these psychological theories has helped to clarify our understanding of leadership in its broadest human dimensions.

THE RELEVANCE OF GROUP DYNAMICS

One area of psychology that has not been appreciated widely beyond academic research of leadership is group dynamics. This is true, not so much in the area of Freudian analysis of groups, but in its assessment of effective leadership of such groups, particularly across ethnic, racial and socioeconomic boundaries. Group dynamics research develops much of its theory from temporary groups brought together specifically for experiential learning in the "here and now." The research and writing on group dynamics may be distinguished according to that body relating to the unconscious, primal (oedipal and preoedipal) elements of the group centered on authority (primarily for therapy) and those writings which relate to the training of interpersonal skills for more effective intergroup cooperative dynamics(T-groups).[35] The former of these schools of group dynamics is recognized most popularly as the London-based Tavistock tradition while the other is associated with the National Training Laboratory (NTL) and the pioneering sociological works of Kurt Lewin.

The literature concerning leadership from the European value system in the Tavistock tradition summons Freudian concepts of "dependency-flight", "counterdependency-fight", "pairing", "oneness" and the "pre-oedipal mother in the group-as-a-whole."[36] Known also as "basic assumptions," these subconscious and unconscious responses are active, yet clandestine in the obvious behaviors of groups as they form, engage in conflict, establish norms and develop in their relationships. In the NTL tradition, more is written about the characteristics of and contextual attributes necessary for a group facilitator/leader to maximize group learning about the dynamics of the experiential process. Although much has been written about the characteristics of and contextual attributes necessary for a leader to maximize group learning and about the effects of leaders upon experiential processes, a paucity of research and writing in organizational behavior exists about the empirical differences in perceptions and manifestations of leadership

---

[35] A.K. Rice, *Learning for Leadership: Interpersonal and Intergroup Relations* (London: Tavistock Pub., 1965, p. 93.

[36] Bion, Wilfrid R., *Experiences in Groups and Other Papers* (New York: Basic Books, 1961), p. 86.

across identity group boundaries of race, age, ethnicity or culture, gender and socioeconomic class.

Nonetheless, these experiential groups process learning from open systems dynamics (where membership is voluntary and fluid), from intimate inquiry and interpersonal vulnerability, and from the direct identities of group members. Therefore, they must address some of the most salient psychodynamics at the intrapersonal, interpersonal and intergroup levels. The often subtle and always complex interplay of basic assumption group psycho-dynamics and the more palpable work group dynamics between leaders and followers has been addressed historically within the group dynamics literature in myriad ways, qualified for group size, group identity and context, group task and phase of group development.

The group dynamics literature speaks of leader/follwer dynamics in terms of boundary protection and spanning, ethnocentrism, Freudian "dreaded primal fathers", authorization and definition in "group-as-a-whole"(i.e. the group as one organism) dynamics, myth and fantasy in groups, parallel processes between authority and subordinate groups, and the derivation of meaning within groups. Interestingly enough, most of these dynamics were considered in the earliest works before the human relations movement and sensitivity training sessions of the forties, fifties and sixties.[37] While it would be interesting to explore several aspects of group dynamics in terms of Black religious leaders, the present interest is in learning about what broad characteristics of effective leadership can be gleaned from a synthesis of experiential group characteristics and the dynamics of Black religions. We look first at leadership in experiential groups.

INSIGHTS ON EFFECTIVE LEADERSHIP FROM GROUP DYNAMICS RESEARCH

Scholars and practitioners of group process inform us that persons in leadership roles for understanding such processes must focus upon modelling a variety of behaviors that maximize individual and group learning instead of maintaining executive privilege. These behaviors may be bifurcated into those

---

[37] See LeBon's, *The Crowd* (1895), Sumner's, *Ethnocentrism* (1906), Freud's, *Group Psychology and the Analysis of the Ego* (1922), Mayo's, *Human Problems of an Industrial Civilization* (1933), Follet's, *The Essentials of Leadership* (1933), and Roethlisberger and Dickson's, *Hawthorne Studies of 1939.*

functional or role requirements for management of group experience and those that refer directly to the personal qualities or attributes of the leader/facilitator.

The group dynamics literature identifies certain requisite skills for the successful leadership of experiential learning within a group process. Exercising authority within such groups requires an ability to recognize the conscious and unconscious processes at work within them. Each type of basic assumption group requires a different set of leadership behaviors to uncover the learning available from it.[38] To exercise authority effectively, group leaders first must be quite clear about their own, personal dispositions toward authority.[39] This is critical because, without a clear understanding of one's experience, interpretation and exercise of authority, it is not possible to establish boundaries or to anticipate one's limitations in a role where others will both attribute and challenge one's leadership authority.[40]

Secondly, effective leadership of spontaneous group processes requires understandings of unconscious processes and other theories of group dynamics including roles, boundaries and social dynamics imported into imbedded contexts.[41] Theoretical grounding requires also that one have a keen sense of the practical importance of one's multiple identities and roles in the function of leadership within such groups. It is here that the leadership functions of boundary management and boundary spanning begin. The effective leader must recognize the embeddness of identities within group, distinguish effective learning practices from environmental norms, be attentive to conscious and unconscious expectations of power and competence from the group and distinguish his/her role as one enmeshed (dependent upon) within these realities.[42]

One critical aspect in the role of leader or facilitator for experiential groups is attention to parallel processes enacted across the boundary of authority figure and novices or learners. In general, parallel processes find the attitudes or

---

[38] Bion, Wilfrid R, *Experiences in Groups and Other Papers* (NY: Basic Books, 1961), p. 93.

[39] Smith, Kenwyn, *Paradoxes of Group Life: Understanding Conflict, Paralysis, and Movement in Group Dynamics* (San Francisco: Josee-Bass, 1987), p. 247.

[40] Hirschhorn, Larry, *The Workplace Within: Psychodynamics of Organizational Life.* (Cambridge, Mass: MIT Press, 1988)

[41] Alderfer, C.P., in Gillette, J. and McCollom, M., *Groups In Context: A New Perspective on Group Dynamics* (Addison-Wesley, Reading, MA.. 1990). p. 293.

[42] ibid, p. 294.

behaviors of authority figures playing themselves out in their subordinate groups. Parallel processes require an appreciation of the particular type of sembiotic dependency (as opposed to equality) extant between groups and leaders as cited in much of the group dynamics literature.[43]

Certain personal qualities also enable the assumption of these role requirements. A culling of the literature finds self-awareness, humility, flexibility and listening skills at the top of the list.[44] While intellectual prowess has been cited already, there is a particular sort of interpersonal intelligence (as per Howard Gardner's multiple intelligence theory) that evidences a high capacity to accept and engage a wide range of emotions in self and others. Effective leaders must use the perception of this data, through themselves as another source of information about group dynamics, then conceptualize the experience of these dynamics in a manner which assists in maximizing learning while minimizing any potential damage to participants within an experiential group.[45] As with any analysis of leadership, it is easy to see the complexity of demands incumbent upon leaders of groups where a significant focus is upon the quality and nature of group process and interactions. Black religion is no exception for, as eloquently stated by Kenwyn Smith, "no one escapes the interpersonal and group dynamics of experiential methods."[46] Much of the Black religious experience is an affective, experiential phenomenon with a central objective of learning for individual and collective spiritual and social development.

ISSUES FROM BLACK RELIGIOUS LEADERSHIP

Like the leaders of experiential training groups, Black religious leaders must accomodate open systems dynamics with their members. That is, religious institutions, particularly in their evangelistic elements, must recognize a fluidity of organizational boundaries. They cannot, ideally, choose the internal motivations of those whom they would have as members of their religion or their

---

[43] ibid, p. 291.

[44] Smith, Kenwyn. *Paradoxes of Group Life: Understanding Conflict, Paralysis, and Movement in Group Dynamics* (San Francisco: Josee-Bass, 1987), p. 253.

[45] Alderfer, C.P. in Gillette, J. and McCollom, M., *Groups In Context: A New Perspective on Group Dynamics* (Addison-Wesley, Reading, MA.. 1990), pp. 254-56.

[46] Smith, Kenwyn *Paradoxes of Group Life: Understanding Conflict, Paralysis, and Movement in Group Dynamics*, (San Francisco: Josee-Bass, 1987), p. 256.

organizations (lest they become cult-like, preferring closed system dynamics). Moreover, Black religious leaders must prepare for the same manner of intimate inquiry, interpersonal vulnerability, and human anxieties as do experiential group leaders. As an alienated and socially-marginalized identity group, however, African Americans may seek to transfer or project upon such leaders forceful expectations of invulnerability, anxiety-free interaction and impersonal authoritarianism denoting control of Black destiny.

In the paradox of their roles as leaders in the spiritual learning and as followers of the whatever word they preach, the Black religious leader must grapple with the fact that the Black Church is perhaps the sole place in American society where they can experience the power of "the leader's inalienable right to executive action."[47] This power, particularly in the broader social context of repressed self-determination, can be a major intoxicant for Black religious leaders. It has been here that the intrapersonal awareness of the deleterious effects of racism and economic injustice for Black religious leaders has been undermined or overwhelmed. The heady experience of exercising parochial power with little or no accountability has been falsely defined as freedom, power, or as some emotionally immature notion of manhood (imitating an inadequate, secular status quo and) shrouded in religiosity. Avoiding this historic pitfall requires many of the same skills that are proposed for effective leadership of experiential group dynamics.

We now know that highly functional leader behavior in group dynamics is characterized by strong influence and the forthright addressing of issues provoking anxiety in the group.[48] This behavior not only alleviates group tension and anxiety, but creates dynamics of "dependency" upon the leader by other group members.[49] Black religious leaders are in role precisely to exercise such strong influence and address the deep-seated anxieties of those who follow their guidance. The critical question for our immediate purposes is *how* leader influence is manifested and exercised and the distinct nature of African American

---

[47] ibid, p. 258.

[48] Gillette, Jonathan, and McCollom, Marion (eds.), *Groups in Context: A New Perspective on Group Dynamics*. (Reading: Addison-Wesley Pub. Co, 1990), p. 94.

[49] Bion, Wilfrid R., *Experiences in Groups and Other Papers* (New York: Basic Books, 1961), p. 94.

anxieties as (literally) opposed to other identity groups. Logically, these anxieties must be related to the dynamics of racism and class oppression perpetrated by the dominant cultural, socioeconomic and racial groups, and perpetuated within the group psychology of African Americans as an historically dependent ethnic minority group.

The duality of consciousness identified by DuBois, Fanon, Memmi and others may be likened to traditional notions of mental illness (i.e. schizophrenia) by western psychology, but its positive affect in the survival of African peoples in the Americas is largely neglected.[50] Moreover, the paradoxical nature of this psychological duality cannot be overstated. African Americans have been born again as a new expression of the African ethos in the social context of an industrialized, globally powerful America. To understand the psychology of leaders in this "new ethnic group", requires a deeper appreciation of the ways in which its core cultural/spiritual ethos is contradicted by the way western, European psychology apprehends humanity through objectification and abstraction.[51] This is especially true for African-centered leadership.

AFRICAN LEADERSHIP: A CONTRAST OF ASSUMPTIONS

Recent writings in organizational behavior have begun to explore the nexus of national cultures and corporate cultures as the respective assumptions prevailing therein are determined as dysfunctional.[52] These works have been effective intellectual tools in the demythologizing of the most popular assumptions concerning the "universality" of western, particularly North American, leadership styles. Geert Hofstede has posited the limitations of U.S. management programs in the context of even European cultural realities for which an affinity might be presumed logically. His proposition was met with forceful opposition from some U.S. scholars.[53] Following Hofstede's diagnoses, it is easier

---

[50] Refer to the wriitings of DuBois, Fanon, and Memmi, too numerous to list here.

[51] Ani, M., *YURUGU: An African-Centered Critique of European Cultural Thought and Behavior* (Trenton, N.J. Africa World Press, Inc., 1994).

[52] Refer to the writings of the following scholars for recent developments in the organizational behavior: Hofstede, 1980; Ahiazu, 1986; Merrick Jones, 1992: Laurent, 1986; Nzelibe, 1986; and Schneider, 1988.

[53] Hofstede, Geert, "Do American Theories Apply Abroad?" in *Culture's Consequences: International Differences in Work-Related Values* (Beverly Hills, Calif.: Sage Publications, 1980), p. 473.

to understand how North American thought, limited within even its *alma mater*, industrialized European contexts, is even more limited when applying such doctrines and practices to cultures and contexts where no shared heritage or cultural affinities exist.

The notion of "rational" behavior in organizational theory and leadership is, itself, culture-bound to western notions and traditions according to Merrick Jones. "What appears to a Western observer of African organizations to be 'irrational', on closer examination, can be seen to reflect a set of values that are different from, but no less valid than those of the West," according to Jones.[54] As prescribed by Jones, leaders of African organizations need a cultural and historical sensitivity, especially in the area of efficient use of organizational resources when weighed against the socio-political networks and socio-cultural expectations of African members, as well as a reflective posture about even those endeavors which seem consistent with collectivist values and participatory management if they are to succeed.

Writers of leadership in the African context have spent a great deal of intellectual capital in a collective expose of the indigenous "African thought system" and its inconsistency with western and North American models of leadership and values as witnessed in the context of management.[55] By relating African "common sense" and theory to the African's interpretation of organizational behaviors, Ahiauzu lays a nice foundation for the further exploration of African thinking on leadership. Quite summarily, Ahiauzu points out that: 1) there is an African thought-system; 2) synthesis, interrelatedness and their consequential expression in symbolism underlie the African thought-system; 3) proverbial wisdom is a preponderant determinant of African common sense and sense-making; and 4) mysticism and ancestral consciousness are parts of the African thought-system which lead to broader than positivistic interpretations of behavior.[56] The implications of this "African thought-system" for interpretations of contemporary leadership are several.

---

[54] Jones, Merrick, and Blunt, Peter. *Managing Organizations in Africa.* (NY: W. de Gruyter, 1992).
[55] Ahiauzu, A.I., "The African Thought-System and the Work Behavior of the African Industrial Man", *International Studies of Management and Organization.*, 1980, Vol. 16, Issue 2, pp. 37-58.
[56] ibid.

Ahiauzu has cited general incongruences between informal, African socialization and the regimented, Eurocentric instruction for easier adaptation to contemporary industrial production as one stark example. By way of another example, he demonstrates how, when African thought-system common sense fails to explain unsatisfactory phenomena, the African is likely to appeal to a mystical source of explanation, especially in industrial settings. Leaders of African-cultured peoples, by implication, need unique appreciation of this cultural imperative less it become a source of additional stigmatization. This is especially true in social contexts where African cultural imperatives are ethnic minority realities. The Black religious experience in America is the vessel carrying this mysticism beyond its African motherland.

FROM AFRICA TO AFRICAN AMERICA: LEADERS, CULTURE, & MORAL DESTINY

From the "hush harbors" of the first African slaves, to the present-day pentecostal Protestantism, the Black religious experience in North America has been the quintessential expression of African culture and spirituality for African Americans. The Black Church, therefore, must be considered the predominant representation and incubator of African cultural dynamics in the American experience.[57] Even in the "highest" religious masses of Black Roman Catholics and Episcopalians, there is an African cultural resonance with the ceremonial and mystical elements of liberation through transubstantiation, humility through genuflection, sacramental symbolism and sanctification by water and wine.[58] Without this cultural resonance, such foreign modes of spiritual development could not have exceeded the tenures of their accompanying imperialistic apparatus (slavery, social terrorism and formal segregation).

We can witness the core cultural imperatives of an Africentric paradigm in the matrifocality of the Black Church in America, where male corporate leadership is lifted up, while female leadership is exercised in essential avenues of the Church's life.[59] Church "mothers" have held an historic role in decision-making and deliberation about the mission of the Black Church. This has been true despite narrow-minded efforts to perceive the Black Church as the sole

---

[57] ibid, p. 89.
[58] ibid, p. 91.
[59] ibid, p. 93.

province of power and authority for men. Moreover, women are increasingly demanded equal access to the formal, corporate leadership roles long regarded as the redemptive bastion of socially-maligned Black men. Even in its most narrowly conceived concerns for equality, it has been a focus on social liberation and empowerment which has driven the Black Church.

Paradoxically, the Black Church has aided and abetted historical efforts aimed at obliterating the African ethos as antonymous to some narrowly presumed "will of God." We have witnessed this perturbing paradox in the historical role of the African American religious experience as it has metamorphised from slave religion, through the Holiness Movement, in the Social Gospel Movement, to Islam and E.Franklin Frazier's *Negro Church*, and into today's *Black Church* of C.Eric Lincoln. Each movement has manifested the continuing duality of the Black psyche in the American context, pursuing a pacifying survivalist ethic with one pastoral hand, and radically reaching for power with the prophetic other.

This pastoral/prophetic dynamic is a defining feature of the African spiritual disposition toward an overwhelming experience of oppression and excellence in America. Black leaders, especially those emerging from the sole autonomous institution of the Black community (the church), have been true representatives of the passification/power paradox that exists in the minds and hearts of all historically oppressed minority peoples. On one extreme, their Black messianism may assume an individualistic zeal that unwittingly divorces them from the collective identification with their core Black constituency and makes them easy targets for some sort of self-delusioned "revolutionary suicide," or repressive murder by a threatened status quo. On the other extreme, an overbearing focus on the redemptive power of suffering historically has rendered Negro leaders as socially impotent as "Uncle Toms" on the "massah's plantation."[60]

What is, perhaps, unique about the African American experience is that the ebb and flow of its putsches for empowerment and passification have marched lock-step and dead-beat with moral and ethical awareness of the United States as a young nation in the global community. In this sense, African Americans have accepted the idea that their moral destiny is inextricable from that of the broader

---

[60] Moses, Wilson Jeremiah, *Black Messiahs and Uncle Toms* (College Station: Penn State Press, 1982).

society. It remains to be seen whether this is merely a manifestation of some "chosen people" groupthink[61] amongst Black Americans or if, indeed, the social and cultural circumstances of this group are uniquely tied to the social progress of the nation in terms of its moral and ethical development. In either event, there is good reason for this belief regardless of its future viability as a social identity. New levels of theological awareness in North America (and beyond) can be attributed to the increased social conscience and activism of the African American community.

The very idea of God has transformed as the social maturity of African Americans has progressed. As the standardbearing minority group in the American Experience, the increasing awareness of African Americans has sparked greater self-awareness of the broader society. Where cries of *"Black Power!!!"* were once frightening to the power structure of the United States, it is not unusual nowadays to hear other groups (e.g. students. senior citizens and other ethnic groups or minorities) attach the *"Power"* epithet to their most salient and marginalized identities. "Women Power", "Student Power", "Green (i.e. ecological awareness) Power" and even "White Power" have become colloquial in the aftermath of the African American popularization of identity-group assertions of self-determination.

Africans in the American context, once evangelized and socialized, initially evidenced no doubts about the existence and providential nature of God. From the early eighteenth to the early nineteenth century, adherence to traditional, passive theological interpretation was proselytized by Black religious leaders in accordance with the laissez-faire economic imperatives of the broader social order in which they were embedded. Reverends such as J.W.C. Pennington of the Colored Presbyterian Church of New York and Lemuel Haynes preached of an "otherworldliness" and rewards in the hereafter that were comforting to most African parishioners and their "superior" European masters/bosses alike.[62] Of particular note was Jupiter Hammond's *"An Address to Negroes in the State of*

---

[61] Janis, Irving, *Groupthink: Psychological Studies of Policy Decisions and Fiascoes* (Boston: Houghton Mifflin, 1982).

[62] Mays, Benjamin, *The Negro's God as Reflected in his Literature* (NY: Athaneum, 1938/1996), p. 57.

New York"(1787) in which he admonished that group to "be content with slavery; obey your masters; God will free you if He so designs."[63]

However, as the social maturity of African Americans progressed (embedded, as they were, within the missionary zeal of Christianity at that time), it is possible to see the penumbra and emanations of this limited perspective. This is particularly true in the African Methodist Episcopal (A.M.E.) experience. A burgeoning consciousness and self-determination began to reveal themselves as African Americans adjusted to the psychosocial exigencies of the era. Bishops Richard Allen, Daniel Coker and Richard Cain began to articulate a divine movement to "make a way" for those oppressed or neglected by legalized racism, economic exploitation and the other (docile) Christian disposition. Hiram Revels and C.T. Walker made pointed statements about a "God of justice" who is categorically opposed to war, slavery and injustice of any sort. Black religious leadership would remain the most viable for African Americans as long as their moral destiny was credibly linked to the themes of messianism and ethnic chauvinism.[64] Later, Bishop Henry McNeal Turner would personify the Black prophetic voice in opposition to the mainstream participation of African Americans in nationalistic efforts ignoring the continued oppression of that group. He and others would offer religious convictions for the full participation of Blacks in national life, primarily to redress injustices and, in the words of one African American poet, make America "...America to me!" In this way, they acknowledged the embedded circumstance of their constituency in ways which may have seemed a betrayal of any pastoral imperative. They may have been asked, "How shall a subordinated people survive, if not in service to the national ethos?"

Theological justifications for rebelling against the continued exploitation of African Americans would prevail amongst Black religious leaders as the moral destiny of the group became an increasingly salient organizational and cultural ethos in the face of rampant hostility from Caucasians. Only international conflicts which threatened the larger society as a whole were compelling enough to convince many Blacks to hold their social justice imperatives in abeyance.

---

[63] ibid, p. 59.

[64] Moses, Wilson Jeremiah, *Black Messiahs and Uncle Toms* (College Station: Penn State Press, 1982), p. 168.

Eventually, the justice delayed would be realized as a justice denied with dire consequences for the African American spiritual focus and the broader social enthusiasm for human rights at home.

Two major American military epochs can be attributed with the advent of atheism and humanism as supplants for Christianity in the African American community. International conflicts amongst Europe and her descendant states effectively exposed the hypocrisy of wars for liberation abroad with domestic conditions of slavery and segregation unaddressed. After concerted efforts by Black religious leaders during both World War I and World War II to quell concerns for African American human rights in the then Negro community in deference to the "greater war" abroad, the logical result of Black disappointment was an abject disgust for the very idea of God as "a useful instrument" in achieving social justice.

In parallel to this disappointment, other leaders were undertaking sophisticated efforts to bring to the world's attention the plight of African Americans under conditions of domestic terrorism. Leaders like Mary Church Terrell and Ida B. Wells (who was mentored by the likes of Frederick Douglass and Booker T. Washington) were appealing to the broader public on behalf of voting rights, women's rights, and lynching victims to the dismay of more conservative leaders within and without the Black community. Wells, in particular, challenged women's suffragists to support her as she sought to demythologize the notion of Black male rapists used to justify lynchings. She also foreshadowed the advent of the National Association for the Advancement of Colored People (N.A.A.C.P.) in 1909 as a multiracial, academic and professionally-credentialled advocacy group for African Americans. The Black human rights agenda had moved beyond the nearly exclusive purview of religious leadership in the community. Women, whites and solidly middle-class characters assumed national leadership roles on a wider array of issues than ever had been promoted.

The Niagara debates of Booker T. Washington and W.E.B. DuBois, leading eventually to the short-lived Committee of Twelve rapprochement of these leaders, were highlighting the paradox of African American identity and ideological contrast. Washington, supported by status quo industrialists, personified the pastoral/assimilationist aspect of a more secular version of Black leadership; DuBois insisted on the internationalization and PanAfrican consciousness that existed within the community. This Panafricanism, however, did not represent nearly the challenge to Black religious leadership that others promoted.

GARVEYISM, ISLAM AND THE LEADERSHIP CHALLENGE OF BLACK NATIONALISM

Black messianism connected with notions of Black moral destiny in powerful ways during the early period of the twentieth century. Perhaps no one epitomized this joining more than Marcus Garvey. Garvey's eloquence and appeal to the lowest common denominator of Panafrican beliefs caught much of Black leadership, especially Black religious leaders, off guard. The virtually instant success of Garvey's Universal Negro Improvement Association (U.N.I.A.) dovetailed neatly with a consistent strain of Black nationalism and moral destiny lifted up by artists and theologians of the day. In marked contrast to Black religious leaders like Rev. J.H. Jones of the Texas Farmers Colonization Association, Bishop Henry M. Turner, and Rev. A.B. Gibson of Georgia whose overtures concerning colonization and cultural repatriation favored remaining in the United States as a "nation within a nation," Garvey played the polemics of colonization and nationalism toward repatriation in Africa itself.

A popular aphorism has it that "when America catches cold, Black folks get pneumonia." With the imminent collapse of the U.S. economy in the 1930's, the palpable disaffection of African Americans became pronounced as social conditions worsened for all citizens. It is in this era that the seeds for unique leadership efforts amongst African Americans such as Garvey's were fertilized. Embedded within a blatant racial hostility rife with lynchings and other legally-sanctioned injustices against them, African Americans experienced an intense collective identification as victims. Garvey spoke immediately to the strata of African Americans who were alienated also by the multiracial, intellectualizing leadership of DuBois' Niagara Movement and its progeny, the N.A.A.C.P. His flamboyance stimulated the imaginations and actualized the fantasies of many. Though eventually brought down by the active enmity of other Black leaders and the U.S. government, Garvey ironically represented the excesses of a messianism and a Black chauvinism that were preached by his very enemies.

Garvey's movement was a mere forerunner of those African Americans that are attracted to the Nation of Islam today. Garvey insisted that leaders "must always be ahead by way of knowledge" and that they must be clean cut, must never reveal personal poverty, must never tell lies to those they lead, and must carry themselves "with dignity", but not be "a snob."[65] Garvey stressed self-reliance and confidence, that the "heart and head must work together" and that leaders must be serious, not extravagant. By articulating a novel form of Black zionism predicated upon personal duty to God, Garvey effectively fused Jewish, Christian and Panafrican symbolism into a program of Black pride and material empowerment. His advice on personal comportment and leader affect spoke directly to a total way of life reminiscent of Islamic traditions and his appeal to Blacks excluded from middle class aspirations was a harbinger of the organizing success witnessed later in Elijah Muhammad's Nation of Islam. Because Islamic Black Nationalism has been presented as a more culturally consistent religious expression for African Americans in contradistinction to that offered by Black Christian leaders, it is useful to reflect upon its history and appeal to Africans, on the Continent and in the diaspora.

Chiek Anta Diop has described the consistency of Islam with fundamental African cultural tenets, particularly the concept of a dual world of material and spiritual manifestations.[66] Diop suggested that only by its appeal to African leaders in the eleventh century, through peaceful introduction, was Islam capable of surviving in indigenous African communities. Subsequent jihads, undertaken by autochthonous Black chiefs, were said by Diop to have masked the colonial imposition intended by the Islamic "marabout" missionaries who gained favor in royal courts and, thereby, received protection for their religious beliefs. Without such protection, without the benefits of intimate royal knowledge of the people, and without a non-violent introduction, the Africans disdain for the tenets of Islam would not have abated over the centuries. It was on the level of rational morality, in the midst of atrophying African religions in the fifteenth century, that Diop attributes the deciding factor of cultural consistency and conversion. Understanding Islam as a "living religion", (requiring a living marabout as the

---

[65] Martin, Tony, *Marcus Garvey Hero: A First Biography* (Dover: Majority Press, 1983).
[66] Diop, C.A., *Precolonial Black Africa* (Westport, Conn.: L. Hill, 1987).

medium between the two worlds) as opposed to Christianity's tendency toward "mere religious custom" is necessary to appreciate fully its success in Africa. Diop goes further to explain how Islam historically has provided the "mystical underpinnings of nationalism" in Africa.

Diop's characterization of Africa's Islamic conversion in the twelfth through nineteenth centuries is immediately relevant to our discussion of nationalism, moral destiny and Black religious leadership in the twentieth century. We have noted the consistency of African thought-systems with contemporary African American cultural imperatives. It is easy to see how Black nationalism and Islam joined with the African sense of moral destiny in America to appeal to those in tune with their core cultural imperatives, mistrustful of well-educated and "race-mixing" Black leaders, and vulnerable to spiritual conversion on the basis of mystical revelations by Islam's leaders here. Since Islam had rooted in Africa, its contemporary appeal was enhanced for African Americans seeing in it an opportunity to exercise their racial and cultural affinities for "the Motherland" in a dialogue with God which did not summon immediately the hypocrisy of Christian justifications for white supremacy and Black suffering.

Wali Fard's appearance in Detroit as "the Great Mahdi—Allah incarnate" spoke directly to the spiritual and social poverty of African Americans in the 1930's.[67] His message masterfully blended the themes of Christianity with a fervent message of self-determination and moral destiny. It was the Nation of Islam that "The Prophet" Fard founded, and there was to be no mistake that the Nation was Black, and the devil was white. Even those (such as Malcolm X after his Mecca pilgimage) who might eschew the narrow Black nationalism of Islam in the United States could find some solace from America's overbearing emphasis on race upon their realization of a spiritual identity that transcends such mundane distinctions around the globe. (The establishment of the World Community of Islam in the West, under the leadership of Imam Warith Dean Muhammad—son of Elijah Muhammad—had this as at least one impetus for its founding in distinction with the Nation of Islam led by Elijah Muhammad, after Fard, and Minister Louis Farrakhan, today.)

---

[67] Lincoln, C.E., *The Black Church Since Frazier*, included in Edward Franklin Frasier's *The Negro Church in America* (NY: Schoeken Books, 1974). Note: *The Black Church Since Frazier* originated as the James Gray Lecture Series at Duke University in 1970.

Like Garveyism, Islam has spoken directly to those without a national voice. Black nationalism, therefore, has always been a threat to that tradition of Black religious leadership which has sought accomodation or assimilation with the predominant national ethos. Even the most Panafrican of Christian leaders may be found less credible to young, rebellious African Americans who find in Islam an alternative to the historic hypocrisy of the "White man's religion" that was used to justify slavery, oppression and colonialism. (Apparently less important to them is the fact of Ethiopia's acceptance of Christianity as early as 343 A.D., a full decade before Constantine so consecrated the Holy Roman Empire and more than centuries before the conversion of Anglo-Saxons.)[68] Black leadership of any religious persuasion has had to recognize the paradox of assimilation/secession in the African American psyche and appeal to one over the other. Black nationalism has been more pronounced when the plight of African Americans has worsened under racial terrorism and economic impoverishment. Today's leadership of the Million Man March by Nation of Islam leader, Minister Louis Farrakhan, is an excellent case in point.

One of the most revealing images from the Million Man March found popular Black religious leaders such as Reverend Jesse Jackson of the Rainbow Coalition, Joseph Lowery of the Southern Christian Leadership Conference, and the leaders of most major Black Christian denominations literally on the sidelines of the dais awaiting a word or a gesture of recognition from Minister Louis Farrakhan. The latter group was even reduced to negotiating on the spot with Minister Farrakhan's staff for what looked like a last minute assignment for a short moment of airtime. They were given their minute at the mike and had to be content with one spokesperson while the others stood behind him as something of an "amen chorus." It was an amazing reversal of popular leadership fortunes. It appeared as though the historically uparallelled success of the Million Man March caught them all off-guard. Despite their decades of experience with Black nationalism and social activism, their political analyses had underestimated the spiritual and psychological needs of African American men to bear witness to their collective condition. They missed also the power of Minister Louis Farrakhan in his personal transformation as a leader for more than the members of

---

[68] Lincoln, C.E., *Race Religion and the Continuing American Dilemma*. (NY: Hill and Wang, 1984)

the Nation of Islam. Indeed, his speech that day referenced more Biblical than Koranic Scripture.

Whether it was the well-publicized disdain for Minister Farrakhan shown by the liberal establishment and the American Jewish community, the alleged sexual harassment scandal leading to Million Man March co-convener Ben Chavis' fall from grace as N.A.A.C.P. president and "one of their own", or their own insulation within comfortably middle class lifestyles, the miscalculation of many Black Christian leaders was painfully obvious. More importantly, the Million Man March, in the near term, raised far more questions about the state of Black America than it provided answers. It was particularly poignant to watch an African American woman, Mrs. Rosa Parks, receive the warmest welcome and intense applause by Black men of all ages. Farrakhan and Chavis succeeded in bringing more diversely Black men to Washington than Martin Luther King brought with a decidedly broader appeal, to an integrated audience, in a more racially segregated society.

A far greater array of ideologically, socioeconomically and religiously diverse African American men arrived in Washington this year than had been witnessed heretofore by the American public. For many, it was an awesome spectacle in every multifarious sense of the word. For Black religious leadership, there was an unmistakable changing of the vanguard. The question for our purposes is whether this is a bona fide paradigmatic shift which will mesh with the new realities of cross-cultural, socio-economic and gender empowerment being sought nationally and internationally by a broader range of groups. Any assessment of its genuine quality as a paradigmatic shift must consider the reality that Islamic orthodoxy is theologically conservative even if articulated as socially progressive in its African American expression. Prescribed Islamic roles for women, clerics and interactions with non-believers mirrors the conservative Christian tradition in terms of its social implications. Yet, Islam offers a distinctive theological brotherhood as a global religion rooted in national and cultural contexts where the Western tradition is generally considered marginal, if not outright anathema.

TOWARD AN EMERGING PARADIGM FOR THE SOCIAL CONTEXT OF BLACK
RELIGIOUS LEADERSHIP

Regrettably, it has not been possible to address the full complexity of
Black religious leadership. Glaring omissions from this chapter are the unique
struggles of Black women in the pulpit and the parish of religious history, Black
pastors of predominantly white congregations, and the experiences of Black Jews.
Admitted also is the myopic nature of this chapter due to the limited background
of its author with respect to African American religious history. The intention has
been to initiate a synthesis of research on group dynamics and traditional
leadership theory with the subject of Black religious leadership. Therefore, this
chapter must be understood as more of an exploration of paradox at the interface
of research paradigms in psychology, leadership and Black Studies rather than an
in-depth exposition of any one of these areas of inquiry.

Thomas Kuhn once posited that the accumulation of knowledge requires a
paradigmatic shift.[69] We believe that broad and significant social change
represents a similar shift. We feel equally emphatic that such a shift is presently in
process as new technologies and and a new global power arrangement occurs
amongst nation-states and multinational corporations jockeying for strategic
influence in an evershrinking world. In this context, static notions of leadership
are no longer useful for capturing the critical dimensions of this global
paradigmatic shift within any cultural context. The traditional models of
leadership logically represent an outmoded paradigm predicated upon a particular
model of U.S. hegemony in global affairs.

Since the days of Mary Parker Follet, the literature concerning leadership
in the North American, European context has focused upon the dissuasion of
popular opinion from the notion that aggression is the hallmark of leadership.[70]
Even so, the behavioral realities of achieving and mantaining global leadership in
various significant arenas may have betrayed these attempts. From several new
realities, leadership theory is beginning to transcend its cultural roots and
transform for more of what Jamake Highwater called a "multiversal" (as opposed

---

[69] Kuhn, Thomas, *The Structure of. Scientific Revolutions* (Chicago: Univ. of Chicago Press,
1984), p. 39.
[70] Graham, Pauline (ed.), *Mary Parker Follett—Prophet of Management: A Celebration of
Writings from the 1920s* (Boston: Harvard Business School Press, 1995).

to "universal") approach to social influence and effective interactions. Emerging areas of research are "symbolic action", "reciprocal interaction" and "interactional psychology."[71] Research on the inherent efficiency of quality leadership rather than control models of management[72], multiple leader roles[73], or "habits"[74], and identity-group behavior differences in leadership[75], and the retraining of privileged castes' perceptions[76] have all surfaced as important areas recently.

Ironically, in the context of empowered work teams, networked organizations with "metastructures" emerging routinely, the writings of Robert K. Greenleaf on "servant leadership" are being rediscovered from the 1970s. [77] Greenleaf stressed service to others, personal development and shared decision-making from a valuing of human differences. These values are directly aligned with new organizational goals for empowerment, total quality management (TQM) and participatory managment in an increasingly global context. They mesh also with the very different values of cultures beyond the male ethos and the North American social context and define well the leaders new role. In fact, they are the hallmarks of a traditional Black religious leadership largely omitted from the increasingly obsolete leadership paradigm.

SUMMARY

The very name African American connotes the cultural embbedness of Africans within the social context of the Americas which are not their indigenous homelands. Their fate is linked almost inextricably to the circumstances of their

---

[71] Griffin, Skivington & Moorhead, "Symbolic and International Perspectives on Leadership: An Integrative Framework", *Human Relations*, 1987, Vol. 40 No. 4, pp. 199-218.

[72] Price, F., "Out of Bedlam: The New Philosophy of Management by Quality Leadership". *International Journal of Quality and Reliability Management*, 1987, Vol. 4, Issue 2, pp. 63-73.

[73] Jaridan & Dastmalchian in *Journal of Applied Behavioral Studies*, 1993, Vol 29, No. 3 pp. 328-342.

[74] Covey, S., *Seven Habits of Highly Effective People.*, (New York: Simon and Schuster, 1989), *Journal of Applied Behavioral Studies*, Vol. 23, Issue 4, Pp. 525-541.

[75] Hearn, J. and Parkin, W. "Women, Men and Leadership: A Critical Review of Assumptions, Practices and Change in the Industrialized Nations", *International Studies of Management and Organization*, 1986, Vol 16, Iss 3/4, pp. 33-60; Renshaw, J.R., "Women in Management in the Pacific Islands: Exploring Pacific Stereotypes", *International Studies of Management and Organization* . Fall/Winter 1986-87, Vol 16, Issue 3/4, pp. 152-173.

[76] Simmons, M., "Creating New Men's Leadership: Developing A Theory and Practice", *Equal Opportunities International*, 1989. Vol 8, Issue 1, pp. 16-20.

[77] Javidan & Dastmalchian, 1993; Lee & Zemke, "Rethinking the Rush to Team Up", *Training*, 1993. Vol. 30, Issue 11, pp. 55-61.

geographical, social, cultural, economic and political contexts. This entwining of destinies creates interesting complexities for leaders of historically oppressed groups. It also informs the religious experiences of those groups in fascinating ways. Embedded in circumstances that have not been self-determined, paradox, contradiction, and dependence define their realities. Leaders in such contexts are forged by forces of which they, themselves, may be unaware.

We have presented evidence here that Black religious leaders, embedded within the American experience, require their own paradigmatic shift for a style and model of leadership befitting a new age of material uncertainty, technological transformation and spiritual promise. From psychological theories that have omitted Black worldviews and values, to global realities and technological innovations that require more interaction amongst increasingly diverse identity groups, leadership of any nature is poised for new challenges. Black religious leaders must recognize and correct any reactionary attitudes and behaviors engendered by the embeddedness of themselves and their core constituencies as victims, belligerents or beneficiaries of a now obsolete status quo within the United States and the broader international community. Living the paradox of their roles as followers, pastors and prophets is expected only to intensify as global complexity further enmeshes the panoply of cultures, ideologies and worldviews.

What is required more than ever by Black religious leaders is a priestly function of clear analyses, founded on the rudiments of their faiths and mindful of the paradoxical interplay of intrapersonal, interpersonal, group, intergroup and interorganizational dynamics in which they and their peoples are embedded. A systems view of the African American experience and ethos is imperative due to a prevailing sociocultural incentive to fragment segments and roles for cultural consistency with external realities or for mere convenience. To understand the interplay of intragroup dynamics in spiritual, material, political, cultural and social dimensions is to place one's finger on the pulse of the African American *elan vital*. This requires a keen sense of history and a willingness to reclaim aspects of an African heritage that have been eschewed and alienated in favor of socio-political satisficing within an oppressive social superstructure. Also required is a willingness and a capacity to discard behaviors, beliefs and assumptions that are culturally inconsistent, representing what Claude McKay once described as "incongruous feathers, awkwardly stuck on."

This entails a revisitation of even the most noble of certainties which have served as guideposts for the social functions of Black religious leadership. The most immediate and difficult of these is the well-worn presumption of a messianic moral destiny on behalf of African Americans. African American ethnic and racial chauvinism in the midst of racism is a difficult characteristic to explicate, precisely because it emerges from a healthy impetus to preserve group self-esteem. However, it can lead easily to the self-centered opposition to input from other racial, cultural or socioeconomic groups whose experiences would be of immense benefit to Black religious leaders today. In a sense, this notion of moral destiny imposes a sort of "groupthink" upon African Americans which well might lead to the dangerous insulation of that group. In such instances, collective psychological defensive routines are more powerful and probable in their protection of a fantasized group sanctity. In a new reality of intercultural exchange and a broader sense of ecumenism, this would be manifestly counterproductive.

Limitations attendant to organizing on the basis of racial victimization, notions of male superiority rationalized on the basis of narrow cultural nationalism or borrowed with "wanna be" motives, economic enrichment to national standards irrespective of global consumption patterns pursuant of Western privilege, or narrow religious dogma eschewing an inescapable ecumenism, also require such priestly discernment. These dynamic realities must be explicated and assessed from a perspective of stewardship, faith and global fellowship. Only then might Black religious leaders be born again, remaining true to their calling, and know when, where and how to invoke their appropriate roles as pastors, prophets and followers of their faithful peoples for a greater wholeness in the future.

CHAPTER II

NOTES ON THE TYPOLOGIES AND POLITICAL STYLES OF BLACK LEADERS IN
AMERICA.

NANNETTA DURNELL
FLORIDA ATLANTIC UNIVERSITY

THE MINISTER

Throughout history, the black church has been one of the most effective means of mobilization and communication in the black community. Morris describes in The *Politics of Black America*, how the church was one of the few institutions exclusively under black leadership and control, and capable of reaching large audiences.[1] Young points out, in *Major Black Religious Leaders*, that black religious leaders and the black church have played a major role in the quest for the freedom and liberation of blacks in America.[2]

Traditionally, Hamilton explains, the black preacher is without question, the one spokesperson for his people with the longest tenure of leadership.[3] Childs discusses in *The Political Black Minister*, how in the 1960s, black preachers began using their leadership and pulpits for "political action" to assist blacks during the Civil Rights Movement—for the black preacher had in his presence people who would respond to him and could spread the word immediately.[4]

Harris describes in *Black Ministers and Laity in Urban Church*, how ministers opened their churches to mass meetings and voter registration drives, and preached sermons that combined the themes of personal redemption through Christ with social justice and protest.[5]

---

[1] Milton Morris, *The Politics of Black America* (New York: Harper and Row Publishers, 1975).

[2] Henry Young, *Major Black Religious Leaders Since 1940* (Nashville: The Parthenon Press, 1979).

[3] Charles Hamilton, *The Black Preacher in America* (New York: William Morrow and Company, Inc., 1972).

[4] John Childs, *The Political Black Minister: A Study in Afro-American Politics and Religion* (Boston: G.K. Hall and Co., 1980).

[5] James Harris, *Black Ministers and Laity in the Urban Church: An Analysis of Political and Social Expectations* (New York: New York University Press, 1987).

Geschwender reports, in *The Black Revolt*, ministers frequently involved their congregations in "social-action" programs. For example, it was not unusual for pastors to have their members support boycotts, voting drives, etc.[6] Witvliet describes in *The Way of the Black Messiah*, that the preachers relied solely on the pulpits to "call on" and "call off" a campaign. For example, ministers met and chose a particular company to boycott; unless or until the company agreed to change its employment policies and hire and promote blacks.[7]

In *The Black Preacher in America*, Hamilton gives a detailed overview of the three distinct types of "political activism" which defines the role of the black preacher in politics: church-based, community-based, and the church-based programmatic. According to Hamilton, the "church-based" minister is influential in the community, town, or city by virtue of being a leader of a rather large congregation.[8] This minister is frequently consulted by the public and private decision-makers of the community (i.e., those in City Hall or the Chamber of Commerce).

The author points out that the politics for this preacher is not a full-time or continuous activity. These preachers may lend their name and support to a particular civil rights cause, but they describe themselves as "simply ministers, not politicians." In fact, "church-based" ministers view their mission as one of "human rights," not politics; viewing politics as basically a dirty business, where people have to make compromises and deals.[9]

The second type of politically involved minister is the "community-based" local activist. Hamilton describes how this preacher takes an active part in local electoral politics, as well as, in mass oriented pressure group politics.[10] This minister may run for office or serve as the leader of a political action group. The church is where these individuals got their start as community-oriented people, but their church office is physically "separated" from their political headquarters.[11]

---

[6] James Geschwender, *Black Revolt: The Civil Rights Movement, Ghetto Uprisings, and Separatism* (New Jersey: Prentice-Hall, Inc., 1971).

[7] Theo Witvliet, *The Way of the Black Messiah: The Hermeneutical Challenge of Black Theology as a Theology of Liberation* (Illinois: Meyer Stone Books, 1987).

[8] Charles Hamilton, *The Black Preacher in America* (New York: William Morrow and Company, Inc., 1972).

[9] Ibid.

[10] Ibid.

[11] Ibid.

Hamilton notes how these ministers are viewed as more "militant" than the "church-based" type, and are less likely to shy away from overt confrontation politics. In fact, if "community-based" ministers local activity becomes very successful or visible, they main gain national prominence. However, it is always understood that their base of support and operation is the particular community from which they come.[12]

One primary example of the "community-based" activist preacher is the Reverend Adam Clayton Powell.[13] Using the Abyssinian Baptist Church in Harlem as his base (with a congregation of more than 11,000), Powell was elected to city council and from there to a seat in the House of Representatives in 1944—a position he maintained until the mid-1960s.[14]

The third type of preacher activist is the individual who uses his church as a specific base to launch and conduct "civic programs." Hamilton identifies this preacher as the "church-based programmatic" activist. Unlike the first type, these preachers are much more public and mass oriented in their actions. Unlike the second type, these ministers might combine their church organization with a specific program of action.[15]

This minister's focus essentially is on organization through the church structure to achieve certain goals; mainly of an economic nature (i.e., jobs, better housing, better health care, and better educational facilities). Such an example would be the Reverend Dr. Martin Luther King, Jr. who was instrumental in several protest demonstrations in the 1950s and early 1960s.[16] In many instances these protest demonstrations were led by local preachers and conducted out of their church buildings which were used as headquarters.

Overall, the black church has been the vanguard of social, economic, and political activism in America. However, as Young points out, each type of black preacher has a unique and distinct conceptualization of the role of the black church in helping blacks achieve their freedom and self-actualization[17]. In

---

[12] Ibid.

[13] Ibid.

[14] Ibid.

[15] Ibid.

[16] Ibid.

[17] Henry Young, *Major Black Religious Leaders Since 1940* (Nashville: The Parthenon Press, 1979).

addition, each preacher defines their own level of protest, and the interrelatedness of the black church to the political, social, educational, economic, and cultural structures of society.

POLITICAL STYLES

Three political styles emerge from a study of black leadership—"the moderate," "the militant," and "the conservative." Wilson points out, that the modes of thinking, speaking, and acting that are characteristic of these styles can be described in the following manner:

(1) the nature of the issues confronting the leader and the values the leader brings to bear on them;

(2) the ends or goal the leader deems it appropriate to seek in the realm of civic action;

(3) the means the leader employs in seeking these ends;

(4) the motives, goals, and attributes of those whom the leader seen in the world about him/her.[18]

Based on the goals, tactics, and rhetoric listed above, the following examples and explanations will provide insight on the major typologies of black leadership in America.

THE CONSERVATIVE

In *An American Dilemma*, Myrdal classified black leaders in terms of "accommodation" and "protest." According to Myrdal "accommodation" or "conservatism" requires acceptance of the caste system; thus, leaders "lead" only in that context by seeking modifications in the life conditions of blacks that do not affect the caste system.[19]

In *Negro Leadership In The South*, Ladd reports that "conservatives" believe that the interests of blacks could best be served by adjusting to the caste system. To them, "accommodation" is regarded as the most practical policy. According to Ladd, conservatives try to alter the prevailing pattern of race

---

[18] James Wilson, *Negro Politics: The Search for Leadership*. New York: Free Press, 1960.
[19] Gunnar Myrdal, *An American Dilemma: The Negro Problem and Modern Democracy* (New York: Harper and Brothers Publishers, 1964).

relations by working within it and its demands. They seek the maximum benefits possible through channels considered legitimate by whites.[20]

Burgess describes in *Negro Leadership In A Southern City*, that the central identifying element of "conservative" leaders is their avoidance—in fact, their rejection—of "direct action" (i.e., boycotts, protest marches, sit-ins, mass protest meetings, and picketing). Instead, "conservative" leaders emphasize negotiations rather than going through barricaded. Because of their stand against "direct action," "conservatives" receive heavy criticism from "militant" leaders.[21]

In *Negro Leadership Class*, Thompson reports, that "conservatives" suggest it is impossible to know what the black masses want, since the community is seen as being sharply divided. Therefore, "conservatives" frequently make reference to common interests, common problems, and the importance of preserving good race relations, thus they do not bring sharp departures from the prevailing pattern of race relations.[22] For the most part, Thompson posits, that "conservatives" no longer command a voice in decision making. They now lead by providing a financial support or occasionally by lending a prestigeful name to a special project.[23]

THE MILITANT

The "militant" or "protest" style is often clearly revealed in the extent to which the leader sees the issues confronting the race and the community. Paris describes in *Black Leaders In Conflict*, that for the "militant," issues tend to be seen in "simplified" terms; where many issues are brought together or agglomerated into a "single" general issue, rather than in parts. With this tendency to "agglomerate issues," rather than to deal with them singularly, the "militant" will present a maximum number of demands to a public agency for solutions.[24]

According to Smith in *Black Leadership: A Survey of Theory and Research*, the central identifying element of "militants" is their emphasis on "direct action." These "militants" are generally envisioned as young men in their

---

[20] Everett Ladd, *Negro Political Leadership in the South* (New York: Cornell University Press, 1966).

[21] Ibid.

[22] Daniel Thompson, *The Negro Leadership Class*. New Jersey: Prentice-Hall, Inc., 1963).

[23] Ibid.

[24] Peter Paris, *Black Leaders in Conflict* (Kentucky: Westminster John Knox Press, 1979).

late twenties and thirties. These leaders are characterized as brash, boisterous, exhibitionistic, and constantly professing impatience with the rate of change.[25]

Fax assesses, in *Contemporary Black Leaders*, that "militants" are more outspoken in the sense that their rhetoric poses racial controversy firmly, clearly, and unavoidably.[26] Geschwender describes in *The Black Revolt*, how their rhetoric frequently serves to dramatize existing racial injustices, and heighten the tension present in racial controversies.[27] The "militant" avoids neutral or conciliatory words, therefore Geschwender adds, any black American who speaks forthrightly and forcefully against racial injustice would be placed in this category.[28]

Holden notes, in *The Politics of the Black Nation*, that the "militant" leader is not one who has achieved something in other areas of life, nor is the "militant" one who merely has a general favorable civic reputation; however, this individual assumes a posture of "protest" and "agitation." Holden describes, how this "protest" leadership involves a rejection of the caste system, and the slower procedures of arbitration and litigation. Instead, "militants" stress that they consider "direct action" an integral part of their program to realize the most vital political objectives of blacks.[29]

According to Brisbane in *The Black Vanguard*, boycotts, protest marches, sit-ins, mass protest meetings, picketing, etc., have become the trademark of the "militant" style of black leadership. And Brisbane notes, since they identify with the suppressed black masses, many "militant" leaders support direct actions because it provides a vehicle for contact and involvement with the masses of black citizens.[30]

---

[25] Robert Smith, *Black Leadership: A Survey of Theory and Research* (Washington, D.C.: Institute for Urban Affairs and Research, 1983).

[26] Elton Fax, *Contemporary Black Leaders* (New York: Dodd, Mead and Company, 1970).

[27] James Geschwender, *Black Revolt: The Civil Rights Movement, Ghetto Uprisings. and Separatism* (New Jersey: Prentice-Hall, Inc., 1971).

[28] Ibid.

[29] Matthew Holden, *The Politics of the Black Nation* (New York: Chandler Publishing Company, 1973).

[30] Robert Brisbane, *The Black Vanguard: Origins of the Negro Social Revolution: 1900-1960* (Valley Forge: Judson Press, 1970).

THE MODERATE

More than either the "conservative" or the "militant" style, the "moderate" style depends upon a level of political involvement. Smith points out, that in contrast to the "militant" style, the "moderate" provides reasons for not taking direct action.[31] Thompson notes, that the "moderate" or "bargainers" perceives race and community issues as ones to which there are no easy solutions, if there are indeed solutions at all.[32] The "moderate" see issues as "complex" and resist agglomerating them into omnibus problems.

"Moderate" leaders are classified as "functional leaders," Thompson explains, and give strong moral and financial support to protest activities. However, "moderate" leaders are more active in the community than the "conservative" leader. Walton describes in *Black Political Parties*, that with the diminishing influence of the "conservative" leadership, many white leaders turn to "moderates" in their search for "official spokesmen." The methods of the "moderates" put whites less on the defensive; for their subtler approach and less strident tones are easier to deal with than the "militants."[33]

To sum, black leadership typologies appear to be based on a composite of goals, tactics, and rhetoric. The categorization of black leaders have basically been structured in terms of (a) acceptance or rejection of the extant race system, (b) style or method of opposition to the extant race system, and (c) style or method of race advancement activity.

For the most part, black leaders in America are classified as either "conservative," "militant," or "moderate." If one is "conservative," that individual is said to be "accommodating" and therefore, "legitimate." If the individual is "moderate," that individual is said to be "responsible" and therefore, "acceptable."

---

[31] Robert Smith, *Black Leadership: A Survey of Theory and Research* (Washington, D.C.: Institute for Urban Affairs and Research, 1983).

[32] Daniel Thompson, *The Negro Leadership Class*. New Jersey: Prentice-Hall, Inc., 1963).

[33] Hanes Walton, *Black Political Parties* (New York: The Free Press, 1972).

And if one is "militant," that individual is said to be "irresponsible" and bears "close watching."[34]

---

[34] Robert Smith, *Black Leadership: A Survey of Theory and Research* (Washington, D.C.: Institute for Urban Affairs and Research, 1983).

CHAPTER III

"SENDING UP SOME TIMBER: ELDERLY SLAVES AND RELIGIOUS LEADERSHIP IN THE
ANTEBELLUM SLAVE COMMUNITY"

STACEY K. CLOSE
EASTERN CONNECTICUT STATE UNIVERSITY

Henry's Hymn
Come ye that love the Lord
And let your joys be known
Join in a song of sweet accord
And thus surround the throne
Let those refuse to sing
Who never Knew the Lord
But servants of the heavenly king
should speak their joys abroad
The God that rules on high
And all the earth surveys
He rides upon the storm sky
And calms the roaling sea.[1]

The baptist hymnal used for devotional ceremonies during the antebellum
period contained the above hymn, "Come Ye That Love The Lord." This hymn
and others reverberated in common meter and short meter from churches in the
South. Such hymns sent up timbers of hope and joy for enslaved people. Sending
up timber was the process by which enslaved people prepared themselves for the
afterlife. The hymns echoed the powerful importance of an omnipotent God in the
lives of enslaved people. Consequently, African American churchgoers sang such
hymns with tremendous pride. Slave owners sometimes recognized such fondness
in their records. Shirley Jackson ("Black Slave Drivers") argued that the recording
of the Henry's favorite hymn was a testimony to the fondness the slave owning

---

[1] Shirley M. Jackson, "Black Slave Drivers in the Southern United States" (Ph.D. diss.: Bowling
Green State University, 1977), 134.

Pettigrew Family had for their old driver.[2] Indeed, it may have been; however, the hymn is also a powerful testament to Henry's religious beliefs.

Along with the family, religion proved to be a major stabilizing factor for enslaved people in the "Old South." Religion led by African Americans offered a challenge to that proposed by slave owners. A portion of that challenge can be found in the Africanness of religion among the enslaved community. In the traditional African religions, the living have a direct link to the dead through the spirits of the ancestors. The old people hold a special role because they are viewed as approaching the time of this spiritual power sooner than others. Floyd M. Wylie argues that "a case could be made for the dropping away of the cultural traditions were it not for the fact that young Africans from their earliest days were inculcated with these values" about ancestors.[3]

---

[2] Ibid.

[3] Floyd M. Wylie, "Attitudes Toward Aging and the Aged Among Black Americans: Some Historical Perspectives," *Aging and Human Development*, (1971), 68; W. Andrew Achenbaum, *Old Age in the New Land* (Baltimore: Johns Hopkins University Press, 1978), 2-3, 193; Pollard, 229; Ibid;Achenbaum, 2-3; see also Southern Historical Collection, Kelvin Grove Plantation Book, Chapel Hill: University of North Carolina; U.B. Phillips, *American Negro Slavery* (Gloucester, Massachusetts: Peter Smith, 1959), 360; Deborah White, *Ar'n't I A Woman?* (New York: W.W. Norton, 1985),130; see also Southern Historical Collection, James Hamilton Couper Papers, Chapel Hill: University of North Carolina; Ibid., Kelvin Grove Plantation Book, Ibid.; Ibid., Kollock Plantation Book, Ibid.; Manuscripts Department University of Virginia Library, Huger Family Papers, Charlottesville: University of Virginia, The plantation listings make reference to the ages of several elderly female slaves on the Huger Plantation near Savannah in 1860 and 1861. The Huger Plantation at Murry Hill contained 87 slaves, 37 males and 50 females. No men were listed in a separate category as old; however, Phillis, Sabrina, Lucy, and Linda were listed as old women. In 1861, Hester is listed as Old Hester, who works in the house. In addition, Sally, Judy, Charlotte, and Granny Phillis have been added to Huger's list of old women making the total of elderly women at 8. Southerners, both white and African American, had some concept of elderly. Some people used the terms aunt and uncle to mean elderly. However, a definition of elderly, even during the antebellum period, was not absolutely clear. W. Andrew Achenbaum stated in *Old Age in the New Land* (1978) that some people considered the elderly to be those people of 50 years of age or older, while others considered those people 60 years of age or older as elderly. In "Aging and Slavery: A Gerontological Perspective," Pollard argued that there are certain inherent problems in defining old age" for the purpose of determining attitudes. Pollard held that "old age defied the magical significance that we today attach to the 65th birthday." For purpose of this study, elderly slaves are those 50 years of age or older. After the slave had reached the age of 50, masters believed the work capacity and monetary value of the slave would decline so drastically that in a short time the worker would be valueless as far as the slave market was concerned. In *Ar'n't I A Woman?*, Deborah G. White stated that women referred to as aunt or granny were "either middle aged or elderly but odds were that they had also had children and some grannies were past childbearing." Slave narratives, autobiographies, and plantation records often make no mention of the actual age of the old slaves; however, they do identify elderly slaves by using such terms as "old," "aged," and "bent."

The elderly were in all likelihood no more religious than other slaves; however, the acquiescence of younger people to the leadership of older, experienced people resulted because of cultural traditions. Religious leadership in the slave quarters provided elderly slaves with their greatest opportunity for influence over other slaves. It was often from the grandparents that children acquired their religious beliefs. Younger enslaved people respected the aged for being old as well as for being religious leaders. Elderly enslaved men and women proved pivotal in sustaining the religious lives of people in the enslaved community.

The African Americans of the antebellum South religiously practiced not only Christianity but also conjuring and the Muslim faith. This Christianity was an African American form of Christianity. Slave owners' version of Christianity involved using religion to control enslaved people. While some owners were effective in establishing Christianity as a controlling entity, such efforts in regards to conjuring did not materialize quite as often. Conjuring came from the Yoruba of Africa, and the older slaves used it to control and influence younger slaves. Conjuring was used by the "old root doctors" to stop masters from whipping slaves and to bring luck, good or bad.

The white southerners often made the assertions that they were pious Christians. Such individuals were quite approving of African American preachers, some of whom were elderly. On Pierce Butler's Georgia plantation, Old Cooper London served as an influential Christian leader in the enslaved community. London taught the African American community the rights and wrongs in a religious sense. In moments of grief, London provided words of comfort for bereaved family members of Shadrach. London eulogized Shadrach (a slave) with remarks from the American Episcopalian prayer book as well as adding several extemporaneous phrases of his own. London proved to be an acceptable religious leader to members of the African American community along with Butler and overseer, Roswell King. On an Alabama plantation, the Methodist preacher was the slave Uncle Sam. In a building near his house, Uncle Sam would gather all the children on Sunday morning to teach them their duty to God and man.[4] Eliza Frances Andrews of Georgia recalled:

---

[4] Katherine M.Jones, *The Plantation South* (Indianapolis: The Bobbs-Merrill Co., 1957), 268; Frances Kemble, *Journal of a Residence on a Georgian Plantation* (New York: Alfred A. Knopf,

Old Uncle Lewis, the old gray haired slave who has done nothing
for years but live at his ease, was coddled and believed in by the
whole family as its religious leader on the plantation. The children
called him not Uncle Lewis but Uncle as if he had really been kin
to them. Uncle Alex (Andrew's Uncle) had such faith in him that
during his last illness he would send for the old man to talk and
pray with him... A special place was always reserved for him at
family prayer and Uncle Lewis was often called upon to lead
devotions. I wasbrought up with a firm belief in him as in the Bible
itself.[5]

Ex-slave Katie Dudley Baumont also related that elderly male slaves were
important in religious life. The slave owner of Baumont allowed the enslaved
community to establish a church of their own. Baumont recalled that "We had a
church about three quarters of a mile down the road." Africanness existed in the
religion of enslaved people, African people challenged mainstream southern
religion. Remarkably, the challenge emerged from within a group of uneducated
people. Much of what the leaders learned had to be memorized over the years.
Reverend William Spotswood White remembered Old Uncle Jack as the pious
Christian leader in Virginia. Jack could not read or write; yet his knowledge of
religious matters resulted from his conversing and sharing his views with other
knowledgeable persons.[6]

The Christianity in the slave community developed into an African
American version of Christianity. The services contained call and response music
and the ring shout, which were brought over from Africa. John Blassingame
reports that a great portion of the religious music, methods, scale, dancing, patting
of feet, clapping of hands, and pantomiming came from Africa.[7] "Call and
response was vital to the progression of the sermon," the spirit uplifted the
congregation to ecstatic response to sermons.[8] Slaves strongly related to the
teachings in the Old Testament, which they had often heard. They connected their

---

1961), 190-91; Frederick Douglass, *Life and Times of Frederick Douglass* (Hartford: Connecticut
Park Publishing Company, 1881), 90-92.
[5] Eliza Frances Andrews, *The War Time Journal of a Georgia Girl 1864-65* (New York: D.
Appleton and Company, 1961), 202.
[6] William Spotswood White, *The African Preacher: An Authentic Narrative* (Philadelphia:
Presbyterian Board of Education, 1849), 47.
[7] John Blassingame, *Slave Community* (New York: Oxford University Press, 1979), 33.
[8] Ibid., 237.

station in life to that of the Israelites during the times of Moses.[9] This belief gave African American slaves a feeling that freedom would one day succeed. Moses Grandy recalled that during his days as a slave in North Carolina, aged slaves and others would often go out into the rain and raise their hands to the heavens during violent rainstorms, while whites hovered beneath the sheets to be safe from the lightning.[10]

The African American version of religion not only provided an avenue to pray for freedom, it also granted slaves religious freedom. Erskine Clarke says in *Wrestlin' Jacob* that the slaves of Charles Colock Jones accepted Christianity as a buffer against the use of guards, guns, and bayonets.[11] Frederick Douglass received religious advice from Uncle Charles Lawson. Lawson served as his trusted counselor, and unknown to his master he even predicted that Douglass had some special calling.

The slave preacher, regardless of age, had to be sure not to preach a gospel of freedom that whites might overhear. Sarah Ford (ex-slave) reported that Uncle Lew spoke to an audience about unity and equality of whites and blacks. The owner moved Uncle Lew into the fields because of his statements.[12] An old preacher, Uncle Tom Ewing, once spoke the words "freed indeed, free from work, free from the white folks, free from everything" in the presence of his owner and found himself threatened with not being allowed to preach. Consequently, Tom never used the words again.[13]

Elderly religious leaders also found other areas in which their knowledge of religious matters might benefit the plantation economy. The ritual elder, Leonard Haynes (originally from Abodoo on the Gold Coast of Ghana) used his religious power to ensure bountiful crops. During planting and harvest periods, Haynes "performed a religious dance of the first fruit," a ritual that insured

---

[9] Albert J.Raboteau, *Slave Religion* (Oxford: Oxford University Press, 1978), 66-67; Blassingame, 22, 138.

[10] James Oakes, *The Ruling Race* (New York: Vintage Books, 1983), 116.

[11] Erskine Clarke, *Wrestlin' Jacob: A Portrait of Religion in the Old South* (Atlanta: John Knox Press, 1979), 58.

[12] Raboteau, 232.

[13] Ibid.

excellent crops for the plantation.[14] Haynes ritual masked those found on the African continent.

There was also a Muslim religious influence among the slaves. A planter on the Georgia coast had a head man, Bu Allah, who was described as being an African of superior intelligence and character. Bu Allah reared his children in the Muslim faith. Three times a day, he would spread his sheepskin prayer rug to the East and pray to Allah. Bu Allah lived to be a very old man and when buried, his Koran and prayer rug were buried along with him. On a visit to the Hopeton plantation, Sir Charles Lyell met Old Tom, an African of Foulah origin who still adhered to his Muslim religion. Tom was not as influential religiously as Bu Allah because most of his offspring declined the Muslim faith and adopted Christianity.[15]

Conjuring was a religion to slaves, and the conjurer held a special role in the slave community. Religion defined in this paper is the belief in supernatural or superhuman forces. Conjuring certainly fits within this definition, even though some slaves considered it superstition. Conjurers were part of a group of significant others, who, unknown to the master, commanded respect in the slave community. Conjurer's had "distinct features such as 'red eyes and 'blue gums,' unusual dress, and the accoutrements of the trade—a crooked cane, charms, and conjure bag ...."[16] Conjuring involved using roots or incantations to bring harm or good luck to slaves down in the quarters. As noted in the *American Slave*, "the lore of conjure men whom negroes looked up to and respected and feared as the equivalent of witches, wizards, and magicians came from African forefathers."[17] Old slave conjurers and persons with medical expertise passed their knowledge down to younger slaves, and not always exclusively to males. Gus Smith remembered that his grandfather passed his knowledge on to one of Smith's

---

[14] William Charles Suttles, Jr., "A Trace of Soul: The Religion of Negro Slaves on the Plantations of North America" (Ph.D. diss.: Univ. of Michigan, 1979), 49.

[15] Caroline Couper Lovell, *Golden Isles* (Boston: Little, Brown, and Company, 1932), 103-4; Sir Charles Lyell, *A Second Visit to the United States of North America* (London: John Murray, 1850), 359.

[16] Ibid., 276.

[17] Rawick, ed., *The American Slave: The Georgia Narratives* (Greenwood, Ct.: Westport Publishing, vol. 3, suppl. series part 1), 232.

female relatives.[18] James Parker's grandfather not only taught him to read but gave him systematic religious instruction in the signs.[19]

Conjuring or fortune telling strongly influenced the slave community. It provided a source of protection beyond the family. One old slave promised that his potions would provide protection from the master's whippings. The charm did not always work. Julia Henderson of Augusta, Georgia, remembered that "old hoodoo man promised no whippings for slaves who chewed on a piece of root, his conjuring failed and as a result he received a good cursing from a slave by the name of Tom for its failure."[20]

Henry Bibb had somewhat better results in his negotiations with an old conjurer to get immunity from being flogged: "It worked the first occasion that he left the plantation without permission. On the second, occasion he was flogged by his master."[21] Bibb had not learned his lesson about conjuring, so he decided to go to another conjurer. This old conjurer told him that the other slave was a quack and if Bibb paid him money, the old man would tell him how to keep from being flogged. Even with the new potion, Bibb was treated no better.[22]

Nicey Kinney, an ex-slave from Georgia, believed that an old witch-man conjured her into marrying Jordan Jackson. A fortune teller told her how the conjuring was done. Kinney said that she preferred not to marry Jordan: "he could not get me to pay attention to him, so he went and got a conjure man to put a spell on me."[23]

An excellent example of the influence that old conjurers wielded is provided by Ellen Belts. Belts recalled that an old man had cursed a group of children who had thrown rocks at him along the road. The man warned a young boy to cease or he would be cursed with death. Kinney and her family members were horrified the next morning as the boy died upon the kitchen floor. Kinney recalled that "nobody ever bother that old man no more, for he sure lay an evil finger on you."[24]

---

[18] Norman Yetman, ed., *Voices from Slavery* (New York: Holt Rinehart and Winston, 1970), 287.

[19] Thomas L. Webber, *Deep Like Rivers* (New York: W.W. Norton Co., 1978), 175.

[20] Rawick, ed., *The American Slave: The Georgia Narratives* (vol. 3, suppl. series part 1), 75.

[21] Gilbert Osofsky, ed., *Puttin' On Ole Massa* (New York: Arno Press, 1969), 70-1.

[22] Ibid., 71.

[23] B.A. Botkin, ed., *Lay My Burden Down* (chicago: University of Chicago Press, 1958), 83.

[24] Ibid., 128.

Frank, a seventy year old fortune teller, resided on the plantation where the fugitive William Wells Brown lived during his enslavement. Uncle Frank was a favorite with the young ladies, who would flock to him in great numbers to get their fortunes told.[25] Although Brown says that he was not a believer in soothsaying, he was at a loss to know how so many of Uncle Frank's predictions came true. Most important to Brown was the fact that his eventual freedom was among the conjurer's many predictions that came about. Brown states that this alone was worth the twenty-five cents he paid the old man.[26]

One old conjurer was believed by ex-slave William Adams to have the power to pass his hands over a wound and heal the wound. The old man miraculously healed a deep cut on a mule's leg. "He came over and passed his hand over the cut. Before long, the bleeding stopped ...."[27]

In some cases, the old conjurers wielded a certain amount of influence over masters. For example, one slaveholder overheard an old conjurer predicting the misfortune that was supposedly to befall an overseer. The overseer had angered the old man in some way, and because of this the old man was going to seek his revenge by riding the back of the overseer. The slaveholder states that "the old man was a conjurer and his wife was a witch. One night the conjurer touched his son with a stick and together they went to ride the backs of the overseer and his son."[28]

Old female slaves also proved quite adept at swaying religious practices in the slave community. On the Sea Islands in 1864, Laura Towne encountered Maum Katie, an African woman, who remembered worshipping her own gods in Africa. Over a century old, she was a spiritual mother, a fortune teller, prophetess, and a woman of tremendous influence over other slaves.[29] "The interpretation of dreams and strange occurrences brought the real world closer to the supernatural realm and offered spiritual guidance to the ill, the troubled, and the lovelorn."[30]

---

[25] Osofsky, ed., *Puttin' On Ole Massa*, 215.

[26] Ibid.

[27] Botkin, ed., 37.

[28] Blassingame, 113.

[29] *Letters and Diary of Laura M. Towne, 1862-1884*, ed. Rupert S. Holland (Cambridge, Mass.: Riverside Press, 1912), 144-45.

[30] Finkelman, ed., *Articles on American Slavery: Women and the Family in Slavery* (New York: Garland Publishing, Inc., 1989), 217.

Although Katie worked on the plantation for a number of years, she still adhered to cherished beliefs from Africa. In this way, Katie resisted in part the culture of her owner. On the Whitehall Plantation of Richard James Arnold, Mum Kate led and influenced the plantation slaves with her ability to recall with great precision biblical lessons from the text of the plantation minister.[31] At the Beaufort Church in South Carolina, elders both male and female exercised religious control over other slaves by inspecting not only reports of death but also the propensity of members of society to backslide.

Although many of the slave preachers were men, the women both old and young were the primary conveyers of spirit possession and the ecstatic Christian religion of the slave community. The female slaves were often the first members of the slave community to shout and praise God.[32] In *Voices from Slavery*, an ex-slave indicated that his "grandmother was a powerful Christian woman, and she did love to sing and shout." The master had her locked up in the loom room because the grandmother would begin shouting so loud and make so much noise that people in the church could not hear the minister. Later, the woman would "wander off from de gallery and go downstairs and try to go down to de white folkses aisles." This behavior continued, and the owner could never stop her from shouting and wandering around the meeting house, after she became aged.[33]

On numerous plantations, the enslaved population appointed old women who cared for children to teach the children their prayers, catechisms, and a few hymns in the evenings.[34] Women, particularly old women had a stronger propensity to practice their religion more openly than men.

Testimonial services emphasized the power of old enslaved women within the Christian faith on other members of the slave quarters. Women usually led the slave community in this religious practice. "Religious testimony was so important

---

[31] Charles Hoffman and Tess Hoffman, *North by South: The Two Lives of Richard James Arnold* (Athens: The University of Georgia Press, 1988), 53.

[32] Margaret Washington Creel, *The Peculiar People: Slave Religion and Community-Culture Among the Gullahs* (New York and London: New York University Press, 1988), 231-32. The middle aged and elderly women were the practitioners and leaders of much of the spirit possession in the religion of the slave community.

[33] Norman R. Yetman, ed., 64.

[34] Albert Raboteau, *Slave Religion*, 176.

that slaves reduced prayers to formulas and taught them to young converts."[35] During these testimonial services, younger slaves learned from old women "old cherished ways of saying and doing things for the edification of their fellow negroes on the slave plantations of the United States."[36] African American women continued to lead most African American evangelical churches in testifying, even after slavery.

Such ecstatic behavior profoundly affected slave children. Some slave children believed that their grandmothers' prayers might produce freedom. Ex-slave Amanda Smith recalled hearing her grandmother pray that God would deliver her grandchildren from bondage. This charge for freedom came along with a desire for Smith and her siblings to have better masters and mistresses.[37]

Some elderly slave women resorted to using religion to gain control of a slave plantation from a white overseer. Old Sinda passed as prophetess among her fellow slaves on the Butler Plantation in Georgia. Sinda acquired so much authority over the rest of the slaves that her prediction of the end of the world became resistance that caused a halt to all work by slaves on the Butler Plantation. Her assertion took such a massive hold upon the African American population that the rice and cotton fields were threatened with an indefinite fallow because of this strike on the part of the workers. The overseer warned the rest of people that he believed that Sinda was mistaken in her prediction and if her prophecy proved false she would be punished. Nevertheless, King had no choice but to wait until the appointed time for the appearance of the prophecy because Sinda had greater influence than King over the rest of the workers during the time of her prophecy. Obviously, Sinda's prophecy failed to occur; consequently, King severely flogged her for causing upheaval on the plantation.[38]

Old Julie, a conjure woman, rivaled the mystical abilities of Sinda. Shortly after the Civil War, freedmen recounted the exploits of Julie. The freedmen

---

[35] Harry P. Owens, ed., *Perspectives and Irony in American Slavery*, John Blassingame, "Status and Social Structure in the Slave Community: Evidence from New Sources," (1976), 145.

[36] William Charles Suttles, Jr., "A Trace of Soul: The Religion of Negro Slaves on the Plantations" (Ph.D. diss.: University of Michigan, 1979), 44.

[37] Amanda Smith, *The Story of the Lord's Dealings with Mrs. Amanda Smith: An Autobiography*, (Chicago: Meyer & Brother, Publishers, 1893), 19-24, 27.

[38] Frances Ann Kemble, *Journal of Residence on a Georgian Plantation* (Chicago: Afro-Am Press, 1969), 84.

recalled that Julie caused much death and maiming on the plantation. As a result the owner responded by selling Old Julie. This sale proved quite difficult. Although the owner personally escorted Julie to a steamboat to carry her far from her home, witnesses reported that the old woman miraculously used her powers and forced the steamboat to reverse its course. To his chagrin, the plantation owner found the boat anchored the next morning at its previous point of exit. This momentous feat supposedly compelled the owner not to part with Julie.[39] The actions of Julie are extremely suspect; however, the fact that the slaves remembered her with such awe is a testament to the power of conjurering within the slave community. An ex-slave in *Weevils in the Wheat* recalled an old woman who instilled fear in a white owner because of her mystical ability. "Ole Aunt Crissy was another slave what was [a] caution. She was, ole she was, ..."[40] "Aunt Crissy was a smart talkin' woman... Ole master got sore, but he ain't never said nothin' Aunt Crissy."[41] This old woman used her influence as a conjuror to usurp the authority of the white owner, thus increasing her power within the slave community.

In some instances, the Muslim faith supplanted the influence of Christianity and conjurering in the lives of older women. Such was the case with the ancestors of ex-slave Katie Brown. Brown recalled that her grandmother staunchly adhered to the Muslim faith during a time in which most slave families were more receptive to Christianity. Katie's grandmother made a "funny flat cake she call 'saraka.' She make um same day ebry yeah, an it big day. Wen dey finish, she call us in all duh chillun, an put in hans lill, flat cake an we eats its."[42] Brown stated that her grandmother and grandfather carefully fasted and feasted in recognition of specific Muslim holidays.

The slave community admired and respected old female slaves because of their staunch religiosity and other actions. They generally were well thought of by the younger slaves and slave children. Frederick Douglass's assessment of the

---

[39] Lawrence Levine, *Black Culture Black Consciousness* (Oxford: Oxford University Press, 1977), 71.

[40] Charles L. Perdue, et. al., *Weevils in the Wheat*, Charlottesville: University Press of Virginia, 1976, 183.

[41] Ibid.

[42] Charles Joyner, *Remember Me: Slave Life in Coastal Georgia*, (Atlanta: Georgia Humanities Council, 1989), 41.

respect granted to old slaves in *My Bondage My Freedom* certainly applied to treatment of old female slaves on other plantations.[43] Douglass stated that there was "rigid enforcement of the respect to elders."[44] The young slaves who resided on the plantation with Maum Katie showed a similar kind of deference to the old spiritual mother that Douglass spoke of in *My Bondage My Freedom*.[45]

Although more old male slaves served as preachers than did elderly female slaves, the old slave women of the plantation South were among the most vocal and open practitioners of the ecstatic form of African American Christianity. Together with old men, elderly women prayed and shouted numerous slaves to near convulsions. Within the realm of the conjurers, the abilities of old slave women reached heights that were unparalleled by the best male conjurers young or old. Women like Old Sinda at times controlled entire plantations, including the white overseers. Along with old male slaves, elderly women sent out timber of freedom and hope for younger people through religious avenues. While many of these individuals no longer performed extensive labor, their presence established a religious leadership that served to keep the "African American community" alive. In addition, religious leadership provided the elderly with a feeling of belonging. This feeling of belonging established a traditonal respected place for elderly African Americans in the antebellum South that transcended time.

---

[43] Frederick Douglass, *My Bondage My Freedom* (New York: Arno Press, 1968), 69.
[44] Ibid., 70.
[45] Letters of Laura M. Towne, 144-45.

CHAPTER IV

WHEN BLACK GODS PREACHED ON EARTH: THE HEAVENLY APPEALS OF PROPHET
CHERRY, DADDY GRACE, AND FATHER DIVINE

BENJAMIN SEVITCH
CENTRAL CONNECTICUT STATE UNIVERSITY

The death of David Koresh, leader of the Branch Davidians, provided a violent end to the latest of a long strand of self-proclaimed messiahs. Koresh, born Vernon Howell, declared: "If the Bible is true, then I'm Christ,"[1] although Wilson Wallis had noted that 144 people had already proclaimed themselves to be Christ, the Son of God, or God Himself.[2] Claims of divinity abounded in many black sects and cults in the first half of the twentieth century. This chapter will examine the messages of three such charismatic leaders, Prophet Cherry, Daddy Grace, and Father Divine, who established followings among the substantial black populations of Northern cities. To their disciples they were, respectively, the chosen of God, the co-equal of God, and God incarnate.[3]

F. S. Cherry, a completely self-educated black man conversant with both Yiddish and Hebrew, claimed to be called by the Lord in a vision to be His Prophet.[4] After experience as a seaman and railroad worker, Cherry established the Church of the Living God, the Pillar Ground of Truth for All Nations, the first black Jewish sect, in Chattanooga, Tennessee, in 1886.[5] Little is known about the movement in the nineteenth century; but Cherry, perhaps despairing of the virulent racism endured by African Americans in the South,[6] relocated his group to Philadelphia where it was called the Church of God; but disciples became more

---

[1] Quoted in Richard Lacayo, "Cult of Death," *Time* 15 March 1993: 36.

[2] Wilson D. Wallis, *Messiahs* (Washington: American Council on Public Affairs, 1943) 32.

[3] Arthur H. Fauset, *Black Gods of the Metropolis* (1944; New York: Octagon Books, 1970) 120.

[4] Fauset, op. cit., p. 32.

[5] Merrill Singer, "The Southern Origin of Black Judaism," *African Americans in the South* , Hans A. Baer and Yvonne Jones, eds. (Athens: Georgia UP, 1992) 128.

[6] See C. Vann Woodward, *The Stranqe Career of Jim Crow*, 2nd ed. (New York: Oxford UP, 1966).

familiarly known as "Black Jews" or "Black Hebrews."[7] His theology held that God, Jesus, Jacob, and Esau were black; conversely, black people are Jews, the descendants of Jacob. White Jews were held in contempt for rejecting Jesus; and consequently only black people could join his church.[8]

Prophet Cherry combined both Jewish and Christian beliefs into this hybrid dogma. As in Judaism the Sabbath began at sundown Friday night and lasted until sundown Saturday.[9] But services were conducted on Sunday and Wednesday evenings as well. Black Jews refused to call their house of worship a synagogue, which they claimed belonged only to whites. They quoted Revelations 3:9 for support: "Behold I will make them of the synagogue of Satan, which say they are Jews, and are not."[10] Baptism and the Ten Commandments were observed, while dancing, drunkenness, and photographs were forbidden. Christian hymns were sung in church, but neither Easter nor Christmas were celebrated as holidays, whereas Passover was.[11] Prophet Cherry referred to the Talmud and Hebrew Bible for scriptual authority , and many of his followers studied Hebrew in Monday night classes. One observer of this practice noted that "it is not uncommon to hear members quote directly from the Hebrew [although it is a question whether they know what they are quoting]."[12]

Central to the faith was the belief that the original inhabitants of the earth *all* were black people. Prophet Cherry rebutted the American Protestant myth identifying the origins of the black race with the curse of Cain by citing II Kings 5 27.[13] The first white man was named Gezahi; his color represented a punishment for his sinfulness.[14] It followed then that "Negro" was a misnomer because all "true Jews are black."[15] This scriptual text provided moral authority for the Prophet's consistently anti-white beliefs. Jesus was the savior of men, but only

---

[7] Wilson J. Moses, Black Messiahs and Uncle Toms: Social and Literary Manipulations of a Reliqious Myth (University Park: Penn State UP, 1982) 185.

[8] Joseph R. Washington, Jr. *Black Sects and Cults* (Garden City, NY: Doubleday ~ Company, 1972) 133.

[9] Charles S. Braden, *These Also Believe* (New York: Macmillan, 1949) 465.

[10] Quoted in Fauset, op. cit., p. 34.

[11] Washington, op. cit., p. 133.

[12] Fauset, op. cit., p. 34.

[13] Fauset, op. cit., p. 34.

[14] Moses, op. cit., p. 185.

[15] Howard M. Brotz, *The Black Jews of Harlem* (New York: Shocken Books, 1970), p. 9.

because Jesus was a black man. Moreover, according to Cherry, "the Gentiles [whites] have taken from the black folk their land, their money, their names, and cursed them with the title 'Negro'."[16] Not until Black Hebrews get into high places would the world be right.

The worship service of the Church of God also reflected Prophet Cherry's singular vision. Swords were hung from the walls, along with various signs with Hebrew letters. The male members of the church wore black skullcaps. Throughout the sanctuary men dressed in military-like garb monitored the proceedings with swords dangling from their sides. Although the church operated without a choir, an orchestra consisting of tambourines, drums, castinets, rattles, and guitars provided accompaniment for the hymns. When the Prophet arrived on the platform he participated in the musical activity by beating a huge drum. After the opening hymn the congregation rose and faced east. With right hands raised a prayer was recited in unison. Prophet Cherry then read, in English, a chapter of the Bible. He annotated his remarks with personal experiences and called upon different members to assist in reading the verses. After a musical interlude the time arrived for the sermon. According to an eyewitness:

> Then the prophet speaks. He castigates preachers, calls them "dumb Dogs," asserts that one policeman is worth twenty-five preachers because a policeman will give up his life to save your property, but preachers want to keep everything good from you, your money, your women, your wine. He flays the white Jews for denying Jesus, and reviles all people who eat pork. He assures his flock that they, not the white Jews, are the true Israelites . He will prove that black folk are not Negroes, coons, niggers, or shines, and he calls out to "all 'niggers' to get the hell out of the place!" He traces the genealogy of black folk, going back to Noah, Shem, Japeth, Ham, Lot Abraham, Isaac, and Jacob. He rails at the Gentiles who "have not left you a spoonful of dirt for yourselves, have taken your name, your religion, and your government." Yet he preaches love for all mankind, asserting that he could not be a child of God if he did not love everybody. He makes fun of a picture of Jesus, embarrassing a Baptist preacher who is sitting on the rostrum by making him get the picture from behind the chair and hold it up to the congregation while he calls out, "I'll give anybody one thousand dollars tomorrow night who can tell me who the hell

---

[16] Quoted in Washington, op. cit., p. 11.

that is!" Thus he goes on for an hour or more. Near the end of his
sermon he is likely to refer to the absence of collections in his
temple, so unlike most Christian churches. "I'll kick the tambourine
to hell out of here," he shouts, "if anybody tries to collect money on
it." Suddenly he calls for a song. The congregation rises. The
prophet beats his drum. After the song the congregation again faces
east, repeats the same words used at the beginning of the service,
and is dismissed.[17]

Cherry injected some non-traditional beliefs into his version of Judaism.
He envisioned three levels of heaven; the first where people lived on earth, the
second in the sky, and the third where God dwelled. Earth, which he believed to
be square, was only six thousand years old, but every two thousand years a
watershed event produced profound changes. The first of these was the Flood
endured by Noah, the second the coming of Jesus, and the third, to come in the
year 2000, would be marked by widespread conversion of African Americans to
their Hebraic heritage, which was denied them by the institution of slavery.[18]
When Prophet Cherry died at the age of ninety-five, his son, Prince Benjamin F.
Cherry, assumed leadership, although the cult never again had the numbers or
stature that the founder created. In fact some members of the congregation denied
that Cherry died and maintained that he had gone "where his people could not see
him."[19]

While the Church of God confined its proselytizing to Philadelphia, other
cults of "Black Jews" were established in Belleville, Virginia, and Washington,
D.C., by Prophet William s. Crowdy;[20] and Rabbi Wentworth A. Matthew led the
Commandment Keepers of the Living God, also known as the Royal Order of
Ethiopian Hebrews, in Harlem. While Orthodox Jews did not recognize these
black sects as legitimate,[21] the Falasha Jews of Ethiopia have immigrated to Israel
under the Law of Return with that government's encouragement. Black Judaism
flourished especially in Harlem during the period 1919-1931 with eight different

---

[17] Fauset, op. cit., p. 37-38

[18] Singer, op. cit., p. 129.

[19] Quoted in Deanne R. Shapiro, "Double Damnation, Double Salvation: The Sources and
Varieties of Black Judaism in the United States," M.A. thesis, Columbia University, 1970, pp. 139-
140.

[20] Washington, op. cit., p. 132.

[21] Brotz, op. cit., p. 5-6.

congregations existing, one with a branch in Brooklyn.[22] Other black Jewish sects were established in Atlantic City, Detroit, and Chicago.[23]

Prophet Cherry's legacy appears to have diminished over time. A contemporary critic praised him for establishing an educational program, encouraging his congregation to open businesses for themselves, and fostering a strong feeling of kinship within the group.[24] But another African American scholar a generation later castigated the "Black Jews" for inventing a culture, a history, and a religion to compensate for rejection by whites. In his opinion "they have succeeded in creating cults which are impressive failures, for they further divide black people and therefore forestall the one thing needed: a black communal sense, a community of enriching differences."[25]

While Prophet Cherry was content to be known as personally called by God, Charles Emanuel Grace had much higher aspirations. Born Marcelino Manoel du Graca, on January 25, 1881, on a Portuguese territory off the West African coast of African ancestry, he immigrated to America around the turn of the century and was employed as a salesman, grocer, and short-order cook on a railroad.[26] After a trip to the Holy Land, he began preaching in 1921 and established his United House of Prayer for All People on the Rock of the Apostolic Faith in Wareham, Massachusetts, a suburb of New Bedford. In the next two years Grace expanded the movement by establishing churches in Charlotte, North Carolina, and Norfolk and Newport News in Virginia. By 1925 Grace had opened a branch in Washington which would become his headquarters. As the cult grew churches were established in Manhattan, Brooklyn, Philadelphia, Stanford, Hartford, and Bridgeport all along the northeastern corridor and as far west as Detroit and even Los Angeles.[27]

---

[22] Brotz, op. cit., p. 10-13.

[23] Hans A. Baer and Merrill Singer, *African American Religion in the Twentieth Century* (Knoxville: Tennessee UP, 1992), p. 115.

[24] Fauset, op. cit., p. 33.

[25] Washington, op. cit., p. 134.

[26] John W. Robinson, "A Song, A Shout, and a Prayer," *The Black Experience in Reliqion*, ed. C. Eric Lincoln (Garden City, NY: Anchor Books, 1974), p. 213.

[27] See Albert N. Whiting, "The United House of Prayer for All People: A Case Study of a Charismatic Sect," diss., American University, 1952.

A tall man with flowing hair, Grace cultivated his towering presence with mandarin-length fingernails which were painted red, white, and blue.[28] A dapper dresser, the Bishop favored cutaway jackets and lots of flashy jewelry. But his followers never objected to his ostentatious appearance. Though he built his church into "one of the largest and wealthiest of all black cult movements,"[29] he adopted a surprisingly patronizing attitude towards his followers, telling them that "when he took on earthly form he chose to lead the Negroes, lowly in state though they are, rather than the members of some more privileged racial group."[30]

First Grace invested himself "Bishop," [31] but then shifted to "Daddy" in order to equate himself with divinity,[32] although he never explicitly claimed to be God.[33] His theology became little more than a play on words. As Daddy Grace described it:

> Never mind about God. Salvation is by Grace only... Grace has given God a vacation, and since God is on His vacation, don't worry Him... If you sin against God, Grace can save you, but if you sin against Grace, God cannot save you.[34]

Every scriptual reference to grace was then interpreted as if it reflected "Daddy" himself. Cult members were expected to genuflect before Daddy Grace's portrait.[35] Daddy even boasted that "he could make the blind see, the lame walk, and cast out evil from the soul."[36]

What really distinguished the United House of Prayer from all other cults was the entrepreneurship of its leader. Each service offered congregants the opportunity to purchase Daddy Grace toothpaste, tea and coffee, men's and women's hair pomade, face powder, soap, talcum powder, shoe polish, and even

---

[28] Robinson, op. cit., p. 213.
[29] Robert Weisbrot, *Father Divine and the Struggle for Racial Equality* (Urbana: Illinois UP, 1983), p. 41.
[30] Fauset, op. cit., p. 23.
[31] Washington, op . cit., p. 127.
[32] Fauset, op. cit., p. 120.
[33] Phil Casey, "The Enigma of Daddy Grace: Did He Play God?", *Washington Post* 6 March 1960: E1.
[34] Quoted in Washington, p. 11.
[35] Moses, op. cit., p. 11.
[36] Sara Harris, *Father Divine,* enl. ed. (New York: Collier Books, 1971; original ed., New York: Doubleday, 1953), p. 50.

Daddy Grace cookies.[37] His assembly line Baptisms, sometimes performed with firehoses, provided a "charismatic touch to Christian worship,"[38] allegedly at a dollar a head. He also pitted branches of his House of Prayer in frequent competitions to raise money for his private use, with the winning collectors receiving such prizes as a seat next to their leader at a banquet. During each service there were several collections taken, as dictated by the "General Council Law, whose Article 48 declared:

> All houses of prayer must raise money in a united drive to buy a car for our Daddy Grace. Each state must do its part.[39]

They did; Daddy Grace rode comfortably in a chauffeur driven limousine. The primacy of money to Grace, as well as his skill in raising, it was clearly delineated in Article 50:

> The state that wins the convocation victory will have an elaborate banquet on the day appointed by Daddy Grace. (The convocation victory is determined by the amount of money turned in.) The convocation King, Prince, Queen, Princess and all of the honorable ministers, officers and members of the victory state will be the guests of Daddy Grace the Supreme. The banquet will be given at the expense of the losing states. Each losing state will have to pay a certain amount which will be named later. Money left over the expenses of the banquet will be presented to Daddy Grace which he will do with as he desires.[40]

Mostly women parishioners attended the typical service in the United House of Prayer. A picture of Daddy Grace decorated the altar, which was referred to as "the mountain." The congregants clapped their hands as an observer noted:

> There are cries of "Daddy! You feel so good!" "Sweet Daddy!" "Come to Daddy!" "Oh, Daddy!" Then there are brief testimonies, usually including references to cures of headache, asthma, or indigestion. More singing and dancing follows. Women become

---

[37] Robinson, op. cit., p. 221.
[38] Weisbrot, op. cit., p. 41.
[39] Fauset, op. cit., p. 28.
[40] Robinson, op. cit., p. 217.

convulsed, contort themselves, cavort through the house of prayer, finally falling in a heap on the sawdust. . . . The minister continues. He extols Daddy Grace soap, which he claims will reduce weight. It has healing properties also, he states. . . . The minister takes a copy of the Grace Magazine, which sells for ten cents, and offers it for sale. "Put this magazine," he cries, "on your chest if you have a cold or the tuberculosis, and you will be cured!". . . More testimony and singing follows; more remarks and Bible references by the minister, more singing, and then dismissal.[41]

Unlike Prophet Cherry, whose long sermons were the focal point of Church of God services, Daddy Grace was a reluctant speaker. His Portuguese accent may have contributed to his reticence, although Norman Eddy, a professor of human relations at Boston University who knew Grace, said of him:

He wasn't much of a preacher, seldom said anything. He was sort of a Buddha. Men such as Father Divine and Daddy Grace have a psychic power. The power was in his personality, not in anything he said or did. [42]

When Daddy Grace died in 1960 his followers numbered in the hundreds of thousands, and his personal estate consisted of several million dollars. He had established 111 Houses of Prayer in 90 cities and towns spanning 14 states and the District of Columbia. His residences included an 84 room mansion in Los Angeles, and smaller houses in New Bedford, New Haven, Philadelphia, Washington, Detroit, and Charlotte, as well as a 22 acre estate outside Havana, Cuba.[43] But the ministry of this self-annointed "Bishop)' did not serve the real needs of his followers. As Joseph Washington has argued:

These adorations are not turned into the assets for the good of individuals or the good of the black community. It is the good of "Daddy Grace" that is the beginning and end of this cult.[44]

Another critic concluded that Daddy Grace did not really conform to the ideal figure of messianism because he had no social program.[45] The sole purpose of this

---

[41] Fauset, op. cit., p. 28.
[42] Quoted in Case y, op. cit., p. E1.
[43] Robinson, op. cit., pp. 213- 218.
[44] Washington, op. cit., p. 127.

cult was to further Grace's financial success. This verdict was even more cynically expressed by Robert Weisbrot, who summarized Daddy Grace's popular mass Baptisms as as "systematically freeing all comers from the burdens of their material possessions."[46]

In sharp contrast to the racist views of Prophet Cherry and the self-serving aggrandizement of Daddy Grace is the career of Father Divine, who eventually declared himself God and was accepted as such by his followers. Although he always refused to discuss the early years of his life, Father Divine was born George Baker, but exactly when or where has always been in dispute.[47]Working as a gardener in Baltimore and attending a black Baptist church, Baker listened to an itinerant preacher named Samuel Morris who interpreted a verse in First Corinthians, "Know ye not that ye are the Temple of God, and that the spirit of God dwelleth in you?"[48] to mean that he, Morris, was God. Morris assumed the name Father Jehovia and Baker adopted his own title, the Messenger.[49] In 1912 Morris and Baker split up; the latter travelled from town to town in the South. His greatest success, and largest crowds, occurred in Valdosta, Georgia, in 1914 where the Messenger told throngs "I be God," which led two jealous black pastors to have Baker arrested as a public nuisance that identified the accused as "John Doe, alias God."[50] Although acquitted of blaphemy but found "of unsound mind,"[51]Baker decided that he had seen enough of Southern justice and arrived in New York with no more than eight disciples.

---

[45] Moses, op. cit., p. 11 .

[46] Weisbrot, op. cit., p. 41.

[47] Various biographers of Father Divine give different dates and places for his birth. The earliest, John Hoshor, *God In A Rolls Royce: The Rise of Father Divine, Madman, Menace or Messiah* (New York: Hillman-Curl, 1936) 30, indicates 1878 and Hutchinson's Island, Georgia, in the Savannah River. Robert Allerton Parker, *The Incredible Messiah: The Deification of Father Divine* (Boston: Little, Brown and Co., 1937) 80, agrees on both date and place; but Harris accepts the place, but gives the year as "around 1880." Harris 5. Kenneth E. Burnham:, *God Comes to America: Father Divine and the Peace Mission Movement* (Boston: Lambeth Press, 1979) 3, claims that "there is no clear trace of the existence of Major Jealous Divine before 1914." The most recent biographer, Robert Weisbrot, *Father Divine* (New York: Chelsea House, 1992) 21, designates 1879 and Rockville, Maryland.

[48] Harris, op. cit., p. 6.

[49] Kenneth E. Burnham, "Father Divine: A Case Study of Charismatic Leadership," diss., U of Pennsylvania, 1963, p. 31.

[50] Harris, op. cit., p. 9.

[51] Weisbrot *Father Divine*, p. 27.

After first living in Manhattan, the Messenger moved to Brooklyn where he lived with his followers who were segregated by sex. This communal arrangement had people turning their wages over to Baker in exchange for room and board. The minister forbade alcohol, drugs, and gambling under his roof and discouraged marriage although he and a woman disciple named Pinnannah were recognized as husband and wife.[52] The movement grew slowly, but in 1919 the Messenger was able to purchase a 12 room house in the allwhite suburb of Sayville, Long Island, when its owner, in an effort to spite his neighbor, inserted the word "colored" in the advertisement.[53] He also changed his name to Major J. Devine which would alternate with Reverend Devine and ultimately metamorphosed into Father Divine, with a minor change in spelling.[54]

In the next decade the cult's membership doubled from 20 to 40 as Father Divine started to publicize himself in Harlem, Brooklyn, and the Bronx. On Sundays the pastor provided elaborate free banquets to anyone who came. When questioned about his bounty, Divine's stock response was that "God will provide."[55] He subscribed to the view that there was but one race, the human race, and objected strenuously to the term Negro. "It is a curse, and a cursed, vulgar name that was given to low-rate you, in short, to DISGRACE you," he preached.[56] And he practiced integration as well as advocating it. In the 1920's Sayville and rural Long Island were overwhelmingly white enclaves, but as newspaper stories and word of mouth began spreading the news of the black minister who gave free Sunday dinners, a few white people started attending, and they were welcomed and treated no differently than the other guests. A Mrs. Withers, who had been a Christian Scientist in Long Island City, became a convert to the movement as "Sister Everjoy." Other early white followers included a widow from Charlotte, North Carolina, a doctor from Chicago, and a young accountant from Kansas City. The most remarkable white convert was a Boston University alumnus, J. Maynard Matthews, who abandoned his automobile agency, donated a Cadillac to Father Divine, and became his executive secretary under the new name of Brother John

---

[52] Weisbrot, *Father Divine and the Struggle*, p. 27.
[53] St. Clair McKelway and A. J. Liebling, "Who is this King of Glory." in St. Chair McKelway, ed *True Tales from the Annals of Crime and Rascality* (New York: Random House, 1950), p. 164.
[54] Burnham, op. cit., p. 48.
[55] Weisbrot, op. cit., p. 37.
[56] Sermon of November 22, 1935 in 7 December 1935: 27.

Lamb.[57] From that time on all of Father Divine's housing, meals, and subsequent businesses would be racially integrated, although blacks overwhelmingly provided the majority of his parishioners.

Anyone among the flock who might have doubted the leader's divinity would be convinced by a 1932 incident. When Sayville residents became incensed by the ever-growing multitudes descending on the Divine residence, and no doubt racially motivated by the integrated audiences of their neighbor, they had the preacher arrested as a public nuisance. After a guilty verdict, Judge Lewis J. Smith imposed the maximum sentence possible, one year imprisonment and a $500 fine. When their leader was being led away a follower comforted a sobbing woman by saying: Don't pity Father Divine but pity the judge who sentenced him. The judge can't live long now, he's offended Almighty God.[58] Four days later, suddenly and unexpectedly, the otherwise healthy fifty-five-year-old jurist died of a heart attack, prompting Father Divine to comment from his cell "I hated to do it."[59] Shortly afterwards the preacher was released on bail and received his vindication the following year when the Appellate Division of the Supreme Court reversed the decision.

The Sayville incident convinced Father Divine to move to Harlem and to greatly expand his movement, now known collectively as the "Peace Mission," a possible allusion to the founder's teachings on inner contentment and interracial harmony.[60] The headquarters, a five-story building on West 115th Street, became known as "Heaven," a fitting repository for a deity. As the cult spread rapidly during the bleak economic conditions of the Depression, the number of branch "Kingdoms, Extensions, and Connections under Father's Personal Jurisdiction" to a peak of 178 by 1941 with centers operating in Canada, Europe, and even Australia.[61] By 1937 *Time* estimated Father Divine to have 50,000 followers,[62] although that figure was thought to be substantially underestimated by the Peace Mission itself.

---

[57] McKelway and Liebling, op. cit., pp. 178-179.
[58] Quoted in Hoshor, op. cit., p. 84.
[59] Quoted in Harris, op. cit., p. 41.
[60] Weisbrot, *Father Divine and the Struggle*, p. 67.
[61] Braden, pp. 12-17.
[62] "Messiah's Troubles," 3 May 1937: 61.

Since Father Divine was accepted as God, no other sacred book was required other than his words, which were faithfully transcribed by groups of secretaries who always accompanied the minister in his travels. His statements in over 10,000 sermons, letters, and interviews were reported in the *Spoken Word*, published weekly from October 20-July 31,1937 and the *New Day*, started on May 21, 1936, and still in circulation long after Divine's death. While scholars have generally accepted the accuracy of the transcriptions of Father Divine's actual words, biographer Robert Weisbrot has cautioned about certain editorial "peculiarities:"

> All words relating directly to race, for example, "White" and "Negro," are replaced by such euphemisms as "light-complected" and "so and so" race. Certain "negative" words with religious connotations are often bowderlized and, in some cases, replaced by their antithesis: thus the "devil" becomes the "other fellow," and "Amsterdam" Avenue becomes "Amsterbless" Avenue.[63]

A typical worship service of the Peace Mission was unlike that of any other religion. The men and women in the audience were segregated, although couples were permitted to sit together. Some of the congregation who sat on an elevated platform in front would rise either to sing hyms or to testify how their lives had been changed by Father Divine's intervention. The lecturn was engraved with the letters A D F D, meaning "Anno Domini Father Divine."[64] The chairperson of the occasion, known in the movement as "Angels," with unusual monikers as Faithful Mary, Miss Love Dove, Miss Beautiful Peace, or Mr. Humility,[65] would speak on various planks of Father Divine's "Righteous Government Platform," which the cult had adopted in 1936. After more testimony spontaneous applause welcomed the entrance of Father Divine, bald, barely five feet-two, and dressed conservatively in a three-piece suit. After a few brief remarks the congregation would be invited to partake of the communal meal in the adjacent banquet room where feasts of Brobdingnagian proportions were served into the early hours of the following morning. A religion professor at Northwestern University described the proceedings:

---

[63] Weisbrot, *Father Divine and the Struggle*, p. 224.

[64] Fauset, op. cit., p. 64.

[65] Harris, op. cit., p. xxvi.

They began first with the serving of vegetables. Each heaping bowlful of well cooked vegetables was brought to Father Divine so that he might bless it before it was passed. This he did by putting in a serving spoon or fork and passing it to his right or left to start it on the long round of all the tables. Each guest served himself as much of each dish as he desired and then passed it on to his neighbor. Eleven different cooked vegetables passed in quick succession . . . . I, not knowing what to expect, had begun by taking a little bit of everything but soon saw that this was not wise and became more selective. Then came platters of meat. It will be recalled that this experience was still in war time and rationing had not yet been lifted. First came three or four cold cuts, including baked ham. Then appeared the hot, freshly cooked meats: roast beef, beef curry, meat loaf, fried chicken, roast duck, roast turkey, beef steak, each heaped high on the platters which were passed around the festive board. . . . The average number of different dishes served at these banquets is around fifty-five.[66]

Notwithstanding the generosity of its leader, no collections of any kind were taken at Peace Mission services. The movement was financed entirely by the generosity of some wealthy benefactors, such as the donation in 1953 by a disciple of a 32 room mansion, for Father Divine's personal use, on 73 meticulously manicured acres in Philadelphia's tony suburbs[67] and the financial acumen of its pastor. Members were permitted to approach their minister with any question or request. Personal interviews with Father Divine lasted long into the morning hours after services were ended. The reverence afforded this black deity was noted by one writer who personally had witnessed Nazi Germany at the beginning of Adolph Hitler's rule, but saw "nothing in the enthusiasm and fanatical worship of Hitler's followers to surpass the intensity and enthusiasm of the followers of Father Divine."[68]

Father Divine's success in his ministry can be attributed to his munificence, social programs, and acceptance as "God,! but not to his skills as a speaker. With no formal training in oratory he disdained preparation in favor of impromptu delivery.[69] Speaking in a high-pitched voice,[70] he fractured English

---

[66] Braden , op. cit., pp.3-4.
[67] Weisbrot, op. cit., p. 219.
[68] Fauset, op. cit., p. 67.
[69] Braden, op. cit., p. 5.

with multisyllabic neologisms, among them "visibilating," "reincarnatable," "metaphiscalzationally," "begation," "lubrimentality," and "anti-supernegation."[71] And Father Divine offered no apologies for his language:

> I AM what I AM; and you see ME as I AM, as I have heard some say, 'I see YOU and YOU is.' It matters not what they say, I understand them. They may make grammatical errors, for I make them for a purpose, that they might understand ME; that I might be with them in their grammatical errors and erroneousness; that I might lift them and they might lift ME. Aren't you glad?[72]

His speeches were peppered with frequent repetitions which stretched normal syntax to its limits. Of his own divinity he once said:

> Because God made himself flesh, it was observable, it was concentratable; in other words, it could be concentrated upon by individuals concentrating on something that was observable, that which was visible being concentratable, individuals concentrating on something, the reaction of such concentrating thoughts caused the reproduction of that which was invisibly incarnated in that on which that individual concentrated, to be transmitted to those who have concentrated on such.[73]

And he seemed to realize that his sermons were really subservient to the theology of his movement. As he once noted:

> I am not preaching emotion; I am not preaching vibrations; I am not preaching inspiration; I am preaching the Inspirator. I am not preaching blessings; I am preaching the Blesser . . . .[74]

In 1937 two events occurred that would eventually produce dramatic changes in the movement. A former follower, Verinda Brown, sued for money that she alleged was given in trust.[75] This was denied by Father Divine, who

---

[70] Marcus H. Boulware, *The Oratory of Negro Leaders: 1900-1968* (Westport, CT: Negro Universities Press, 1969), p. 207.

[71] C. B. Crumb, "Father Divine's Use of Colloquial and Original English," *American Speech*, 15 (October, 1940): 327.

[72] *New Day* 1 September 1938: 23.

[73] *New Day* 20 August 1934: 11.

[74] *New Day* 19 May 1951: 4.

[75] Weisbrot, *Father Divine and the Struggle*, p. 209.

swore in a lengthy affidavit that no follower in his entire career had ever given him money. But another disgruntled "Angel" testifying for the plaintiff claimed that the weekly take from all the Peace Mission businesses was between fifteen and twenty thousand dollars and that Divine personally "handles all that money and he keeps it for his own purposes."[76] The court entered a judgment in the amount of $4476 plus costs, which was immediately appealed. Recognizing the danger posed by having other greedy or disgruntled disciples filing similar suits as well as the embarrassing slight to his "Godly" reputation, Father Divine decided never to acquiesce to the court's decision. Although the verdict was twice upheld on appeal, he refused paying an "unjust" judgment; and under threat of imprisonment for contempt of court, Father Divine moved permanently to Philadelphia in 1942 to escape the jurisdiction of New York authorities.[77]But the majority of his businesses and followers were now permanently deprived of the physical presence of their charismatic leader; and as the economy of the nation improved with the war effort of the forties, the Peace Mission never attracted the same number of adherents in the city of Brotherly Love as it had in Harlem.

The other turning point in 1937 was the death of Pinninnah,[78] now known in the movement as Mother Divine, which was kept secret from all but Father's inner circle for many years. This contradicted the teaching that "a person of perfect faith would always have perfect health"[79] as well as the ethos of an omnipotent deity. Moreover, Father Divine had preached that "God is the life and length of your days; therefore you should live and never die."[80] But the cult suffered an even greater shock when, in 1946, the then sixtyseven-year-old leader married a twenty-one-year-old blonde white woman, Edna Rose Ritchings, of

---

[76] Quoted in Harris, op. cit., p. 94.

[77] Weisbrot, *Father Divine and the Struggle,* p. 210.

[78] Biographers of Father Divine differ on the spelling, origin, and date of death of Father Divine's first wife. Harris claimed that "Peninah," also known as "Sister Penny," was a follower of Father Divine when he preached in Valdosta, Georgia. Harris 11. She claims that Peninah died of cancer in Kingston, New York, "some six years or thereabouts" before his remariage. Harris 266. If accurate, this would date Peninah's death in 1940. Burnham spells the name "Penninah," accepts her Valdosta origins, but does not speculate upon when she died. Burnham, 7. Weisbrot claims that "Pinninnah," about whose origin he does not speculate, died in 1937. Weisbrot, *Father Divine and the Struggle* 213. In yet another version, "Pinninah" hailed from Newark.

[79]McKelway and Liebling, op. cit., p. 164.

[80] Weisbrot, *Father Divine,* p. 108.

Vancouver, Canada, who now assumed the name of "Sweet Angel."[81] Father Divine explained that his first wife decided that she needed a new body and that "Mrs. Divine presently, as you see her," was the "reincarnation of the spirit and the nature and the characteristics of Mother Divine."[82]

When the leader of a religion is recognized as "God" by his following, plans for succession become moot. As Father Divine aged and his health deteriorated, personal appearances became less frequent. One memorable one was the visit, in 1953, of another famous black cult leader, Prophet Jones, whose sect, "Universal Triumph, The Dominion of God, Incorporated,"[83] accepted the notion that God spoke directly through their pastor.[84] This meeting of two spiritual potentates had the potential of testing the faithful, but that was diffused when Divine greeted his guest with "I am happy to meet you, Your Holiness," to which the Prophet responded, "God bless you, Your Godliness."[85]

While Father Divine, who had championed integration since the 1920s, lived long enough to see the civil rights movement successfully pass legislation in Congress, he was too old and too frail to play any significant part. In 1965, at the age of 86, he died, and the ever-decreasing numbers of followers were led by the second Mother Divine, who continued at the helm into the 1990s.[86]

Although Prophet Cherry, Daddy Grace, and Father Divine were by no means the only religious leaders claiming Messianic status in the first half of this century, their heavenly appeals were representative of this genre. As Arthur Huff Fauset has observed of all cults, there is in adherents "the desire to get closer to some supernatural power, be it God, the Holy Spirit, or Allah."[87] The three sects studied here all had singing, shouting, and hand-clapping in the worship service, another characteristic of black religion.[88] The Great Depression also produced "an apparent vacuum of church leadership which was filled by flamboyant Messiahs and cultists like Father Divine and Daddy Grace, whose promise of utopias and

---

[81] *New Day,* 1 September 1945: 26.

[82] Harris, op. cit., p. 268.

[83] *New Day,* 24 August 1946: 17.

[84] Washington, op. cit., p. 117.

[85] Boulware, op. cit., p. 208.

[86] Quoted in Weisbrot, *Father Divine and the Struggle,* pp. 217-218.

[87] Weisbrot, *Father Divine,* p. 113. Fauset, p. 76.

[88] Boulware, op. cit., p. 203.

provision of social services to the abject poor caught the attention of the press and the imagination of the people."[89] Another reason that Messianic appeals were favorably received by black parishioners can be found in the blatant prejudice and discrimination endured by African Americans in the first half of this century. Prophet Cherry constantly reminded his congregants of the degredations inflicted by whites; his theology offered the faithful the prospect of being the "Chosen People," with all the accoutrements of Old Testament martyrdom.

Daddy Grace, who in the opinion of one historian of cults "prostituted" the institution,[90] was universally considered to be a mountebank.[91] Historian Robert Weisbrot concluded that "Grace seems to have differed from many other cultists chiefly in the scale of his rapine."[92] Still, one observer argued, not without merit, that "many of the magnates in the secular world reversed the Bishop Grace process by becoming ardent sponsors of the Christian church after they had achieved material success."[93]

Of the three religious leaders examined here, Father Divine has received the most favorable reviews from historians and social critics. A biography of him in the *Black Americans of Achievement* series focuses on his charitable endeavors and efforts to reform society.[94] It is not difficult to understand why this black Messiah's heavenly appeals would gain acceptance. Long before there was a national civil rights movement in this country Father Divine was both preaching and practicing integration and racial tolerance. Before government could respond to the needs of the downtrodden, Father Divine ministered to their bodies and souls. As one biographer summarized:

> Ecstasy reigned among the poor, the racially outcast, and the troubled in spirit so long as the good Father remained to inspire them. Twice a day, every day, the banquets broke through the

---

[89] C. Eric Lincoln and Laurence H. Mamiya, *The Black Church in the African-American Experience* (Durham, NC: Duke UP, 1990), p. 121.

[90] Washington, p. 127.

[91] Moses, op. cit., p. 11.

[92] Weisbrot, op. cit., p. *Father Divine and the Struggle,* p. 92.

[93] Fauset, op. cit., p. 89.

[94] Weisbrot, op. cit., p. 57.

monotony of their lives to bring them what they knew with deepest belief was the Kingdom of Heaven on earth.[95]

As Mohandus Gandhi once observed, "God Himself dare not to appear to a starving man except in the form of bread."[96]

---

[95] Weisbrot, op. cit., p. 57.

[96] Quoted in Winston C. Brembeck and William S. Howell, *Persuation: A Means of Social Influence,* 2nd ed. (Englewood Cliffs, NJ: Prentice-Hall, 1976), p. 85.

CHAPTER V

FATHER DIVINE'S PEACE MISSION MOVEMENT IN THE GREAT DEPRESSION

BENJAMIN SEVITCH

CENTRAL CONNECTICUT STATE UNIVERSITY

Although Father Divine's career spanned over six decades from 1912, when he toured the South as "the Messenger,"[1] until his death in 1965, the Peace Mission movement reached its zenith in the 1930s, both in the number of adherents and also in the diversity of its activities and programs. Estimates of membership varied remarkably. Divine himself kept no records, but acknowledged 22 million followers, clearly a gross exaggeration, in 1936.[2] The earliest biographer, John Hoshor, estimated 2 million disciples in that same year.[3] The fewest number of followers in the mid-thirties, less than 2 thousand, was suggested by St. Clair McKelway and A. J. Liebling.[4] Robert Weisbrot, the most thorough of Father Divine's biographers, believes that 50,000, the estimate that Time made in 1937, "becomes plausible."[5] Notwithstanding the wide range in estimating the number of believers, all who have written about Father Divine are agreed that the apogee of his Peace Mission movement occurred in the depths of the Great Depression.

When Father Divine was released on bail on June 24, 1932, after his conviction of being a public nuisance in Sayville, Long Island, the news of Judge Smith's untimely death and the minister's declaration that he "hated to do it,"[6] spread quickly through the black neighborhoods of New York. The very next day

---

[1] Robert Weisbrot, *Father Divine and the Struggle for Racial Equality* (Urbana: Illinois UP, 1983), p. 68.

[2] The estimate of membership is contained in the Preamble of the Peace Mission's "Righteous Government Platform," in *Spoken Word* 14 January 1936: 7-16.

[3] John Hoshor, *God in a Rolls Royce: The Rise of Father Divine, Madman, Menace or Messiah* (New York: Hillman-Curl, 1936), p. 139.

[4] St. Clair McKelway and A. J. Liebling, "Who is this King of Glory," in St. Clair McKelway, ea., *True Tales from the Annals of Crime and Rascality* (New York: Random House, 1950), pp. 185-187.

[5] Weisbrot 69. See "Messiah's Troubles," *Time* 3 May 1937: 61.

[6] Quoted in Sara Harris, *Father Divine*, enl. ed. (New York: Collier Books, 1971; original ea., New York: Doubleday, 1953), p. 41.

7,000 people packed the Rockland Palace at 155th Street and Eighth Avenue for a rally. Before his incarceration Divine's audiences and followers had been counted at most in the hundreds. Now he faced both faithful and potential converts who had all the proof of his "divinity" they needed. He did not disappoint:

> You may not have seen my flesh for a few weeks but I was with you just the same. I am just as operative in the mind as in the body. There were many who thought I had gone some place but I'm glad to say that I did not go anywhere. I held the key to that jail all the time I was in it and was with you every time you met. They can prosecute me or persecute me or even send me to the electric chair but they can never keep me from you or stop me from doing good.[7]

Divine realized that his movement had now outgrown his capacities in Sayville, and in 1933 he moved his headquarters to Harlem at 20 West 115th Street, which he leased from Lena Brinson, a disciple.[8] From this moment on all property used by the movement would be owned by members; nothing would be listed in Father's name. Divine never derived any income from his ministry and businesses; consequently he never even filed an income tax return.[9] While he did accept contributions from members of the Peace Mission, he never solicited money from anyone, and he refused to take any collections at any of his services. He also returned any financial contribution from non-believers, usually with a letter explaining that "God provided for his needs."[10] Unlike other black cult leaders, such as Daddy Grace and Prophet Jones, who used religion as a means to self-aggrandizement, Father Divine was a model of personal rectitude who set a high ethical standard for his disciples. He even turned town paid speaking engagements because he thought it morally repugnant to charge for preaching the word of God.[11]

---

[7] Quoted in Harris 43. Also see *New York Amsterdam News* 29 June 1932: 1.

[8] Robert Allerton Parker, *The Incredible Messiah: The Deification of Father Divine* (Boston: Little, Brown and Co., 1937), p. 109.

[9] Harris, op. cit., p. 4.

[10] Moses Fickler, an industrialist from Montreal, attempted to make a contribution valued at $460,000, which Father Divine returned. See *New Day* 26 September 1940: 83.

[11] Henry Santrey, an executive of the Cox Steel and Wire Company of Dallas, offered $10,000 to engage Divine for a one-month lecture tour. The minister refused, stating that taking money for speaking "is against my policy, as I am a free gift to the world, gratis to mankind." *Spoken Word* 16 June, op. cit., p. 1936: 23.

Once in Harlem the Peace Mission movement began to respond to the needs of its poorest residents. Father Divine's arrival came just one year after the large black migrations from the South. By 1933, 50 per cent of Harlem's black families had no employment and were forced to apply for governmental relief. The tuberculosis death rate in Harlem was four times higher than for the city as a whole. Only one hospital was open to service a black population which exceeded 350.000; other city hospitals had policies of racial segregation.[12] So desperate were conditions for blacks that in 1932 the National Urban League reported that "in a single block in Harlem 70% of the tenants were jobless, 18% were ill, 33% were receiving either public or private aid and 60% were behind in their rent." [13] Father Divine recognized that the most basic need of hungry people is food. All day long at 20 West 115th Street good hot meals were served to all that came. Hundreds of hungry people at a time were fed in waves as Divine told his visitors "Do not fast. . . . Eat your fill."[14] No one was turned away. Father Divine's staff would work late at night until the last person was fed. The lavish meals were offered free of charge to those unable to pay, and for fifteen cents to those who could.[15] The majority of Divine's diners belonged in the former group. Outside the building was a large sign stating that "all people, languages and races, all are welcome."[16] Of course, Father Divine's movement and meals had been integrated a decade before when the minister lived in Sayville; still the Peace Mission may have been the only public place in America in the 1930s where blacks and whites could be seen eating together. As the movement grew and more buildings were acquired in Harlem and other cities, the practice of providing free meals to poor people continued. Looking back upon the depths of the depression Father Divine reflected:

> Yes, we had 2500 to 3000 fed daily in our places in 1935 and '34
> and 1933—around that time—and about 2500 to 3000 daily in
> New York City absolutely gratis, as those of the people that did not

---

[12] Harris, op. cit., pp. 46-48.
[13] Hoshor, op. cit., p. 89.
[14] Quoted in Harris, op. cit., p. 50.
[15] Keith V. Erickson, "Black Messiah: The Father Divine Peace Mission Movement," *Quarterly Journal of Speech* 63 (1977) : 434.
[16] Hoshor, op. cit., p. 126.

have employment—and also thousands, untold thousands, fed at ten and fifteen cents a meal.[17]

While one biographer, Sara Harris, thought that Divine may have overestimated the figures, but conceded that the minister "is not exaggerating very much."[18] Another writer accepted the count as between "2,500 and 3,00 meals daily for 1933 to 1940."[19]

In the Great Depression, as well as in any other period of history, man did not live by bread alone. Shelter was the next human need to be addressed by Father Divine. In his Sayville days the innermost core of the Peace Mission became known as "Angels," with new names bestowed by "God" himself.[20] They donated their wages, private property, and labor to the movement; in return Father Divine provided food, lodging, and clothing. At his Harlem headquarters on 115th Street, the "Angels" and Father lived in what was now known as "Heaven." On the second, third, and fourth floor between 50 and 75 "Angels" lived dormitory style, strictly segregated by sex, although not by race.[21] Father Divine lived in an appartment on the top floor, which was adjoined by offices of his administrative aides and secretaries, many of whom were white. The entire crew worked late hours answering mail, transcribing speeches, and dealing with finances, sometimes well into dawn.[22] As was the case in Sayville, Father Divine was a puritanical moralist who imposed strict rules of conduct and behavior in Peace Mission properties. A hand painted sign admonished residents, "Notice— Smoking—Intoxicating Liquors—Profane Language—Strictly Prohibited."[23] Other proscribed behaviors included gambling, which Father viewed as "trying to do something for luck, getting something for nothing," and drugs.[24] Anyone who breached these rules of conduct risked expulsion.

---

[17] Quoted in Harris, op. cit., p. 51.

[18] Harris, op. cit., p. 51.

[19] Erickson, op. cit., p. 434.

[20] John Maynard Matthews, a white automobile dealer from Boston, converted in the 1920s and emerged as "Brother John Lamb," Father Divine's chief administrative assistant. Weisbrot 65. Viola Wilson, an emaciated prostitute who came to Father Divine in 1933, was reborn as "Faithful Mary," one of the most important "Angels" of the 1930s. Harris, p. 73.

[21] McKelway and Liebling, op. cit., p. 184.

[22] Weisbrot, op. cit., p. 73.

[23] Weisbrot, op. cit., p. 35.

[24] *Spoken Word* 1 June 1935: 10.

The most unusual of Father Divine's moral values was his strict insistence upon sexual abstinence. He discouraged marriage, although married couples who joined the Peace Mission were not required to divorce. Single people were segregated by sex not only in the dormitories but also in the dining rooms. When asked whether his disapproval of marriage or procreation wouldn't lead to extinction, Divine responded

" Well, of course, when we learn to live, we unlearn to die. Men have been learning to die from their earliest existence, instead of learning to live. Why should we go on increasing and multiplying and replenishing the earth with more misery?[25]

One biographer contended that Divine's sole motivation in maintaining a policy of chastity was to pave the way for "complete, social, political, and individual intermingling of the white and colored races."[26] According to this argument Divine knew that his times would not tolerate a religious movement that fostered, or even permitted, miscegenation. But this explanation is undermined by the fact that Father Divine advocated chastity from his first days in New York City in 1915,[27] which preceded the time when whites became followers. What is indisputable, however, is that religious movements that foster celibacy will eventually face extinction themselves, since their ability to recruit new members never keeps up with losses due to death. Even though the Peace Mission still has some aged adherents in the 1990s, it is destined to follow the same fate as the Shakers.

One building was obviously inadequate to meet the needs of Harlemites. The Peace Mission grew rapidly in the Great Depression, acquiring, always in the names of followers and never owned by Father Divine, three apartment houses, nine private residents, between 15 and 20 flats, and several meeting halls which contained dormitories on the upper floors. The cult became the largest hostelry in Harlem, providing at its peak sleeping quarters for more than 1,500 persons.[28] Most of these were not "Angels," for whom Divine provided housing free of

---

[25] Quoted in Hoshor, op. cit., p. 111.

[26] Hoshor, op. cit., p. 112.

[27] Kenneth E. Burnham, "Father Divine: A Case Study of Charismatic Leadership," diss., U of Pennsylvania, 1963, pp. 40-46.

[28] McKelway and Liebling, op. cit., p. 186.

charge; the movement now created another category of followers, called "Children," who lived in Peace Mission properties called "Extension Heavens," and paid one to two dollars a week as room rent. [29] Meals cost roomers ten or fifteen cents;[30] consequently room and board for Divine's lodgers were cheaper than comparable places in Harlem. Each "Extension Heaven," though Spartan but clean and safe, had full occupancy or close to it. A laundry was available in each rooming house and the larger ones contained a barbershop and a beauty parlor. The large number of residents, who did not mind sacrificing privacy in the dormitory conditions and who did not complain of overcrowding, enabled each residence to turn a profit for the movement; if it did not, then a different "Angel" was put in charge of operations.[31] An example of just how profitable the "Extension Heaven" system was can be deduced by analyzing the economics of a cluster of Peace Mission properties on 126th Street in Harlem. The main building leased for $300 a month and was inhabited by "Angels" who lived rent-free. Six other brownstone houses cost $75 monthly, but 300 "Children" paid one to two dollars a week to live there. This arrangement produced upwards of $15,000 in gross revenue and netted at least $6,000 annually, but this figure excludes whatever monies that were contributed by the "Angels" or derived from the low cost meals that were sold to the "Children" [32]

While Father Divine's success in feeding and housing people brought him fame and increasing numbers of converts, he believed that gainful employment and business offered the best opportunities for his followers to live meaningful lives. In Sayville he had operated a licensed employment agency;[33] in Harlem he began first in the landlord and restaurant endeavors. Quickly the Peace Mission branched into other enterprises as well. By the mid-1930s Father Divine's followers in Harlem operated 25 restaurants, 10 barber shops, 10 cleaning establishments, 24 wagons selling vegetables or sea food, 6 groceries, and a coal business that ran 3 trucks from mines in Pennsylvania to Harlem houses. One "Angel" alone was responsible for operating meat stores, a bakery, and a tailor

---

[29] Weisbrot, op. cit., p. 74.
[30] Harris, op. cit., p. 50.
[31] McKelway and Liebling, op. cit., p. 190.
[32] Weisbrot, op. cit., p. 74.
[33] Burnham, op. cit., p. 48.

shop.[34] Most of the profits from such businesses were donated to the movement, although Father Divine never made this a requirement. Since some of the "Angels" or other volunteers worked for no wages other than transportation and similar job-related expenses, Peace Mission businesses had much lower costs than their competitors and could afford to charge less for goods and services. In 1936, for example, a ton of coal could be purchased from the movement for $7.50 a ton, which was exactly one dollar less than the regular market price.[35] Each business was clearly identifiable to patrons as "Father Divine's Grocery," or "Peace Shoe Shine Parlor," or had the telltale logo "We Thank You Father" displayed prominently in the windows. Most workers wore "Peace" buttons. In 1939 a black educator, Gordon B. Hancock, who was generally critical of the cult, noted: "I am waiving Father Divine's 'divinity,' but as a business genius, we must lift our hats to him."[36]

It might be assumed that Father Divine would recommend that the faithful should patronize the businesses that his followers operated. He did, but in a very oblique way, and in a manner that reflected his honesty and life-long conviction of getting value for money:

> See what I am doing for you. You can come to these different auditoriums and dining rooms and follow ME around wheresoever you will—not one penny have you been requested to give ME, nor any other individual connected with ME, unless you get more than that penny's worth, for the penny you are requested to give—for food, for shelter, or for rainment. From the dress shops and other places, I have told you and I have shown you, if you cannot get things as reasonable and more reasonable in the dress shops under the Spirit and Guidance of the Peace Mission, go elsewhere and buy. I have shown you conclusively, MY work must be absolutely independent, it must be competent and must be reliable and it must be profitable. By working on the cooperative it can be profitable and can be much more profitable than others.
>
> You can earn more and clear more than others by cooperation and harmonization, and by MY Spirit and MY Presence and MY INFINITE BLESSINGS. Groceries and all the places of business, those places that claim to be representing

---

[34] Weisbrot, op. cit., p. 123.

[35] Robert Weisbrot, *Father Divine* (New York: Chelsea House, 1992), p. 84.

[36] *Baltimore Afro-American* 20 September 1939: 12.

ME,—they cannot and will not give you more than what others can
and will give you, do not patronize them, do not give them your
patronage; for MY Spirit has come to give the best and always the
best for the least.[37]

While Macy's may never have sent a customer to Gimbel's, Father Divine
was more than willing to tell his disciples to shop wherever they got the best
price.

Harlem remained Father Divine's headquarters and the largest single
concentration of Peace Mission enterprises throughout the 1930s, but the cult
experienced exponential growth during the decade and became international in its
scope. Whereas previously only the African American press had covered Father
Divine and the Peace Mission, now stories about his movement appeared in such
mainstream journals as the *New Yorker*, *America Magazine*, *New Republic*,
Saturday Evening Post, *Christian Century*, *Newsweek*, *Time*, as well as the *New
York Times*.[38] Articles also appeared in academic periodicals, although the
scholars tended to take a rather disparaging attitude.[39] Initially expansion began in
the areas closest to New York City. "Extension Heavens ' took root in Newark,
Jersey City, Bridgeport, CT, Philadelphia, and Baltimore.[40] Within less than ten
years the cult had operations in Washington, D.C., Chicago, California, Seattle;
and over two dozen Peace Mission centers operated outside the United States,

---

[37] *New Day* 14 April 1938: 17.

[38] From 1931 until 1963 the *New York Times* had over 300 articles covering Father Divine. In that
same period *Newsweek* published 12 and *Time*, 14. Burnham, op. cit., p. 62. See St. Clair
McKelway and A. J. Liebling, "Who Is This King of Glory," *New Yorker* 13 June 1936: 21-28; 20
June 1936: 22-28; 27 June 1936: 22-32; Hubert Kelley, "Heaven Incorporated," *American
Magazine* 221 (1936): 40-41,106-108; Henry Lee Moon, "Thank You, Father So Sweet," *New
Republic* 16 September 1936 147-150; Jack Alexander, "All Father's Chillun Got Heavens,"
Saturday EVENING Post 18 November 1939: 8-9, and Frank S. Mead, "God in Harlem, "
Christian century 26 August 1936: 1133-1135.

[39] The very titles of the articles in scholarly journals often revealed the negative slant of the
author(s). See James Brussell, "Father Divine, Holy Precipitator of Psychosis," *American Journal
of Psychiatry* 92 (1935): 215-224; Laura Bender and Zuleika Yarrell, "Psychoses among Followers
of Father Divine," *Journal of Nervous and Mental Diseases* 87 (1938): 418-449; Hadley Cantril
and Muzafer Sherif, "The Kingdom of Father Divine," *Journal of Abnormal Psychology* 33
(1938): 147-167; and Laura Bender and M. A. Spalding, "Behavior Problems in Children from the
Homes of Followers of Father Divine," *Journal of Nervous and Mental Diseases* 91 (1940): 460-
472.

[40] McKelway and Liebling, op. cit., p. 191.

mostly in Canada, Europe, and Australia.[41] Many of the foreign branches were led by English-speaking people who had visited Father Divine or had read his sermons. The followers in Germany even produced a German language translation of the *New Day*, the Peace Mission weekly that reported all of Father Divine's utterances.[42]

The demographics of Father Divine's movement in the Great Depression reflected distinct and sometimes surprising patterns. Almost one third of the branches were located west of the Mississippi, with the largest concentration by far residing in California. This state was receptive to Utopian movements in the 1930s, such as muckraker Upton Sinclair's nearly successful gubernatorial bid and Francis E. Townsend's pensions for the elderly. Unlike the racial composition of Father Divine's East coast operations, 70% of Californian members were white.[43] Women greatly outnumbered men, by a margin of three to one, a phenomenon common to black cults of this era.[44] Ironically, the area of the country that had the fewest Peace Mission outposts comprised the states of the former Confederacy, which still had the largest concentration of African Americans in the depression years. In 1938, for example, the *New Day* reported 112 properties existing in 23 states and the District of Columbia; however, only 9 of these were in the Deep South.[45] Most likely Father Divine's advocacy of complete racial integration would have met its stiffest resistance in the part of the country that gave birth to the Ku Klux Klan and Jim Crow laws. Even though a Southerner by birth, Father Divine showed no inclination to revisit the South, where in 1914 in Valdosta a court had found him insane and banished him from Georgia.[46]

Since the Peace Mission was both profitable and growing as the decade progressed, Father Divine was always looking for new ways to expand the movement. The masses of Southern blacks who migrated to Northern cities came mostly from rural environments and possessed agricultural experiences in their

---

[41] Weisbrot, *Father Divine and the Struggle*, p. 71.

[42] Burnham, op. cit., p. 123.

[43] Weisbrot, *Father Divine and the Struggle*, p. 70.

[44] Daddy Grace's United House of Prayer for all People also had predominately female worshippers. See Arthur H. Fauset, *Black Gods of the Metropolis* 1944; New York: Octagon Books, 1970), p. 29.

[45] *New Day* 20 October 1938: 100.

[46] McKelway and Liebling, op. cit., p. 157.

backgrounds. Because the cult operated numerous restaurants and sold foodstuffs retail in its groceries and huckster wagons, Divine concluded that farming would serve the Peace Mission in more than one capacity. Toward this end the minister's minions started, in 1934, accumulating property in rural Ulster County, New York, about 70 miles northwest of Harlem in the fertile Wallkill Valley. Ironically, the very first purchase, a very old house, Hasbrouck Manor, once had been used for Klan activities.[47] The next two years saw farms and other real estate purchased in Olivebridge, Stone Ridge, High Falls, Krumville, New Paltz, Kingston, and Saugerties.[48] Collectively these rural outposts were known in the movement as the "Promised Land."[49] The most prominent acquisition, Spencer's Point, a luxurious 500-acre property, was located just across the Hudson River from another well known landmark, Hyde Park, the mansion of President Franklin D. Roosevelt.[50] By 1939 the "Promised Land" contained 22 properties covering 2,000 acres. Some were estates, most were farms; others included rooming houses, stores, garages, and even resort hotels. Not one had an outstanding mortgage on it.[51]

As was true for all Peace Mission activities, Father Divine had big plans for the "Promised Land." In 1936, at the very apogee of his career, he announced at "Divine Lodge" in Samsonville:

> Upon this Foundation we shall continue to expand, and as I say, the Agricultural Department in Ulster County will produce chickens and ducks and guineas and geese, horses and cows, turkeys and pigs, and everything necessary to eat. They will increase them and multiply them. As I Said this Afternoon at one of the smaller Farms, I Said, 'You should produce at least a thousand pigs as these larger pigs you have here, next year—and the larger Farms should produce from two to three thousand pigs weighing from two to five hundred pounds each. That is what you should do! Chickens and pigs should be multiplied the same as you have ever heard of locusts for the wicked. Turkeys and cows, and all of the things, or animals whichever, for the sustenance, and comfort and

---

[47] Weisbrot, *Father Divine*, p. 74.

[48] Parker, op. cit., p. 285.

[49] Hoshor, op. cit., p. 253.

[50] Weisbrot, op. cit., p. 74.

[51] Weisbrot, op. cit., p.126.

convenience of the body, and for the children of men collectively. Your crops should increase, and multiply and produce much more than men can produce, more than they can develop, because they are under the curse and they are living for self.[52]

The pastor's dreams did not materialize completely. The New York Board of Health did not permit "Kingdom" milk to be delivered to Harlem, while meat and poultry continued to be purchased from a New York City supplier.[53] But a reporter from the *New York Herald Tribune* toured the "Promised Land" in 1936 and observed "Father Divine has bought no rundown farms. Rather they are going concerns, equipped with electricity and baths, and completely furnished from radios to old pewter." The journalist also noticed one feature of the "Promised Land" that its leader had adopted in his Harlem operations: "Father Divine is a great one for economizing on space and, by putting up partitions and squeezing in beds, he can double the accomodations of the average house."[54]

On August 20, 1936, two Hudson River steamboats, the *City of Keansburg* and the *Calvert*, were chartered as "Gospel Ships" to permit Harlemites to visit the "Promised Land." For one dollar the 3,500 ticket purchasers booked a round-trip passage to Kingston. Father Divine was in his glory, even taking credit for the good weather:

> As the cosmic forces of nature are brought into harmony and become to be My servants, even so will the conscious mentality of all humanity, and their destructive tendencies and their energy, be brought into subjection harmoniously, and none shall hinder the Infinite.[55]

The same low prices that prevailed at the Peace Mission's Harlem hostelries and restaurants also were in force at the "Promised Land," notwithstanding its obviously more pleasant surroundings. One visitor, not part of the cult, stayed for a while at an "Extension Heaven" at Greenhill Farms outside of Kingston and reported being "cordially received and allowed to partake of all the privileges of a member." The only difference in his treatment was that he was

---

[52] Quoted in Parker, op. cit., pp. 289-290.
[53] Parker, op. cit., p. 290.
[54] *New York Herald Tribune* 6 April 1936: 13.
[55] Quoted in Parker, op. cit., p. 291.

required to pay "a fee of two dollars a week for lodgings and approximately fifteen cents a meal" for board.[56] Because Father Divine owned no property, drew no salary, and lived modestly, there was no need to charge high prices for anything. What he asked of his followers, as he expressed it, "If you love ME as much as you say you do, let your love and devotion become to be practical, profitable, and good-for-something."[57]

That Father Divine was a strict moralist was apparent; that he would apply his morality to government was not. For three days, January 10-12, 1936, six thousand followers, including several from California and Europe, gathered in Harlem's Rockland Palace to endorse Divine's political testament, "The Righteous Government Platform of Father Divine's Peace Mission Movement."[58] It began with a preamble and an introductory statement of principles supported by fourteen specific planks. Ten of these dealt with correcting racial inequities, particularly in employment decisions. One plank advocated what would eventually would become American law in the 1960s:

> Immediate legislation in every state in the Union, and all other states and countries, making it a crime to discriminate in any public place against any individual on account of race, creed, or color; abolishing all segregated neighborhoods in cities and towns, making it a crime for landlords or hotels to refuse tenants on such grounds; abolishing all segregated schools and colleges, and all segregated areas in churches, theatres, public conveyances and other public places.[59]

Another plank advocated universal disarmament and stated that followers of Father Divine would be conscientious objectors in the event of war.[60]

---

[56] Fauset 59. Father Divine's insistence upon low prices in all Peace Mission businesses is illustrated even more dramatically when in the early 1950s, a reporter seeking an interview, checked into the Divine Lorraine Hotel in Philadelphia. She noted: "I was shown to an impressive suite which had a huge living room, bedroom and bath, and for which I paid the same price as out-of-town followers would have been charged—fifty cents a night." Harris, op. cit., p. xxi.

[57] Quoted in Hoshor, op. cit., p. 254.

[58] *Spoken Word* 14 January 1936: 7-16.

[59] Charles S. Braden, *These Also Believe: A Study of Modern American Cults and Minority Religious Movements* (New York: Macmillan, 1949), p. 21.

[60] Kenneth E. Burnham, "Father Divine and the Peace Mission Movement," in *Black Apostles*, eds. Randall K. Burkett and Richard Newman (Boston: G. K. Hall & Co., 1978), p. 35.

Adherence to nonviolence gave rise to planks opposing lynching and capital punishment.[61]

Father Divine's proposals on economic issues ranged all over the political spectrum. One plank called for "repeal of all laws or ordinances providing for compulsory insurance: employers' liability, public liability, or any other form of compulsory insurance,"[62] suggesting a Libertarian bent. Yet in other parts of the document Divine called for "control of all idle plants and machinery," as well as "THE establishment of a minimum wage scale." [63] The minimum wage proposal was incorporated into the Fair Labor Standards Act passed by Congress two years later. Other ideas suggested by Father Divine were more improbable: the adoption of one world language, the abolishment of welfare, the elimination of all tariffs and other obstacles to free trade, and the destruction of all counterfeit money.[64]

After the Righteous Government convention of 1936 dispersed, the Peace Mission decided that a parade through Harlem would be appropriate. This homage turned into an annual event, with Lenox Avenue providing the parade route. Thousands marched carrying banners proclaiming:

God
Father Divine

Has Brought
Righteousness
Justice
Truth[65]

The 1938 parade, as usual, extolled the divinity of Father Divine, but one black woman's sign merely stated "Stop Persecution of the Jews in Germany."[66] Clearly some people believed Divine's teaching that there was but one race—the human race. Whether the Righteous Government Platform was viewed as a

---

[61] Braden, op. cit., p. 21-22.
[62] Burnham, *Father Divine and the Peace Mission* , p. 34.
[63] Ibid.
[64] Burnham, op. cit., pp. 34-35.
[65] Weisbrot, op. cit., p. 42.
[66] Weisbrot, op. cit., p. 66.

blueprint for governmental reform or the Utopian musings of a religious fanatic, conventional politicians of every stripe coveted Father Divine's endorsement during the Great Depression. In the New York City mayoralty campaign of 1933, both major candidates trekked to Harlem to visit the Peace Mission. John O'Brien, the Democratic incumbent, made sure he was recorded in favor of Divine's "great work."[67] But the liberal Fusion candidate, and eventual winner, Fiorello La Guardia, was more effusive:

> I say, Father Divine, no matter what you do, I will support you. I came in that spirit, and I came here tonight, not to ask but to give, for I believe, Father Divine, in what you say.
> This city must be cleaned up and I am willing to clean it up, and I ask for Father Divine's help and counsel, because he knows the spots that have to be cleaned. I want to pay my tribute to Father Divine, and say peace be with you.[68]

Neither candidate got Divine's blessing. Even as late as 1940 the chairman of the Republican National Committee, Joseph Martin, Jr., "wrote Divine to inform him that Willkie's platform 'embodies all the virtues and principles that you request' and that Willkie 'asks that you, Father Divine, urge your followers to register and to vote for him and the Republican party'.[69]

Notwithstanding the economic dislocations of the Great Depression and their correspondingly greater effects upon African Americans,[70] the Peace Mission's position on welfare never wavered. Father Divine was against it. Welfare and other forms of public or private philanthropy, robbed individuals of their pride; and he admonished that "there is more respect for a person who can respect himself independently than that person who is dependent on charity"[71] While he did not oppose the New Deal program of public works jobs, Divine objected to the provision of the law that required those seeking them to first apply for unemployment relief. He recommended that his followers should seek

---

[67] *New York Times* 6 November 1933: 3.

[68] *New Day* 4 November 1937: 12.

[69] Weisbrot, op. cit., p. 167.

[70] One scholar noted that "forty percent of Harlem's work force was on relief and those finding work generally earned seventeen percent less than whites holding similar positions, while paying twenty percent higher rents." Erickson, op. cit., p. 431.

[71] *Spoken Word* 26 January 1935: 2.

employment, but not "go on the welfares as beggars and as incompetent and unreliable people."[72] The Peace Mission's position on charity had more than just philosophical or theological implications. One New York City official estimated that during the Great Depression Divine's admonitions had saved the city over $2 million in welfare payments alone.[73]

After the 1930s the Peace Mission movement waned in both numbers and programs. Many factors contributed to the diminution of Father Divine's influence. The 1937 lawsuit by Verinda Brown, a former disciple who claimed that money was given to Father Divine in trust and not returned, resulted in a financial award that would be twice upheld on appeal.[74] Rather than pay the judgment which would tarnish his reputation and possibly encourage similar claims, Divine moved permanently to Philadelphia in 1942. He now could return to the Empire State only on Sundays or otherwise risk contempt of court; consequently the city that had previously been headquarters to the cult and the state with the most businesses and properties were now deprived of the hands-on supervision that Father Divine had formerly provided. The death of Divine's wife in 1937, while not known to most members of the movement until several years later, certainly undercut the omnipotence expected of a deity.[75] But this paled when compared to the cultural shock that must have accrued to cult members when, in 1946, at the age of sixty-seven, Divine married a white Canadian woman almost a half-century his junior.[76]

The non-traditional aspects of Divine's cult ran counter to much of the African American religious experience. Here was a minister who, though twice married himself, discouraged marriage and procreation and enforced the separation of the sexes on his movement's properties. While religion provided a haven from the institutional segregation and second-class status that American society offered blacks, Father Divine welcomed whites into his church, made one his executive secretary, and placed others in high level positions. For many, these actions ran counter to their own perceptions and experiences. Even Marcus

---

[72] *Spoken Word* 11 February 1936: 17.

[73] *New York Daily News* 6 August 1939: 16

[74] Weisbrot, op. cit., pp. 209-210.

[75] Harris, op. cit., p. 266.

[76] Weisbrot, *Father Divine*, p. 108.

Garvey, who was willing to accept contributions from whites for his African repatriation scheme, questioned the sincerity of Father Divine's white supporters and Divine's integrity for accepting their aid.[77] Perhaps the largest impediment to the future growth of the Peace Mission movement stemmed from Divine's acceptance as "God." That living person would be venerated as deity contravened the teachings of Baptist and Methodist congregations, whose membership comprised over 61 percent of church going African Americans living in Northern cities during the 1920s and 1930s.[78] Even in 1936, at the very peak of Divine's popularity and favorable press coverage, Adam Clayton Powell, Jr., pastor of the Abyssinian Baptist Church, one of the largest and most prestigious congregations in Harlem, called Divine "the colossal farce of the twentieth century." Powell, who would later represent Harlem in Congress, went on to describe Peace Mission members as existing "on the fringes of life, hanging between sanity and insanity."[79]

Finally, it should be remembered that the rapid growth of Father Divine's movement came at a time when economic conditions for blacks were at their very worst. He fed them, provided housing, and offered jobs and self-respect. Divine himself worked hard, lived an exemplary life free from personal scandal, and preached positive virtues. As the Depression ended and the country moved towards a wartime economy, conditions for African Americans, while certainly a long way from parity with whites, were improving. By the 1940s Father Divine was in his seventh decade and no longer possessed the strength, vitality, and good health of his earlier years.[80]

For years scholars have struggled with the proper location of the Peace Mission movement in various taxonomies of African American religion. Melville J. Herskovits believed religiosity to be a controlling factor in the life of the average African American to the point that it "causes them, in contrast to other underprivileged groups elsewhere in the world, to turn to religion rather than to

---

[77] Wilson J. Moses, *Black Messiahs and Uncle Toms: Social and Literary Manipulations of a Religious Myth* (University Park: Penn State UP, 1982), p. 170.

[78] Hans A. Baer and Merrill Singer, *African-American Religion in the Twentieth Century* (Knoxville: Tennessee UP, 1992), p. 54.

[79] Adam Clayton Powell, Jr., "The Soapbox," *New York Amsterdam News* 6 June 1936: 12.

[80] Father Divine contracted diabetes in his later years, but this fact was not made known until 1960. See Footnote 7, Weisbrot, *Father Divine and the Struggle*, p. 222.

political action or other outlets for their frustration."[81] Yet Father Divine's Righteous Government Platform was precisely a declaration of political action. Arthur Huff Fauset, perhaps the most introspective and detached student of black cults of the 1940's, theorized that "American Negro cults practice forms of endogamy, in some instances proscribing even with regard to race." Yet Fauset was forced to admit that "in the Father Divine cult, where marriage is strictly forbidden, there is much greater social catholicity within the cult."[82] One of the foremost authorities of black sects and cults, Joseph R. Washington, Jr., has written eloquently about the role of prophet or Messiah which characterized the leadership of many religious groups during the Great Depression. Yet Washington concluded that:

> Prophet or messiah does not fit with the meaning of Father Divine or Daddy Grace. These men are God to their people, the black God who has come to deliver black people from white rule. In this, the cult-type does not fall between the black church or sect types, but transcends them.[83]

Disagreement also prevails about the Peace Mission's leadership. "Divine was concerned with the material welfare of his followers," Wilson Jeremiah Moses argues, "although in a peculiar way. He seemed to have the ability to manage the financial affairs of an apparently large group of persons who lacked the ability to cope with the mundanities of economic life in modern urban society." Divine, Moses concluded, could be lumped in the same category as Daddy Grace and Prophet Jones, all "opportunistic, egotistical charlatans, who elevated themselves for purposes of self-aggrandizement."[84]

While this writer would agree with the depiction of Grace and Jones, I would argue that Father Divine's career should be considered *sui generis*. Not lacking in ego, Divine claimed responsibility for the deaths of Will Rogers, Hitler, and Tojo, plus numerous national disasters such as hotel fires and tornadoes.[85] But

---

[81] Melville J. Herskovits, *The Myth of the Negro Past* (New York: Harper, 1941), p. 207.

[82] Fauset, op. cit., p. 108.

[83] Joseph R. Washington, Jr., *Black Sects and Cults* (Garden City, NY: Doubleday & Company, 1972), p. 16.

[84] Moses, op. cit., pp. 11-12.

[85] *New Day* 25 November 1950: 26-27.

there is little doubt that he genuinely believed in his own divinity. "I have come to give you victory over difficulties, over races, creeds, and colors, over segregation, over prejudice," he said.[86] Few could deny that in the Peace Mission movement Divine delivered on these promises. "Self-aggrandizement" does not seem appropriate for a religious leader who provided free meals to the faithful and non-believers alike and who never took up collections of any kind. The Peace Mission movement acquired property in the 1930s and later because it was managed prudently and efficiently. If Father Divine is to be criticized, as Garvey did, for accepting aid from white followers, it should be noted that everything belonging to his cult was communally open to all members. When Father and Mother Divine moved to Woodmont, the spacious French Gothic estate that John Devoute, a wealthy white disciple, had donated to the movement, its building and grounds served as "a mecca for followers from all over the world.[87]

The complexity of Father Divine's movement is especially reflected in the typology that Hans A. Baer and Merrill Singer have given to African-American religion. They identify four basic varieties: "(1) the mainstream denominations or established sects, (2) the messianic-nationalist sects, (3) the conversionist sects, and (4) the thaumaturgical sects,"[88] and saw in the Peace Mission "aspects of all of the four categories."[89] Like the mainstream denominations, Divine was committed to social reform programs. The segregated schools of the South had left many ghetto residents mostly illiterate. Twenty percent of the students enrolled in night schools throughout New York City in 1935, a figure totally out of proportion to the membership of his movement, were followers of Father Divine.[90] As did the mainstream churches, Divine urged his disciples to register and vote. Resembling other "messianic-nationalistic sects," such as the Nation of Islam and Black Judaism, the Peace Mission demonstrated, according to Baer and Singer, "a religious counterhegemonic tradition that rejects the label 'Negro' as an oppressive white invention and seeks to replace it with a more satisfying self-definition based on a belief in the unparalleled spiritual and historic significance

---

[86] *New Day* 18 October 1955: 23.
[87] Burnham, "Father Divine" in *Black Apostles*, p. 38.
[88] Baer and Singer, op. cit., p. xxiii.
[89] Baer and Singer, op. cit., p. 215.
[90] *New York Times* 8 December 1935, sec. 2: 9.

of African Americans."[91] What better "self-definition" than a God who took on the appearance of a short, bald, black man who preached integration and had white worshippers? Just as the conversionist sects, primarily the Holiness and Pentecostal groups, advocated salvation through profound change in oneself, the Peace Mission banquets witnessed such characteristic practices as "dancing, shouting, clapping, testifying, and joyous singing" while members also "were expected to abide by a strict code of conduct prohibiting alcoholic beverages, smoking, social dancing, gambling, theatergoing, and most notably, all forms of sex."[92] Finally, the thaumaturgical sects, which stress "magico-religious rituals," such as the numerous black Spiritual Associations, found representation in the sheer opulence of Peace Mission banquets. It was, as Robert Weisbrot noted, "a repast without end, for Divine was continually welcoming new guests and blessing new rounds of food and drink."[93]

Throughout his career Divine was criticized, by blacks and whites alike.[94] From humble origins he rose to become one of the most influential African American religious leaders. Despite all the despair of the Great Depression, he helped thousands of people and gave them that most precious of all intangibles, hope. The closing words should be his:

> If causing millions to become prosperous and independent where they were once in poverty and underprivileged; if causing millions to be lifted from the Relief Rolls and from the bread lines; if causing those millions by the Spirit of fanaticism to return all stolen goods and to pay for all just debts, causing them to live soberly, righteously and Godly, being honest, competent and true, refusing even slightly to indulge in intoxicating liquors and beers,

---

[91] Baer and Singer, op. cit., p. 112.

[92] Baer and Singer, op. cit., p. 217.

[93] Weisbrot, *Father Divine and the Struggle*, p. 35.

[94] See Endnote 39 for representative criticisms by white writers. The first biographies of Father Divine are more critical than complimentary. Hoshor ridicules blacks throughout his text; the chapter devoted to Divine's followers is titled "GOD'S STOOGES." Hoshor, op. cit., pp. 156-176. Parker, while not guilty of the overt racism of Hoshor, considers the Peace Mission an aberration, as in the observation that "the career of Father Divine, from earliest childhood, seems to follow the pattern of the paranoid reaction type, as defined by modern psychiatry. " Parke, op. cit., p. 203. Black writers were usually more balanced in their approach, but could be caustic as well. See Roi Ottley 'New World A-Coming': Inside Black America (Boston: Houghton Mifflin, 1943), pp. 82-99; and Claude McKay, "There Goes God! The Story of Father Divine and His Angels," *Nation* 6 February 1935: 151-153.

smoking and using obscene language, or gambling on horse races, playing the numbers and all types of gambling rackets be insanity, then bring the perfect person or persons who have sanity and intelligence and let them teach us something.[95]

In the opinion of this writer, that "perfect person" of whom Divine spoke, has not yet appeared.

---

[95] *New Day* 13 March 1941: 76.

CHAPTER VI

THE AME CHURCH AND AMERICAN POLITICS

LARRY LITTLE

VILLANOVA UNIVERSITY

The age of imperialism marked a time of increasing racial tensions in the United States. The problems of segregation, discrimination, and disfranchisement caused grave and considerable debate within the AME church and the African American community. In 1876, northern Republicans, in what historian Rayford Logan characterized as "the betrayal," abandoned the cause of liberty and equality for African Americans in exchange for the presidency, symbolically and substantively ending Radical Reconstruction. Although southern Democrats promised to respect the rights of African Americans in the compromise that brought Rutherford B. Hayes to the Oval office, once Hayes removed federal troops from the South, white southerners escalated efforts at intimidation, violence, fraud, and bribery to deny the franchise to black southerners. Southern states readily adopted dubious legal devices such as the literacy test, the poll tax (introduced in Mississippi in 1890), and the "grandfather clause" (developed in Louisiana in 1897) to relegate African Americans to permanent second-class citizenship. Moreover, the failure of Congress to pass the "force bill" in 1890 revealed the increasing powerlessness of African Americans at the national level to secure legislation that would guarantee self-determination through the franchise. In *A Revolution Gone Backward* (1987), Bess Beatty details the erosion of African American political rights from 1876 to 1896 and includes the political thought and actions of many AME members. Emphasizing the active participation of African Americans in the debate over their political future, Beatty demonstrates that many African Americans continued to fight for political rights, a battle that united black America across class, sectional, and political lines. Throughout the era, leaders and members of the AME were active in attempting to preserve the rights of African Americans.[1]

---

[1] Rayford Logan, *The Betrayal of the Negro from Rutherford B. Hayes to Woodrow Wilson*, (London: Collier Books, 1969); Thomas Gossett, *Race: The History of an Idea in America*, (Dallas: Southern Methodist University Press, 1970), 266; Bess Beatty, *A Revolution Gone*

Meanwhile, in the wake of Booker T. Washington's Atlanta Exposition speech in 1895 that seemed to sanction segregation and the *Plessy v. Ferguson* decision by the Supreme Court in 1896, discriminatory "Jim Crow" laws and restrictions increased in both the North and the South, creating two Americas, one white, one black. In the *Negro Thought in America* (1963), August Meier examines African American efforts to build a viable black community through racial solidarity and self-help. Meier concludes that during times of increased racial hostility, African Americans emphasized economic and moral development rather than political action and civil rights as the best strategies for racial progress. Nevertheless, by the turn of the century, African Americans and, particularly, AME members ascribed to a full spectrum of solutions to the "Negro problem"— from assimilation to racial solidarity, from agitation and political activity to economic and moral advancement, from the desirability of segregation and the "accommodation" of Jim Crow to emigration. Still, two basic schools of thought dominated the debate. One school, identified with Booker T. Washington, promoted what has been termed an accommodationist stance on political issues and emphasized moral, social, and economic development through self-help and gradual integration into American society. The other school, associated with W. E. B. DuBois, stressed political and social equality through politics and agitation and immediate integration into American society. Leaders of the AME internalized elements of both philosophies, both of which aimed for the same goal of inclusion in American society.[2]

Moreover, although strategies differed slightly in emphasis on gradual and immediate integration, economic and political development, and industrial and liberal arts education, both were rooted in American traditions. Indeed, a major difference in the philosophies of Washington and Dubois was their visions of American society that formed their vision of the role of African Americans in that society. In the Jeffersonian tradition, Washington envisioned a more democratic American, especially southern, society of independent, black yeoman farmers working and living beside white yeoman farmers in self-sufficient communities

---

Backward: The Black Response to National Politics, 1876-1896, (New York: Greenwood Press, 1987), xi, 173.

[2] Meier, *Negro Thought in America*, 24-25; For similar themes and conclusions and the development of the physical and institutional urban, black community see Spear, *Black Chicago: The Making of a Negro Ghetto*.

that could feed the world. On the other hand, in the Hamiltonian tradition, DuBois envisioned a more republican American society that included an elite led community of educated, middle-class African Americans who functioned as an interest group within the larger society. Consequently, much of the inconsistency in black political ideology stemmed not only from the hopelessness of the African American condition, as several scholars have illustrated, but also from the inconsistencies inherent in American political ideology since the conception of the nation. Moreover, both visions included autonomy for the African American community to insure liberty and equality in a plural society, and both expressed a firm faith in American ideals and institutions. Still, as Beatty suggests, "revolution" for African Americans rather than progressing "had gone backwards," and African American leaders continued to employ the rhetoric of the revolution. Americanism, racism, and ethnicity created a duality of consciousness in individual African Americans as well as the community—the "twoness" that W.E.B. DuBois examines in *Souls of Black Folks* (1903). This duality allowed African Americans to continue the revolution by absorbing the philosophies of Washington, DuBois, and others and espousing one or the other or all to varying degree depending upon any number of factors. Leaders within the AME, like most African American leaders in the struggle for liberty and equality, practically applied whatever philosophy seemed to best fit the nation's evolving racial attitudes and condition.[3]

Church members had always expressed a doctrine that was similar that of Booker T. Washington. Washington's success gospel for economic advancement through hard-work, diligence, thrift, and good, individual moral character originated from Protestant ethics that had been the cornerstone of AME teachings. Moreover, the unique social welfare role assumed by members the church as early as the African Free Society in 1787 often relied on the strategies of self-help and racial solidarity. Founded as a separate institution where all could worship in equality, the AME Church, for many African Americans, proved that separate institutions not only worked but were necessary and that African Americans could be self-governing and economically viable. Thus the AME publications,

---

[3] The best sources for the philosophies of Washington and Dubois during this era remain Booker T. Washington's *Up From Slavery* (1901) and W. E. B. DuBois' *The Souls of Black Folks* (1903), both reprinted in *Three Negro Classics*, (New York: Avon Books, 1965).

successful black businesses that depended on African American readership for survival, often featured articles that embraced the philosophies of economic chauvinism and separate institutions. Members of the AME espoused much of the Washington ideology. Although the physical mobility required for upward mobility within the denomination made regional generalizations difficult, some regional trends were evident. Even with the radical Turner, based in Atlanta, in terms of political participation, the most conservative voices in the AME came from the South. In the north, the voices of radicalism centered in Philadelphia and Chicago. The Midwest, especially in Ohio, tended to be moderate with flashes of both conservatism and radicalism.[4]

Perhaps the most ardent supporters of the Washington philosophy was Bishop John Wesley Gaines, also based in Atlanta. A self-educated former slave, Gaines emphasized individual uplift and proclaimed that African Americans "must rise as individuals and not as a race." At the 1900 South Florida Conference, Gaines called for "friendly race relations" and "the maintenance of law and good government, and the eternal overthrow of vice and crime." A favorite strategy of Washington followers was to hold agricultural, business, and educational conferences throughout the South, designed to disseminate information, create unity, and promote moral and economic advancement. In 1902, AME members helped organize the Negro Young People's Christian and Educational Congress held in Atlanta to formulate a plan for the future of African Americans. Gaines served as president, and Washington, also a major organizer of the conference, served as keynote speaker. The apolitical work of the Congress pleased Gaines who noted that the Congress "recognized the truth that mere political agencies are powerless to change our status or remedy the evils of our situation." Instead, the conference predictably offered educational and economic solutions to the "Negro problem" and eschewed political activism.[5]

Another former slave, Bishop Abram Grant, based in Texas, also consistently supported Washington as did transplanted Canadian Charles S. Smith who helped to increase the influence of the Nashville region within the AME

---

[4] Meier, *Negro Thought*, 218;

[5] W. J. Gaines, "How We Learn Wisdom," *AME Church Review*, 18 (January, 1902), 273; *Minutes of the 8th Session of the South Florida Annual Conference of the AME Church, February 21-26, 1900*, (West Palm Beach, FL: Dean Bros., 1900), 16; Garland Penn, ed., *The United Negro: His Problem and His Progress*, (Atlanta: D. E. Luther, 1902), 491.

church. Smith maintained that the "best way to help the race is through self-help, self-support and self-culture." Such rhetoric promoted a brand of black nationalism that sought autonomous inclusion into American society. Although Washington's greatest support within the denomination came from the South, many northern AME members also supported much of Washington's outlook. By 1904, after years of greater militancy, delegates of the Ohio Conference had fully developed much of the rhetoric surrounding this philosophy. The delegates recommended "moderation in public speech and manner and political demand; frank and honest admissions in debate of privileges and benefits" and "less pessimism, more hope, development, cautious prudence in the so called 'up-to-date' idea [talented tenth], less imitation and more genuine character." The delegates of the conference, as many church members, adopted what detractors considered an accomodationist stance to political rights and promoted individual, moral character to solve the "Negro problem." Moreover, the supporters of this stance, rather than displaying resignation, demonstrated an optimism that American ideals would eventually overcome racism.[6]

Still, for other members of the AME, the secondary status assigned to acquiring political and civil rights was the least appealing aspect of the Washington philosophy. For instance, as late as 1900, editors of the *Review* continued to call for bipartisan support for a new federal elections (force) bill. Moreover, delegates at the 1901 Philadelphia Conference spoke for many in the AME:

> Others argue that we must refrain from all part in the political affairs of government, but to this we are compelled to answer that our duties are the common duties of American citizens, and we cannot be content to take any course other than that held by our brother citizens of other race varieties.

Ironically, just as the more republican Federalists coopted the rhetoric of the American Revolution from the more democratic Antifederalists to ratify the Constitution, the advocates of the more republican DuBois ideology seized that same rhetoric from advocates of the more democratic Washington ideology to

---

[6] Quoted in Wright, *Bishops of the AME*, 321, 191-192; *Minutes of the 73rd Session of the Ohio Annual Conference of the AME Church, September 30-October 4, 1904*, (Hamilton, OH: Whitaker and Brown, 1904), 68.

oppose Washington and demand political inclusion. Moveover, for many, participation in American politics was the true test of "manhood." In 1896, Bishop Turner proclaimed that "for the Negro to stay out of politics is to level himself with a horse or a cow." DuBois maintained that "silent submission to civic inferiority," as advocated by Washington, eventually would "sap the manhood of any race in the long run." Thus DuBoisian philosophy linked manhood to suffrage which led to self-determination, the ability to make decisions based on African American experiences and values.[7]

Members of the AME, consistently pointed to themselves and their denomination as proof that African Americans could govern themselves and thus were worthy of equal citizenship. In *History of the AME* (1891), senior bishop Daniel Payne asserted that the existence of the AME church was "a flat contradiction and triumphant refutation" of the tendency to prove African Americans incapable of self-government and self-support, which was a "slander so foul in itself and so degrading in its influence." A year earlier in an 1890 *Recorder* article, elder A. B. B. Gibson similarly maintained that "if you doubt this assertion you will first have to snatch the A. M. E. Church out of existence." African Americans had governed themselves successfully within the AME Church since 1816, and many church members agreed with elder Albert Jackson who asserted in 1896 that the AME church was a perfect proof that the "Negro is in possession of that power to govern." Even in the apolitical atmosphere of the Negro Young People's Congress, AME financial secretary E. W. Lampton proclaimed that the "AME Church is a perfect government in all its ramifications." Thus, even the most conservative of church members of the AME believed that African Americans could govern themselves. To believe otherwise would have denied their own accomplishments.[8]

Beyond rhetoric and ideology, throughout the period, members of the AME also helped to establish and actively participated in local, regional, and

---

[7] "The Federal Elections Bill (Force Bill)," *AME Church Review*, 7 (October, 1900), 221-3; *Journal of Proceedings of the 85th Session of the Philadelphia Annual Conference of the AME Church, May 22-27, 1901*, (Philadelphia: AME Publishing House, 1901), 66; DuBois, *Souls of Black Folk*, 252, 247; Quoted in Beatty, *A Revolution Gone Backward*, 158.

[8] Payne, *History of the AME*, 10; A. B. B. Gibson, "Is the Negro Capable of Self-Government," *Christian Recorder*, 26 June 1890, 5; Albert Jackson, "The Negro's Capacity for Self-Government," *Christian Recorder*, 13 January 1898, 2; Garland, *The United Negro*, 314.

national organizations that espoused political rights for African Americans. Foremost among the national organizations were the Afro-American League, National Federation of Colored Men of the United States, Afro-American Council, and National Association for the Advancement of Colored People. In 1890, influential lay journalist T. Thomas Fortune finally organized his dream, the Afro-American League, formed in part to protest and take legal action against disfranchisement. An original goal of the League was to bring African American leaders together before elections to decide which candidates would get the black vote. League members, however, attempted to create an all black political party, one of several attempts during the period, but lack of support led to the organization's demise within a few years. Although short-lived, the National Federation of Colored Men, organized in 1895, continued the tradition of political protest and agitation to promote the "welfare, progress and general improvement of the race." Led by lay attorney D. August Straker, the Federation sought involvement in Republican party politics. The Afro-American Council, organized by Fortune and powerful AME Zion Bishop Alexander Walters in Chicago in 1897, also stressed African American involvement in the political process to alleviate African American grievances. Bishop Grant served as first vice president, and Turner, Arnett, Derrick, and Ransom all served as members on the Council. Like its predecessor Afro-American League, the Council promoted active political participation, even after coming under Washington's influence in 1901. Still, ideological differences between Washington and his critics eventually led to the Council's downfall in 1908. Moreover in 1905, critics of Washington, led by DuBois, organized the Niagara Movement to press for immediate political and economic equality. Founders of the Movement, including the radical and highly political Reverdy Ransom, issued a "Declaration of Principles" that demanded progress, suffrage, civil liberty, and economic opportunity. By 1909, a coalition of black Americans and sympathetic white Americans had transformed the Niagara Movement into the National Association for the Advancement of Colored People. The NAACP, like the other organizations, sought to improve conditions for African Americans through litigation and legislation, yet at times, all of the organizations employed tactics of protest and agitation. Members of these agencies refused to concede political power and asserted that active involvement in politics was the best way to solve the "Negro problem."[9]

Many within the AME, especially within the clergy, remained active in American politics, and like most African Americans of the period, AME leaders and members maintained close ties to and supported the Republican party, the party of Lincoln. Vigorous supporters of abolition, after the Civil War, African Methodist ministers, along with other black ministers, played a central role in Reconstruction politics in the South, supporting important legislation on education and economic improvement. Historian Eric Foner notes that nearly every AME minister in Georgia was reported to be active in Republican organizing, and Clarence Walker identifies twenty-three AME preachers, all Republicans, who became politicians during Reconstruction. Walker maintains that the ministers, all educated and including sixteen former slaves, were among the brightest and most talented that the AME had to offer. This group included United States senator Hiram H. Revels from Mississippi and congressman Richard H. Cain, future AME bishop from South Carolina. Most of the others served in various state legislature or state constitutional conventions. Even more AME clergy participated in the postwar black convention movement in the South that helped to encourage the passage of the 14th and 15th Amendments. Other future bishops who served in southern state legislatures were Josiah Armstrong in Florida, Charles S. Smith in Alabama, William H. Heard in South Carolina, and Henry M. Turner in Georgia. These AME ministers envisioned a color blind American society in which African Americans could participate fully and equally.[10]

Nevertheless, the betrayal of 1876 placed political power in the hands of southern Democrats and initiated the removal of African Americans from southern politics. In 1877, Democrats in Georgia expelled Turner and the other black state legislators, and by 1880, all the AME ministers and the majority of

---

[9] Beatty, *A Revolution Gone Backward*, 90-91, 130-31; D. August Straker, "The Organization, Object and Aim of the National Federation of Colored Men of the United States," *AME Church Review*, 12 (April, 1896), 510-12; Meier, *Negro Thought*, 121-138; *Voice of Missions*, 1 September 1899; Frazier R. Thomas, ed., *Afro-American History Primary Sources*, (Chicago: Dorsey Press, 1988), 209-212.

[10] Eric Foner, *A Short History of Reconstruction, 1863-1877*, (New York: Harper and Row, 1990), 41-42, 49-52, 125; Walker, *A Rock in a Weary Place*, 116-125; Wright, *Bishops of the AME*, 27-28, 77, 214, 317.

other black legislators had been unseated. Moreover, the 1884 election of Grover Cleveland, the first Democratic president since the Civil War, produced an atmosphere that caused some AME leaders like Frances Harper to warn against too much reliance on politics. Indeed, some within the denomination began to question whether AME ministers should become involved in politics at all. In 1885, two Floridian elders, A. J. Kershaw and future bishop Morris M. Moore, engaged in a mini-debate over the role of AME ministers and politics. Kershaw maintained that political preachers "have done more to retard the advancement of our church than any other cause, ignorance excepted." He asserted that "air blown bubbles of fame and the 'almighty dollar' drive men into politics," and that ministers of the AME should stay out of the political arena. In reply, Moore questioned what Kershaw meant by "political preachers" and then declared that AME ministers in southern politics were the "sole means" by which African Americans learned to understand their rights and the their worth in American society.[11]

In the wake of the 1900 presidential elections, a *Recorder* contributor defended what he considered the bishops' "right and duty" to be involved in politics. Defending Bishops Arnett, Grant, and Derrick, stalwart Republicans, the writer maintained that being a "high dignitary in the Church does not bar one from being a man." Again, the writer linked participation in politics to manhood. Throughout the period, AME members rejected periodical efforts to officially restrict the political involvement of the church hierarchy. Expressing prevalent AME attitudes on the political role of ministers, the representatives of the 1916 Pittsburgh Conference maintained that the "divine 'call'" to the ministry was not intended to preclude "our concern for the temporal welfare and prosperity of the people and race." They declared that it was among their civic rights and duties to serve as "watchmen" for the people. During the age of imperialism with the political and civil rights of people of color under siege throughout the globe, AME members steadfastly sought to remain actively involved in American politics and, indeed, international politics. As Americans, political participation was their duty

---

[11] Beatty, *Revolution Gone Backwards*, 74; A. J. Kershaw, "The A.M.E. Church: Political Preachers Vs Its Progress," *Christian Recorder*, 4 June 1885, 1; Morris M. Moore, "Reply to Rev. A. J. Kershaw," *Christian Recorder*, 32 July 1885, 1.

as well as their right; it was a question of "manhood," which could only be achieved through self-determination.[12]

Though most of the church hierarchy remained loyal to the Republican party, the degree of loyalty fluctuated, and support often differed regionally along lines similar to the support for the Washington or DuBois philosophy. In the South, those most loyal to the Republican party and the Washington philosophy identified with the John Wesley Gaines faction in Atlanta. Many, with the notable exception of Charles S. Smith, were former American slaves, self-educated and self-made, who maintained close relations with the party of Lincoln. Although not as politically active as their northern counterparts, this group, which included Abram Grant, Evans Tyree, and Edward W. Lampton, still sought to influence Republican party politics. A few from this group, like W. H. Mixon of Alabama, served at Republican party conventions as "tan" delegates from an increasingly segregated Republican party in the South. In the North, the most loyal and active AME Republicans centered around Benjamin W. Arnett in Wilberforce, Ohio, the only AME minister elected to a state legislature, Ohio, 1886, in the post-Reconstruction era and William B. Derrick in New York. This group included Benjamin Franklin Lee and lay educator William S. Scarborough in Ohio and Richard R. Wright and AME journalist J. M. Henderson in New York. George W. Prioleau and Theophilus G. Stewards, AME army chaplains whose views often ranged beyond the borders of the United States also identified with this group. Although loyal, deteriorating conditions for people of color often forced these leaders to criticize individual Republicans and Republican party politics.

Those within the Henry McNeal Turner circle based in Atlanta were the most outspoken southern critics of the Republican party and the Washington philosophy of political disinvolvement. Turner surrounded himself with several of the rising stars in the denomination who were extremely critical and, at times, preached complete separation from the party. Moreover, this cadre leadership, which included William H. Heard, William D. Chappelle, Henry B. Parks, and Joseph Simeon Flipper, in a form of black nationalism and emigrationism often

---

[12] M. W. Thornton, "Bishops and Politics," *Christian Recorder*, 29 November 1900; Wright, *Bishops of the AME*, 25-26; *Journal of Proceedings of the 49th Session of the Pittsburgh Annual Conference of the AME Church, October 4-9, 1916*, (Philadelphia: AME Book Concern, 1916), 77.

preached a solution to African American problems that lay outside the borders of the United States. In the North, Philadelphia provided the greatest voices of dissent and dissatisfaction with the party. Though not as inclined to break with the party as their southern counterparts, Levi J. Coppin, Benjamin T. Tanner, Cornelius T. Shaffer, AME editors Hightower Kealing and Henry T. Johnson, publisher James Embry, and other members of the Philadelphia based AME Minister Association often encouraged black voters to consider the worth of individual candidates rather than their political affiliation. Reverdy Ransom and the much less radical but equally political Archibald J. Carey also led greater voices of dissent in Chicago. Still, the mobility required for advancement tended to blur regional differences, and the coalitions and friendships that formed within the denomination depended on many issues beyond American politics. In addition, there were some black Democrats within the hierarchy like journalist and missionary H. C. C. Astwood and lay attorney and educator C. H. J. Taylor, considered the most influential black Democrat of the period. Although not a significant force within the church, black Democrats, nevertheless, constantly reminded members that the Republican party had failed to deliver on the promise of liberty and equality for African Americans. Still, most within the AME continued to support and work through the Republican party to try to obtain a political solution to the problems of racism.[13]

Based on patronage as well as the promotion of political and civil rights, the relationship between the members of the AME church and the Republican party became increasingly tenuous as the party became less interested in issues concerning African Americans. In the years between the betrayal of 1876 and the election of Grover Cleveland in 1884, African Americans, particularly members of the AME, had supported three successive Republican administrations, which compiled lackluster records on racial matters. Leaders and members of the church enthusiastically continued to support Republican candidate James G. Blaine in the 1884 election, accusing the Democrats of having a "white man's party." Editors of the *Recorder* warned against election fraud by the Democratic party in the South and maintained that there could "be no certainty that the election will be free or

---

[13] Wright, *Bishops of the AME*; Wheeler, *Uplifting the Race*; For more on African Americans in the Democratic Party see Beatty, *A Revolution Gone Backward*; August Meier, "The Negro and the Democratic Party," *Phylon*, 17 (Second Quarter, 1956), 182-91.

honest." Many feared that a Democratic victory at best would reverse the gains of radical reconstruction and at worst return the nation to American slavery. With the election of Cleveland, however, AME leaders began to regard the Democratic president with guarded optimism, noting that Cleveland was a better man than most in his party. The January, 1885, *Review* contained a seminar on the election in which fourteen prominent African American leaders viewed the election with varying levels of optimism. Cleveland contributed to this atmosphere by making the traditional appointments of African Americans as ministers to black nations, including C. H. J. Taylor to Liberia and H. C. C. Astwood to San Domingo. Indeed, as Bess Beatty points out, the number of black Democrats increased after the election of Cleveland, never to return to the Republican fold.[14]

Nevertheless, the overwhelming majority of AME members continued to view the Republican party as the best hope for equality and liberty, and the election of Benjamin Harrison in 1888 renewed hopes for a legislative solution to African American problems. The failure of Congress to pass the elections and education bills in the early 1890's, however, caused many African Americans to search for political alternatives. One such alternative was the populist movement. Thus, church members closely scrutinized the goals of populism and were very tentative about supporting the movement. For a short time, a coalition between black and white farmers and workers seemed possible. Although C. H. J. Taylor was unsuccessful in his bid for the Kansas legislature on the Populist-Democratic ticket in 1890 and 1892, such a coalition did make noteworthy gains in Georgia and North Carolina. Nevertheless, racism doomed any chances of a lasting coalition. White populists, especially in the South, considered African Americans socially inferior, and although they may have allowed a degree of political equality to resolve economic problems common to both black and white farmers, they never advocated social equality. Black populists did not belong to the same alliance organizations as the white populists but instead forged their own alliance organizations. W. D. Chappelle summed up many AME attitudes on populism when he maintained that peaceful relations only came about because of the ability of white southerners to impose their wills. He concluded that such relations

---

[14] "The Democratic Convention," *Christian Recorder*, 17 July 1884, 3; "The Figures," *Christian Recorder*, 3 July 1884, 3; "The Republican Platform," *Christian Recorder*, 19 June 1884, 1; Beatty, *Revolution Gone Backwards*, 23-24, 66-77.

"depended on a mutual respect that did not exist in the South." By 1900, populism had proved to be a disaster for African Americans, who bore much of the blame for the failures of the movement. Many deemed the Republican party as the only alternative.[15]

The height of AME involvement in the Republican party came during the McKinley administration from 1896 to his assassination in 1901. During this period, AME members maintained a faith in the American political system and supported the patronage system that symbolically represented equality and citizenship for African Americans. Though symbolic, often self-serving, and beneficial mainly to the black middle class, as Martin Kilson points out in "Political Change in the Negro Ghetto," the patronage system did benefit the entire African American community. Through clientage politics, African American leaders maintained access to government officials and institutions, provided public services, and built a network of important appointive positions, tax boards, school boards, teaching, and post office among others. Not only did individual church members serve as black clients but the church itself served as a black political interest group that provided a collective and united front on political issues. Thus, AME members sought to transform political support for the Republican party into patronage. Even the defeat of Harrison in 1892 failed to dampen the optimism of many. Republican loyalist W. B. Derrick asked if the Republican party had a future; answered the question, "Yes;" and concluded that the Republican party was the best "hope" for African Americans. Indeed, the Republican party made considerable congressional and statewide gains in the 1894 elections, and church officials such as R. A. Adams in Louisiana reminded party leaders not to forget party supporters when time for appointments came around. With the 1896 elections looming, AME members like the editors of the *Review* increasingly condemned the Democratic party efforts to disfranchise African Americans and maintained that in the face of such adversity the "colored

---

[15] For more on African American involvement in the populist movement see Gerald Gaither, *Blacks and the Populist Revolt: Ballots and Bigotry in the "New South,"* (University, AL: University of Alabama Press, 1977); Hanes Walton, Jr., *The Negro in Third Party Politics,* (Philadelphia: Dorrance and Company, 1969); Quoted in Wheeler, *Uplifting the Race,* 79.

man" would remain "a law-abiding citizen; true to the American flag, true to American institutions."[16]

Indeed, after four years of Democratic rule and increasingly successful efforts by southern Democrats to disfranchise and segregate African Americans, the 1896 presidential nomination of William McKinley, who as governor of Ohio used the national guard to put down a series of lynchings, seemed to hold special promise for black America. Moreover, African Americans played a crucial role in the nominating process at the 1896 Republican Convention held in St Louis and expected some type of patronage should McKinley defeat Democrat William Jennings Bryan. African Americans and AME church members in particular were extremely visible at the Republican Convention with more than seventy-five black delegates from the North and South and an even larger number of black political lobbyists and interest groups. Bishop Benjamin W. Arnett, former Ohio state legislator and political ally of McKinley, served as chaplain for the convention. During the convention, AME church members helped to exert pressure on the convention to force St. Louis hotels to admit African American guests. Moreover, AME members, led by D. August Straker, supported the efforts of the National Federation of Colored Men of the United States to insert a plank against lynching into the Republican party platform. With great difficulty according to Straker, the Federation succeeded, and the Republicans placed an anti-lynching provision in the final platform.[17]

After the nomination of McKinley, AME members lent overwhelming support to his election. For many, as a fellow Methodist, McKinley represented the foremost opportunity to improve conditions for African Americans. Both the

---

[16] Martin Kilson, "Political Change in the Negro Ghetto, 1900-1940," in Nathan Huggins, Martin Kilson, Daniel Fox, eds., *Key Issues in the Afro-American Experience*, (New York: Harcourt Brace, 1971), 167-92; W. B. Derrick, "Has the Republican Party A Future?," *AME Church Review*, 10 (October, 1893), 220-25; R. A. Adams, "Remember Us," *Christian Recorder*, 8 November 1894, 3; "Editorial," *AME Church Review*, 12 (October, 1895), 309.

[17] Everett Walters, "The Governors of Ohio," *William McKinley Papers*, (Columbus, OH: Ohio Historical Society, 1970), 1; For details on the African American role at the 1896 Republican Convention see Hanes Walton, Jr., *Black Republicans: The Politics of the Black and Tan*, (Metuchen, NJ: Scarecrow Press, Inc., 1975); Jasper Leroy Jordan, compiler, *Benjamin W. Arnett Papers at Carnegie Library, Wilberforce, Ohio*, (Wilberforce, OH: AME Archives, 1958), 1; "Editorial," *AME Church Review*, 13 (July, 1896), 149; D. August Straker, "How the Anti-Lynching Plank Was Put Into the Republican Platform," *AME Church Review*, 13 (October, 1896), 201-10; idem, "The Organization, Object and Aim of the National Federation of Colored Men," 510.

Recorder and the *Review* endorsed McKinley's candidacy and "the strong work" of the Republican party. Several AME annual conferences also endorsed the nominee. The members of the 1896 Pittsburgh Conference resolved that "We believe Major McKinley to be the highest type of statesmanship, the most able exponent of American protection and strong advocate of sound money." Wilberforce University conferred an honorary LL.D. degree upon McKinley who, the *Recorder* reported, received the degree with "sincere expressions of his appreciation." Members worked tirelessly to elect McKinley and enthusiastically acknowledged McKinley's victory, concurring with *Recorder* editors that "Hail to the Nation's new Chieftain, the Advance Agent of righteousness, prosperity and protection, should thereby be the refrain on every patriotic lip from Yankeedom to Dixie." "In McKinley," the editors wrote, "American citizens of all classes and in general are to have an advocate, and the Afro-American especially a trustworthy friend." Members reiterated the constant theme that McKinley would protect the rights of all American citizens, regardless of race, color, or religion. At his inauguration, McKinley took the oath of office with a bible given to him by the AME bishops. The president-elect requested the bible, which close friend and political associate Arnett presented on behalf of the bishops. Arnett later served as a key advisor on African American affairs and appointments throughout the McKinley administration. Thus, the association between the AME church and the Republican party was as close as it had ever been since Reconstruction, and members looked to McKinley for protection and patronage.[18]

Political patronage was a major concern to members of the church. The author of a March, 1897, *Recorder* editorial noted "the evils connected with the political service prize system" but maintained that there were "greater evils" in considering patronage as a peace offering to those who did not support McKinley. The author contended that a "good Republican" would better serve the McKinley

---

[18] "Editorial," *AME Church Review*, 13 (July, 1896), 152; *Minutes of the 29th Session of the Pittsburgh Annual Conference of the AME Church, October 8-14, 1896*, (Philadelphia, AME Publishing Co., 1896), 44; "Episcopal Address," *Christian Recorder*, 11 March 1897, 1; "Editorial," *Christian Recorder*, 4 March 1897, 2; "The New President and His Inauguration," *Christian Recorder*, 11 March 1897, 2; "The Bible That Was Used," ibid., 1; Meier, *Negro Thought in America*, 57; For more on McKinley-Arnett relationship see David Gerber, *Black Ohio and the Color Line*, (Urbana, IL: University of Illinois Press, 1976), 355-56; and Richard Sherman, *The Republican Party and Black America from McKinley to Hoover, 1896-1933*, (Charlottesville, VA: University Press of Virginia, 1973).

administration than a "good Democrat," and that African Americans had proven to be "good Republicans." The author realized that the patronage system was flawed, yet as long as it existed, African Americans needed to be considered. McKinley's record of appointment of African Americans was mixed. On one hand, his appointments were highly visible, symbolic gestures that fell short of what black Republicans, especially those in the North, expected. On the other hand, as *Recorder* editors noted in March, 1897, "Up to date, the present Republican administration has outranked all predecessors in the matter of giving representative appointment to citizens of color, either North or South." McKinley believed his record of appointment was "of consequence" and noted that because of his thirty or so appointments, "the colored man has a fair share of representatives in Federal service." No doubt because of Arnett's influence and the relationship between the church and the political party, AME members received an unprecedented amount of appointments during the McKinley administration. Leaders within the AME such as Judson W. Lyons and Henry Y. Arnett received important domestic positions while others like William Heard and Campbell Maxwell received overseas appointments.[19]

Nevertheless, AME members were not completely satisfied. For instance, while praising the selection of Richard T. Greener as consul to India, *Recorder* editors maintained that the president "should see fit" to assign church members D. August Straker and H. C. C. Astwood to positions as well. Ironically, some appointments of AME church members caused conflict with other African American leaders. The nomination of Bishop Abram Grant to the United States Labor Commission produced negative responses from within the African American community. Writers in both the New York *Age* and the Washington *Colored American* complained about the nomination and the appointment of AME clergy to civil positions. Grant, citing the demands of his duties as bishop, diffused the potential rift by rejecting the nomination. Still, political patronage solidified the relationship between the AME church and the Republican party, and

---

[19] "Political Spoils," *Christian Recorder*, 18 March 1897, 2; Lewis L. Gould, *The Presidency of William McKinley*, (Lawrence, KS: The Regents Press of Kansas, 1980), 154-59; George Sinker, *The Racial Attitudes of American President, From Abraham Lincoln to Theodore Roosevelt*, (Garden City, NY: Doubleday, 1971); "Editorial," *Christian Recorder*, 7 October 1897, 2; Quoted in Gould, *William McKinley*, 154; *Christian Recorder*, 14 March 1901, 7.

again, most members supported McKinley in the rematch against Bryan in the 1900 elections.[20]

Yet, during the 1900 elections, dissatisfaction over a variety of issues from imperialism to disfranchisement caused members of the AME to increase criticism of McKinley and the Republican party. The greatest voices of dissent originated from the Turner faction that outright endorsed Bryan. Typical was presiding elder W. D. Chappelle who supported Bryan and maintained that "it must be evident to every Negro that the Republican party is a party of money, and has clearly proven that the Negro is not wanted in their ranks." The monthly AME missionary newspaper, the *Voice of Missions*, edited by Turner, printed articles that severely criticized the motives and record of McKinley and the party. Moreover, several AME leaders concluded that African Americans should not blindly support either party. Many within the Philadelphia faction, such as Coppin and Tanner, took this approach, not completely breaking from the party while counseling caution. Tanner explained that "The white man has given us the cue. He goes for the party that goes for him. Let the Afro-American do the same ... The Negro should be tied to no party. He should vote for the party that will do the most good."[21]

Nevertheless, most decided the political party that would do the "most good" was the Republican party and, therefore, denounced such attitudes and refused to swap "the tried and safe steed of Republicanism for the bucking bronco of deteriorated Democracy." Some members maintained that even though as an individual, McKinley "may not have pleased us all, but in the party to which he belongs are to be found the most of our friends." In October prior to the elections, a *Recorder* contributor found it difficult to believe that Turner had gone Democratic. Indeed, Turner's rhetoric was so vehemently anti-Republican that Derrick traveled to Atlanta to try to get him to soften his tone. The ill-fated mission, however, caused more damage than good and provided Turner an opportunity for greater criticism in the next edition of the *Voice of Missions*. Such

---

[20] "Editorial," *Christian Recorder*, 20 January 1898, 2; *Christian Recorder*, August 1898; *New York Age*, August 1898; *Washington Colored American*, August 1898.

[21] W. D. Chappelle, "Signs of the Times," *Christian Recorder*, 27 September 1900, 2; *Voice of Missions*, 1 October 1900; *Voice of Missions*, 1 November 1900; Benjamin Tanner, "Bishop Tanner and Democracy," *Christian Recorder*, 23 November 1899, 1; also see "Editorial," *AME Church Review*, 11 (January, 1895), 430.

rhetoric fueled mounting pressure for Turner to resign his position as editor of the *Voice of Missions*, which he did at the end of the year. Even the more moderate stance of Tanner came under fire. In an unnamed *Recorder* article, the author maintained that Tanner's advice only proved the "current adage that 'politics makes strange bed fellows."' The author asserted that the bishop's questionable advice, which would not be heeded, harmed both himself and others and that African Americans would continue to support the Republican party. Moreover, much of that support was rooted in the desire for self-determination through the franchise for African Americans. Editors of the *Review*, in assessing the "lessons of the [1900] elections", concluded that members of the Democratic party had defeated themselves by advocating African American disfranchisement in the southern states. The editors declared that "to the Negro the paramount issue was the question of his own political salvation."[22]

   Although neither party championed the cause of African Americans or, more importantly, had ready made solutions to the pressing economic, social, and political problems of the age, support for the Republican party reached a pinnacle with the presidential elections of 1904. Indeed, after the assassination of McKinley, AME members found little difficulty supporting Theodore Roosevelt. Several members of the AME believed that the Republicans would have gained even greater support from the black community in 1900 if the presidential ticket had been reversed with Roosevelt running for president rather than McKinley. The year before the 1904 elections, delegates at the 1903 North Ohio Conference unanimously resolved to endorse Roosevelt's "wise and patriotic administration." The delegates also believed "that the peace and prosperity of this country will be enhanced by his continuance as the chief executive of the government." *Review* editor H. T. Kealing was extremely pro-Roosevelt. He maintained that Roosevelt represented "progressiveness vs stagnation, Americanism vs Provincialism, the reign of all the people vs the tyranny of a favored class." Delegates at the 1904 Ohio and Pittsburgh Conferences formally endorsed Roosevelt. At the Pittsburgh Conference, delegates declared that Roosevelt had "a spirit of fairness relative to

---

[22] "McKinley or Bryan," *Christian Recorder*, 19 July 1900, 2; "Think Before Acting," *Christian Recorder*, 25 October 1900, 2; "We've Said Enough," *Christian Recorder*, 4 October 1900, 2; *Voice of Missions*, 1 October 1900; *Voice of Missions*, 1 November 1900; Bishop's Advice to Voters," *Christian Recorder*, 9 November 1900, 2; "One of the Lessons of the Election," *AME Church Review*, 17 (January, 1901), 287.

all that is allied to the highest and best interest of humanity, without regard to race or condition." After the inauguration of TR, at which several African Americans organizations reportedly marched in the parade, *Review* editors echoed a constant refrain: "Mr. Roosevelt does not stand for the Negro as a Negro, but for him as a man: and his stand would be just the same if the oppressed were a Jew, an Irishman or a native Mississippian."[23]

Nevertheless, AME criticism of the Republican party began to expand during the second Roosevelt administration, and the annual conferences, which more often had taken more conciliatory tones, became more vocal in reproaching the party. Roosevelt contributed to this atmosphere by apologizing for inviting Booker T. Washington to the White House, condemning the entire black regiment rather than individuals in Brownsville incident, and generally ignoring the plight of African Americans. The Republican nominee William H. Taft inherited much of that criticism during the 1908 elections. Although, editors of the *Review* reluctantly maintained that Taft ought to win, they did not outright endorse Taft and acknowledged that "work must be done." The representatives of the 1908 Illinois and Indiana Conferences endorsed Taft, but only after downplaying the Brownsville incident and severely reprimanding the party for losing sight of its principles and not living up to the standards set by the founders. The delegates of the 1908 Iowa Conference refused to support Taft and maintained that continued affiliation with the Republican party had failed to protect African American rights and privileges as citizens. Even after Taft's victory, the delegates of 1910 Pittsburgh Conference found little difference between the parties, and the delegates at the 1911 Indiana Conference advised that "instead of casting it (sacred ballot) for party and party fealty, cast it for men and measures." A year later, the Indiana Conference maintained that the nation was in the "throes of a great political upheaval" and refused to support any candidate in the five candidate race for the presidency. Indeed, no annual conference officially

---

[23] "A Strong Ticket," *Christian Recorder*, 28 January 1900, 2; *Minutes of the 22nd Session of the North Ohio Annual Conference of the AME Church, October 7-11, 1903*, (Hamilton, OH: Brown and Whitaker, 1903), 55; H. T. Kealing, "The Convention That Nominated Roosevelt in Chicago," *AME Church Review*, 21 (October, 1904), 125; *Minutes of 37th Session of the Pittsburgh Annual Conference of the AME Church, October 12-17, 1904*, (Philadelphia: AME Book Concern, 1904), 101; *Minutes of the 74th Session of the Ohio Annual Conference of the AME Church, September 28-October 2, 1904*, (Hamilton, OH: Brown and Whitaker, 1904), 40, 43; "President Roosevelt's Inauguration," *AME Church Review*, 21 (April, 1905), 333; "At the Old Stand," Ibid., 396.

endorsed a candidate in the 1912 elections, and the *Review*, now edited by Reverdy Ransom, ran articles supporting all the major candidates, admonished the Republican party platform, remained non-committal, and praised the twenty percent of African Americans who voted for Wilson.[24]

By 1912, the dependency on the Republican party became easier to overcome. The Republican party and prior Republican administrations failed to enforce laws that protected African American rights and privileges, stood mute in the face of mounting violence against African Americans, and helped fashion American apartheid in the South and North. Accordingly, AME members increased their criticism of the party and government policies, yet they did so by keeping an enormous faith in the American political system. They did not voluntarily remove themselves from American politics and continuously sought to participate in the political process by whatever means at their disposal. Although they had much in common with the Washington philosophy, members of the AME steadfastly believed that the franchise in the United States meant manhood, self-determination, and equal citizenship. Moreover, the political differences between Washington and DuBois concerning political participation was in degree of emphasis, and the AME publications often reported efforts by Washington to halt disfranchisement and influence the American political process. Members of the AME internalized the doctrines of Washington and DuBois, and throughout the period, sought to participate in a plural American society as an autonomous African American community. Indeed, providing a national forum, the AME functioned as a political interest group concerned with racial matters that transcended class, economic, and even political lines. Members of the church

---

[24] Sinkler, *Racial Attitudes*, 318-19; "Editorial," *AME Church Review*, 25 (July, 1908), 75; *AME Church Review*, 25 (October, 1908); *Journal of Proceedings of the 37th Session of the Illinois Annual Conference of the AME Church, 1908*, 44-45; *Journal of Proceedings of the 70th Session of the Indiana Annual Conference of the AME Church, September 16-21, 1908*, (Seymour, IN: Graesdale-Mercer, Co., 1908), 64; *Minutes of the 26th Session of the Iowa Annual Conference of the AME Church, September 9-14, 1908*, 65; *Minutes of the 43rd Session of the Pittsburgh Annual Conference of the AME Church, September 28-October 2, 1910*, (Philadelphia: AME Book Concern, 1910), 38; *Minutes of the 73rd Session of the Indiana Annual Conference of the AME Church, September 6-10, 1911*, (Philadelphia: AME Book Concern, 1911), 78-79; *Journal of Proceedings of the 74th Session of the Indiana Annual Conference of the AME Church, September 11-16, 1912*, (Philadelphia: AME Book Concern, 1912), 76; "The Negro's Political Consciousness," *AME Church Review*, 29 (July, 1912), 84-85; *AME Church Review*, 29 (October, 1912); "Editorial," *AME Church Review*, 29 (January, 1913), 264-67.

established a client-patron relationship with the Republican party that was both detrimental and beneficial to the African American community. Moreover, during the age of imperialism, African Americans were among the few people of color in the world who could address the problems and racial implications of imperialism at an international as well as national level. Ironically, in the United States, the party most associated with imperialism was the Republican party. Thus, the relationship between the AME church and the Republican party conditioned the way in which church members would respond to international affairs and issues during the age of imperialism, often causing dilemmas and contradictions for AME members.[25]

---

[25] For an example of an article highlighting BTW's efforts to halt disfranchisement see "On Time," *AME Church Review*, 18 (July, 1901), 94.

CHAPTER VII

ONE CHURCH, INDIVISIBLE: THE POLITICAL STRUCTURE OF THE AME

LARRY LITTLE
VILLANOVA UNIVERSITY

I

The AME Church is one of the best examples of African American religious institutional development. Founded in 1816, the AME Church is the oldest and, for much of the nineteenth century, was the largest African American religious denomination. By 1890, the AME had a membership of 466,202, a number that had increased to 673,700 by 1900. The AME church reached every corner of the United States with more than 4,000 churches and parsonages valued at 6.8 million dollars and located in every major city. In 1890, the church leadership consisted of ten bishops, seven general officers, 196 presiding elders, and more than 16,000 pastors, ministers, and local preachers. Extremely influential and political, AME church members, beyond the prominent clergy, included businesspeople, educators, journalists, and politicians. Especially in urban areas, the AME drew from the black middle class for leadership and support.[1]

In 1890, the church also supported twenty-three educational institutions including five colleges (such as Wilberforce University in Ohio, the oldest African American college; Allen University in South Carolina; and Morris Brown College in Atlanta) as well as eighteen other schools, academies, and seminaries valued at $425,000. Church members participated in the debate concerning liberal arts and industrial education for African Americans and produced a great deal of rhetoric that supported both sides of the argument. Nevertheless, the meager funds allocated and lack of viable curricula for industrial education supports James Anderson's conclusions in *The Education of Blacks in the South* (1988) that the

---

[1] *Journal of the Proceedings of the 21st Quadrennial Session of the General Conference of the AME Church, May 7-25, 1900*, (Philadelphia: AME Book Concern, 1900), 63; Benjamin W. Arnett, *The Budget*, (Xenia, OH: 1890) 83-84.

AME placed a "low priority" on industrial education. Instead, the primary stimulus for building schools came from the need and desire to have an educated ministry. Thus, curricula for all AME schools included a significant emphasis on moral and religious training. Delegates at the 1896 North Ohio Conference illustrated this concern when they maintained that "Our first care should be to provide for the training of educated ministers, teachers and leaders of the people." William Gaines, an AME presiding elder who lectured at Fisk University and Gammon Seminary in Georgia, further maintained that education was an important requirement for interpreting the Bible. Delegates at the 1900 General Conference displayed the importance of education by fighting to get more money for schools in their districts, accusing one another of prejudice toward certain parts of the country. By 1900, the number of AME schools, colleges, universities, and seminaries had increased to more than forty-one, and between 1884 and 1899, AME members had raised $1,140,013 for education.[2]

The AME church as an institution was an active and integral part of the African American community, responding to its physical as well as spiritual needs. The age of imperialism marked a period of transition for society in the United States. Technological changes initiated a drive toward industrialization and urbanization that, along with racism and nativism, fortified rigid social, economic, and political hierarchies in American society. The vast imbalance in the distribution of wealth left millions of Americans unable to share fully in the fruits of scientific and technological advances. American institutions underwent profound changes, and AME members constantly devised and amended institutional goals to respond to a transitional American society. Thus, AME leaders consistently sought answers to the economic downturns that adversely

---

[2] Ibid.; All of the general and annual conferences of the AME published educational reports that included summaries of expenditures and curricula; James Anderson, *The Education of Blacks in the South, 1860-1935*, (Chapel Hill, NC: University of North Carolina Press, 1988), 67, 135; Joseph McMillan, "The Development of Higher Education for Blacks during the Late Nineteenth Century: A Study of the African Methodist Episcopal Church; Wilberforce University: the American Missionary Association; Hampton Institute; and Fisk University," (Ed.D. diss., Columbia University Teachers College, 1986), 53, 57; E. Franklin Frazier, *The Negro Church in America*, (New York: Schoken Books, Inc., 1963); *Minutes of the 15th Session of the North Ohio Annual Conference of the AME Church, September 24-31, 1896*, (Philadelphia: AME Publishing House, 1896), 41; Edward L. Wheeler, *Uplifting the Race: The Black Minister in the New South, 1865-1902*, (Lanham, MD: University Press of America, 1986), 103; *1900 General Conference*, 189-190, 241.

affected the African American community and to the racism and discrimination that polarized American society.

Indeed, the AME church members displayed the reform traditions of the progressive era, primarily seeking change within the parameters of American society. Consequently, AME members engaged in a variety of reform and social welfare activities to benefit the African American community. For instance in Chicago in 1900, the radical and highly political AME minister Reverdy Ransom, whose church was bombed in 1903 after sermons denouncing political corruption, organized the Institutional Church and Settlement House based on the moral and social redemption tenets of the social gospel. Incorporating the themes of racial solidarity and self-help, the AME church established old folks' homes, orphanages, and mutual benefit societies. The denomination operated kindergartens and libraries, lecture and literary societies as well as penny savings banks and employment agencies. For much of the period, the black church in general provided the major source of social welfare activities for the African American community. Members of the AME realized they lived in an era of reform and, as seen in a speech by W. H. Council, president of an AME normal school in Alabama, searched for their place within the movement.[3]

Not only did AME members participate in the reform and social welfare traditions, they also exhibited much of the impulse toward organization and efficiency that characterized the era. Historians of progressivism who ascribe to what is known as the organizational synthesis maintain that organization building—with its new and innovative forms of bureaucratization, integration, and marketing and its drive toward professionalization—constituted the primary process of change in America's basic institutions. They further assert that this process involved a fundamental shift by a new middle class to values that stressed efficiency, continuity, systematic controls, and group action. Unfortunately, these

---

[3] For more on the social welfare activities of the black church see August Meier, *Negro Thought in America, 1880-1915*, Ann Arbor, MI: University of Michigan Press, 1963) and Allan Spear, *Black Chicago: The Making of a Negro Ghetto, 1890-1920*, (Chicago: University of Chicago Press, 1967), 92-96, 63; Donald Albert Dewitt, "Ransom on Race and Racism: The Radical and Social Thought of Reverdy Cassius Ransom—Preacher, Editor and Bishop in the African Methodist Episcopal Church, 1861-1959," (Ph.D diss.: Drew University, 1988), 112-129; "The Negro and Reform Movements," *AME Church Review*, 15 (July, 1898), 557; Editors of the *AME Review* did not support church financing of the Institutional Church and Settlement House. For more on the debate see the editorial sections of the July, 1900 and the July, 1901 editions of the *Review*.

scholars have overlooked the organizational synthesis in efforts at organization building in the African American community. Moreover, these historians tend to view African Americans as essentially victims, targets of both scorn and reform. Yet, members of the AME church displayed many of the attributes of the synthesis. In 1900, participants at the North Ohio Conference maintained that African Americans could best improve their positions through organization building, while members of the Indiana Conference maintained that "we must perfect organizations already in existence rather than create new ones. Though they seem at odds, nevertheless, they both stressed the importance of organizations. Meanwhile at the 1900 General Conference, church officials made efforts to centralize finances and to departmentalize and consolidate various functions in the name of efficiency. Such actions suggest that African Americans actively sought to bring more order to their institutions and make them more efficient and that members of the AME actively sought to improve the organizational structure of their church.[4]

The ministry of the AME Church also became more professional during this period. Indeed, the clergy of the AME could be viewed as leading the way in the professionalization of Protestant ministers in America. In "Military Professionalism and Officership in America," Allan Millet asserts that during the nineteenth century, the authority and dominance of Protestant ministers declined because congregations began to demand that ministers justify their social usefulness more than their religious functions. Accordingly, ministers sought to gain their former status and authority through the social gospel and by applying skills of occupations such as youth or social worker, teacher, sociologist, and social psychologist. The clergy of the AME did not suffer a corresponding decline in authority. On the contrary, an increasingly hostile and divided American society enhanced the status of ministers in the community. Buoyed by an African helping

---

[4] Louis Galambos, "The Emerging Organizational Synthesis in Modern American History," *Business History Review*, XLIV (Autumn, 1970), 279-290; Louis Galambos, "Technology, Political Economy, and Professionalization: Central Themes of the Organizational Synthesis," *Business History Review*, 57 (Winter, 1983), 471-493; Robert H. Weibe, *The Search for Order, 1877-1920*, (New York: Hill and Wang), 133-163; *Minutes of the 19th Session of the North Ohio Annual Conference of the AME Church, October 3-7, 1900*, (Hamilton, OH: Brown and Whitaker, 1901), 17; *Journal of Proceedings of the 60th Session of the Indiana Annual Conference of the AME Church, August 30-September 4, 1899*, (Hamilton, OH: Brown and Whitaker, 1900), 44; *1900 General Conference*, 114

tradition, AME ministers, as all black ministers, had long been accustomed to providing for the social needs of the African-American community that other segments of American society ignored. Discrimination and segregation intensified those needs. The AME also fulfilled another prerequisite to professionalization by creating an educational system designed to produce a learned and professional ministry, capable of teaching as well as preaching. Rather than victims, members of the AME sought to participate in the transitional American society, regardless of racial limitations.[5]

The organizational structure and, more specifically, the political structure of the AME church played an important role in the manner AME members responded to international events and world affairs. Founded on principles of self-determination, the church provided a political framework that allowed political participation and the growth of leadership outside the norm of American politics and encouraged the development of a political rhetoric that was strongly rooted in the traditions of American republicanism. In many ways, the AME church functioned on the representative principle. The five levels of conferences— general, annual, district, quarterly, and church—performed the legislative functions, representing national, regional or state, and local divisions within the denomination. They also performed some judicial functions. At the highest level were the general conferences, which, from the founding of the church in 1816, AME officials held every four years. The 1900 General Conference was the 21st Quadrennial Session, and included 267 ministerial and 127 lay delegates from eleven episcopal districts and sixty-five annual conferences. A different bishop presided over the conference each day. The general conference formulated official church policy and, according to the by-laws, had "full power to make rules, regulations and modifications under certain limitations and restrictions." Although influential, the bishops had no veto power over the decisions of the conference, which, as all the conferences, operated on the one person one vote method to reach decisions. Members of the annual conferences elected delegates to the general conference. The ministers of each annual conference elected one representative for every twenty of their number. Meanwhile an electoral college

[5] Allan Millet, "Military Professionalism and Officership in America," (Mershon Center, The Ohio State University, 1977); Joanne and Elmer Martin, *The Helping Tradition in the Black Family and Community*, (Silver Springs, MD: National Association of Social Workers, 1985).

composed of an elected lay official from each church within the bounds of an
annual conference elected two lay representatives for the general conference.[6]

The episcopal districts were divided into annual conferences, representing
a particular region or state and presided over by the bishop of that region. The
annual conference made rules and regulations within the region as long as they did
not conflict with rules established by the general conference. The annual
conferences varied in size. For example in 1900, the Pittsburgh conference had
seventy-nine delegates; the Ohio conference had fifty-seven, while the California
conference had only twenty. Composed of all the traveling ministers, pastors, and
elected local preachers as well as elected lay officials from the circuits and
churches within the conference, representatives at the annual conferences often
displayed a degree of independence from the presiding bishop who did have a
veto power. The annual conferences were divided into district conferences
composed of several circuits, stations, or missions. Presided over by an elder and
occasionally a bishop, the district conference conducted AME business within the
various districts. The quarterly conferences, which met four times a year, and the
church conferences, which met at least once a month, conducted religious and
secular business for the individual circuits and churches within the district.
Although all ministers automatically served in the district, quarterly, and church
conferences, congregations elected the local preachers and lay members who
participated. Working under the premise of one person one vote, the various
conferences illustrated the democratic spirit that ran deeply within African
Methodism.[7]

The ministry served as the executive and judicial branches of the AME.
The Council of Bishops, composed of all the bishops and headed by the senior
bishop, met semi-annually to manage administrative affairs. The general
conference assigned bishops to the various episcopal districts; however, the
Council of Bishops annually reviewed those assignments and could and did make
changes when necessary. It was not uncommon for bishops to rotate assignments
yearly. Still, bishops had authority over the entire connection and were not
confined to particular districts; they were pastors-in-chief of all the churches in

---

[6] *1900 General Conference*, 1-5; Henry M. Turner, *The Genius and Theory of Methodist Polity*,
(Philadelphia: AME Publications, 1885), 41-45.
[7] Ibid., 46-72.

the connection. Although such a system enhanced the bishops' power at a national level, it also contributed to greater autonomy by regional and local leaders. The bishops, assisted by presiding elders, managed the day-to-day activities of the church within the episcopal districts. Indeed, the word "Episcopal" in the name denoted rule by bishop. Every four years at the general conference, church delegates elected new bishops, if needed because of expansion, death, or retirement. Bishops were answerable to the general conference, which could suspend, expel, or reprimand them for improper or imprudent behavior. As overseers or superintendents of the church, their duty was to travel at large and conduct the spiritual and temporal affairs of the denomination.[8]

Presiding elders were assistant bishops, a sort of sub-episcopate. Bishops appointed presiding elders who governed in local districts just as bishops did in episcopal districts; they were pastors-in-chief for all the churches within the district. Presiding elders could not serve in the same district for more than four consecutive years and likewise traveled throughout their districts conducting the spiritual and temporal affairs of the church. At the general conference the presiding elders of each episcopal district formed Episcopal Cabinets that made recommendations and suggestions on appointments and other church matters to the bishop of their district. Presiding elders were answerable to the annual conference as well as the bishop, both of whom had powers of removal. Members of the AME church considered the presiding eldership system "a system of power, strength, and forcibleness to the Methodist Church." The bishops and presiding elders wielded an enormous amount of power within the AME, and in *The Negro Church in America* (1963), E. Franklin Frazier likened the hierarchy of black Methodist denominations to czars who rewarded and punished subordinates to extract loyalty. Nevertheless, the lack of bishop veto power, the removal powers of the conferences, and the required mobility in appointments insured that the general conference was the final authority and hampered the ability to consolidate power in any one specific area.[9]

---

[8] Ibid., 114-133; Richard R. Wright, *The Bishops of the African Methodist Episcopal Church*, Nashville, TN: AME Sunday School Union, 1963), 25-28.

[9] Turner, *Genius and Theory*, 134-146; A. S. Jackson, "The Presiding Elder System," *AME Church Review*, 10 (October, 1893), 301-06; Frazier, *Negro Church in America*, 49.

Ordained traveling ministers, pastors, deacons, and licensed local preachers exercised executive duties at the local level. Pastors and local preachers remained at home and could find secular employment although pastors who did such did not receive full pay. Traveling minsters could not pursue a secular occupation and were expected to devote their full energies to the church and be ready to do any work and travel anywhere the church sent them. In a sense, the AME considered the entire ministry as traveling ministers, and the ability to travel was an important prerequisite for advancement within the ranks. Each ministerial position, with the exception of presiding elder, required some type of election from one the conferences. Because of the highly competitive nature of positions within the AME ministry, members of the clergy consistently projected themselves in a manner that would improve their chances for advancement and leadership roles in the church and thereby the African American community.[10]

Lay officials also contributed essential administrative duties, especially financial and legal. The various lay positions, as the ministerial positions did for the ministry, offered the opportunity for political competition and upward mobility among the laity. Congregations elected or approved most lay officials, providing mass participation within the AME political process and structure. Church congregations elected three to nine trustees whose primary duties included holding legal title to church property. In theory, women, who also voted for trustees, could serve as trustees although the church discouraged such practice. Trustees also cared for and improved church property, represented the church in legal matters, and generally managed all secular affairs not already provided for. The extent of the powers and duties of the trustees was a source of debate within the AME. At times, as AME attorney D. August Straker noted in 1887, trustees found themselves suing the church rather than representing it in matters that concerned "property owned by the people."[11]

Other lay officials included stewards and class-leaders who were considered spiritual officers with temporal duties. Nominated by the pastors and elected by the quarterly conferences, stewards served as advisors to the pastors

---

[10] Turner, *Genius and Theory*, 95-114;

[11] Turner, *Genius and Theory*, 147-157; D. August Straker, "The Origins of the Powers and Duties of Trustees of the African Methodist Episcopal Church," *AME Church Review*, 3 (April, 1887), 359.

and performed such duties as opening and preparing the church, providing for janitorial services, and collecting church donations. Three to nine stewards per church comprised Boards of Stewards who chose the official church recording secretary and treasurer from their ranks. Class-leaders, appointed by the pastors and charged with teaching the doctrine, conducted religious classes, administered relief to the sick and poor, and collected church donations. The stewards and the class-leaders met weekly to form an Official Board, which the pastor chaired and which made decisions on the day-to-day operation of the church. The lay officials served as valuable links between the congregation and the ministry and more directly represented the congregations on the various boards, councils, and conferences within the AME. The participation of the congregations within the political process added to the democratic and republican spirit of the AME. Congregations elected the electoral colleges which chose the lay delegates to the general conferences, and the 127 lay delegates at the 1900 General Conference represented a significant voting force. Moreover, the system was designed so that the ministry and laity formed checks on one another that preserved the constitutional rights of both. Congregations not only elected and approved lay officials, they also voted on many decisions concerning individual churches from financial matters to capital improvements to new membership, further adding to the democratic spirit.[12]

II

Women also participated in the organizational and political structure of the AME, which likewise provided women the opportunity to develop critical political skills and leadership outside the norm of American politics. Not only did women participate as equal members in elections at the congregational level, they also formed conferences to support the missionary activities of the church. In 1874, the wives of seven bishops founded the Woman's Parent Mite Missionary Society, and two years later, the 1876 General Conference officially recognized the society's role within denominational affairs. The Parent Society established conferences that corresponded with the principal general and annual conferences. This allowed the wives of the ministers to be in conference at the same time as their husbands. Local auxiliaries of the society elected delegates to the annual

---

[12] Turner, *Genius and Theory*, 133, 157-177.

conferences who elected delegates to the general conference. The membership of the Parent Society, however, was entirely from the North; therefore, in the early 1890's, AME women in the Midwest and South formed the Home and Foreign Missionary Society. The separate societies created some sectional tensions, and leaders of both societies failed to agree to efforts to unite the two at the 1900 General Conference. The two eventually united in 1944. The primary charge of the women's missionary societies was to raise funds for home and foreign missions, a function they performed expertly.[13]

The question of whether women could or should serve as ordained ministers received considerable debate within the AME. Bishops like William B. Derrick and Henry M. Turner supported licensed female preachers but not ordained ministers. Turner maintained that there were "too many, drunkards, gamblers, liars, lynchers, mobs, Sabbath breakers, blasphemers, slanderers and sinners in the land to stop and quibble over women preachers." The 1884 General Conference recognized female preachers and allowed them to become licensed. Several AME women preachers were active in states in the North and South and as such were automatic voting members in the quarterly conferences. Nevertheless, although Sarah A. Hughes became the first ordained woman minister in 1885, the church eschewed such action throughout the period. Instead, the 1888 General Conference created the office of deaconesses, a sort of quasi-ministerial position for women. Certified by the church, deaconesses performed an array of duties, prime among which was "to minister" to the poor and sick. Each annual conference formed a nine-member Board of Deaconesses that included at least three women and that certified deaconesses recommended by the quarterly conferences. Some women in the AME defined the word "minister" quite literally and considered deaconesses the equivalent of ordained ministers, noting as Mary Louise did in the August, 1899, *Voice of Missions* that deaconesses "conducted revivals, saved souls and built churches." Nevertheless,

---

[13] Stephen Angell, "Henry McNeal Turner and Black Religion in the South, 1865-1900," (Ph.D. diss., Vanderbilt University, 1988), 343, 502-03; David Wood Wills, "Aspects of Social Thought in the African Methodist Episcopal Church, 1884-1910," 171; *Minutes of the 3rd Session of the Conference Branch of the Woman's Mite Missionary Society of the AME Church of the 4th Episcopal District, Indiana, 1900*, (Crawfordsville, IN: The Journal Co., Printers, 1900), 20; *1900 General Conference*, 202.

most members of the AME regarded deaconesses in a similar light as stewardesses.[14]

Stewardesses were lay officials of the church who assisted stewards, class-leaders, and pastors in spiritual and temporal affairs. The pastor of each church nominated and the Board of Stewards elected a three to nine member Board of Stewardesses. Although they had no legislative or judicial power, stewardesses performed administrative duties that kept the church smoothly functioning. Most of the women who were active in church affairs were the wives of the bishops, presiding elders, and ministers, and as Cynthia Neverdon Morton concludes in *Afro-American Women of the South* (1989), women often implemented the programs and plans that men devised. Several women involved in denominational affairs, like Ida B. Wells, Frances Ellen Walker Harper, Fanny Jackson Coppin, and Josie D. Heard, were active in social and political affairs outside of the church. Heard, speaking for the Parent Missionary Society, maintained that "whenever the conditions of the American negro is discussed, or wherever any effort is put forth for the bettering of his condition, that there we also have an interest." On behalf of the Society, she sent a communication to the 1899 meeting of the National Afro-American Council pledging the Society's support. Politically active women such as Josephine Turpin and Mary Church Terrell maintained close relationships with the AME and were constant speakers at AME events and contributors to the various AME publications. Although women suffered sexism within the denomination, the AME church, nevertheless, provided a political structure in which women participated and offered a more egalitarian atmosphere than the rest of American society.[15]

III

Indeed, the organizational and political structure of the denomination furthered the democratic and republican nature of the AME and allowed

---

[14] Angell, "Turner and Black Religion," 492, 524; "Editorial," *Voice of Missions*, 1 May 1897; "Our Greatest Women," *Voice of Missions*, 1 October 1896; Turner, *Genius and Theory*, 101, 168-69; Mary Louise Brown, "A Word for My Sex," *Voice of Missions*, 1 August 1899.

[15] Turner, *Genius and Theory*, 165-68; Cynthia Neverdon Morton, *Afro-American Women in the South and the Advancement of the Race, 1895-1925*, (Knoxville, TN: University of Tennessee Press, 1989), 8; *Proceedings of the 2nd Connectional Convention of the Women's Parent Mite Missionary Society, November 8-16, 1899*, Philadelphia; Dorothy Sterling, *Black Foremothers: Three Lives*, (New York: The Feminist Press at City University of New York), 82, 85.

participation in decision making at nearly every level. Members were consistently concerned with the type of people who would represent them at the various levels. Church members and officials, like presiding elder Walter Thomas, repeatedly reminded one another to elect to the various conferences delegates "who are true African Methodist" and "who are not political tricksters and wire pullers." Viola Caliman, delegate to the 1901 Pittsburgh Missionary Society Conference, warned members to avoid "a selfish ambition for office and honor . . . [and] cliques and rings" that only have "their own selfish interest in view." In Henry M. Turner's *The Genius and Theory of Methodist Polity*, which the 1888 General Conference accepted as the official guide book for the ministry and laity, the senior bishop outlined the qualifications for various church positions. Beyond education, piety, character, and honesty, Turner cited assertiveness, business practicality, impartiality, judgement, and broad views as ideal qualifications for officials of the AME. Such qualifications suggest that the AME sought to enlist people who could deal with the challenges of a secular world.[16]

Members competed fiercely for the highly coveted and influential positions within the various conferences and the AME bureaucracy, and it was likely that people voted for those who represented their views. Moreover, each member of the clergy had to pass through three elective positions in order to be positioned for an appointment to presiding elder. With more than 16,000 members in the clergy in 1900, many of whom actively pusued advancement within the church, the AME was a very political organization. In an era of discrimination and disfranchisement, these delegates often constituted the only African Americans for whom African Americans voted. Moreover in the South, the church provided the only opportunity for many African Americans to vote for anyone. Not bound to follow the opinions of the presiding bishops or elders, the delegates made decisions based on their views and the views of their constituents.

Members of the AME also used the church as a national and international political forum from which they addressed issues that affected the African American community, the nation, and the world. In several ways, many of the

---

[16] Walter Thompson, "The Work of the Coming Conference," *Christian Recorder*, 2 February 1899, 2; *Minutes of the 5th Session of the Woman's Mite Missionary Society of the Pittsburgh Annual Conference of the AME Church, July 11-14, 1901*, (Wilkes Barre, PA: Harold and Fernsler, 1901), 23-24; Turner, *Genius and Theory*, 84, 142, 158, 171.

women and men of the AME functioned as members of what black political theorist and activist W. E. B. Dubois termed as the "Talented Tenth," educated people capable of leading the African American community in a plural American society. Thus, they functioned as leaders of one of the interest groups that James Madison beleived was so necessary to keep democracy from becoming tyrannical. As the age of imperialism encompassed more people of color, many within the AME extended their leadership roles to represent and identify with opressed people in a plural international society. In a world of increasing political alienation for people of color, the AME stood as one of the few voices of color within an emerging world power that could speak out against the national and global subjugation of liberty.

Accordingly, the political-minded ministry and laity of the AME developed a political ideology and rhetoric that was strongly rooted in traditions of American republicanism and in the African American struggle against American racism. During the late nineteenth and early twentieth centuries, AME members sought self-determination as the means to liberty and equality for African Americans and indigenous people of foreign lands. Much of world history has developed around the concept of self-determination—the ability to make choices, to be self-governing, and to act according to independent beliefs and values. Self-determination has been both motivation and goal in American society since the earliest colonists who linked self-legislation with liberty and equality. Synthesizing Whig ideology, Lockean philosophy and other seventeenth century political theories, the promoters of the American Revolution espoused a political rhetoric that promised a republican government with full participation by all citizens. Full participation, however, did not come as white Americans placed limits on black Americans through racism.

Meanwhile, during the early national period, AME founder Richard Allen and others, influenced by racial restrictions and the need to express Christianity through black theology initiated a black religious separatist movement that contributed to the democratization of American religion as described by Nathan Hatch in *The Democratization of American Christianity* (1989). Indeed, Hatch maintains that African American preachers were the "most striking evidence of the democratization of Christianity" because they were able "to infuse ordinary existence with profound spiritual meaning," making them natural leaders in the black community. Black ministers manifested much of that "spiritual meaning" in the black theological gospel of liberation, developed in response to two hundred years of slavery. Thus, buoyed by the liberation gospel in the ideological struggle against racism, African Americans and, specifically, members of the AME began to develop political rhetoric and action that reflected the spirit of the American Revolution and that, in part, led to the Civil War and the passage of the 13th, 14th, and 15th Amendments.[17] Members of the AME during Reconstruction, as Clarence Walker illustrates in *A Rock in a Weary Place* (1982), through a version of American "civil religion," attempted to ensure full equality and participation by educating former slaves in the South to be good American citizens and Christians. Moreover, as God's chosen, it was the duty of the church to participate in the liberation of African Americans and the realization of American democratic ideals by eliminating racism. During the age of imperialism, AME leaders continued to practice and expand this version of American civil religion to oppose international as well as national racism that limited access to self-determination for people of color in the United States and across the globe. Also during the age of imperialism, members of the AME displayed elements of the five themes of black political thought described by Charles Hamilton in *The Black Experience in American Politics* (1973)—constitutionalism, sovereign nationalism, plural nationalism, leftist thought, and pan-Africanism. Plural nationalism stressed racial consciousness and cohesiveness and cooperative action to avoid complete assimilation or separation. The traditions of racism and republicanism and the autonomous nature of the AME led the majority of politically active members to

---

[17] Joseph H. Kupfer, *Autonomy and Social Interaction*, (Albany, NY: State University of New York Press, 1990), 3, 9-10; For more on the psychology of self-determination see Edward L. Deci, *The Psychology of Self-Determination*, (Lexington, MA: Lexington Books, 1980) and Malcolm Walcott, *The Psychology of Human Freedom: A Human Science Perspective and Critique*, (New York: Spinger-Verlag, 1988); There are many studies on the development of republicanism and the American Revolution including Bernard Bailyn, *The Ideological Origins of the American Revolution*, (Cambridge, MA: Belknap Press of Harvard University Press, 1992), Robert Middlekauf, *The Glorious Cause: The American Revolution, 1763-1789*, (New York: Oxford University Press, 1982); and Gordon Wood, *The Creation of the American Republic, 1776-1787*, (Chapel Hill, NC: University of North Carolina Press, 1969); Nathan O. Hatch, *The Democratization of American Christianity*, (New Haven, CT: Yale University Press, 1989), 112-13; For more on black theology and the liberation gospel see James Cone, *Speaking the Truth: Ecumenism, Liberation, and Black Theology*, (Grand Rapid, MI: Eerdmans Publishing Co., 1986); and James Raboteau, *Slave Religion: The "Invisible Institution" in Antebellum South*, (New York: Oxford University Press, 1978).

pursue a course toward plural nationalism in the United States. Meanwhile, imperialism and its racial implications led members to expand their thought into a plural internationalism that would export American ideals and institutions without American racism.[18]

Hamilton stressed that black political thought sought the implementation of constitutional theories. Moreover, the rhetoric and actions of AME members suggest that implementation of the ideals imbedded in the *Declaration of Independence* and the American Revolution also was a major theme of black political thought. Throughout AME literature, members often quoted from the "Declaration of Independence"—"life liberty, and the pursuit of happiness" and "all men are created equal;" the preamble to the Constitution—"We the people...;" and the Gettysburg Address—"of the people, by the people and for the people." The rhetoric of liberty and equality permeated AME political rhetoric and consciousness. In 1898, members reveled at the paintings by Henry Tanner, Bishop Benjamin Tanner's son, that the French government displayed at the Luxembourg Gallery. Symbolically, one presiding elder maintained that the featured painting, "Resurrection of Lazarus," and the fact that an African American had paintings on display at a European art gallery represented the "dawning of liberty." In an 1887 *Review* article, a Baltimore attorney compared the 13th, 14th, and 15th Amendments to the Magna Charter, "that Pallium and Gibraltar of English Liberties." He also quoted from the French Constitution of 1793 and Alexander Hamilton, "Can this be free government if partial distinctions are tolerated or maintained." A year later in the *Review*, one of the clergy voiced a tenet of civil religion and called for support of the Blair bill, national aid to education, because educating "the people" was the best way to insure the vitality of American republican institutions. The social gospeler Reverdy Ransom believed that the African American right to liberty, equality, and justice was part of God's evolving plan and was inherent in the nation's democratic heritage. Such rhetoric held Americans accountable for American ideals and was echoed beyond individual members.[19]

---

[18] Walker, *Rock in Weary Place*, 8-9; Charles V. Hamilton, *The Black Experience in American Politics*, (New York: G.P. Putnam's Sons, 1973), xxv.

[19] Ibid.; J.E. Brock, "The Dawning of Liberty," *Christian Recorder*, 13 January 1898, 6; E.J. Waring, "The Colored Man Before the Law," *AME Church Review*, 3 (April, 1887), 496-503; F.C.

Not only the state of the country committees at the AME annual conferences but many of the other committees like education or missions used the language of the American Revolution to express their views. Quoting the Gettysburg address and asserting that "we are part of the people," the delegates at the 1885 North Ohio Conference declared that the "right and duty of self government devolves upon us in common with the other people of this country." The conference thus linked self-determination to being a part of American society. Representatives at the 1899 Ohio Conference maintained that the worse feature of the African American condition was the "unjust limitations put upon our freedom in the exercise of our rights as American citizens." They argued that "the negro has free and equal chances only to enter the saloon, penitentiary, jail, workhouse, idleness, ignorance, disease and death." The representatives defined the limits placed on their ability to secure self-determination. Placing the struggle for liberty within an international perspective, members of the 1915 Virginia Conference continued to stress the importance of "Christian education as a levelling effect upon the world" that would eventually "strike down all caste and superficial distinction." To drive home their point the delegates quoted de Tocqueville— "Despotism may govern without religious faith, but liberty may not."[20]

Throughout the era, representatives of the Illinois Conference illustrated the continuity of political rhetoric and thought within the AME. At the 1890 conference, delegates resolved that since "taxation without representation is tyranny and the elective is one of the fundamental principles of our christian civilization," they therefore supported a national elections bill. In 1897, the delegates maintained that it was "the duty of the church to inquire into the cause or causes of this condition . . . [and] bring within reach of the people the equal distribution of the benefits of our republican form of government or that our government shall be indeed and in truth 'a government of the people for the people and by the people.'" By 1911, little had changed in the delegates' rhetoric which

---

Long, "Vitality of Republican Institutions," *AME Church Review*, 5 (October, 1888), 133-140; Morris, *Reverdy Ransom*, 2.

[20] *Minutes of the 4th Session of the North Ohio Annual Conference of the AME Church, September 23-28, 1885*, (Xenia, OH: Gazette Office, 1885) 35-36; *Minutes of the 69th Session of the Ohio Annual Conference of the AME Church, September 14-19, 1899*, (Hamilton, OH: Brown and Whitaker, 1899), 79-80; *Journal of Proceedings of the 49th Session of the Virginia Annual Conference of The AME Church, April 22-26, 1915*, Nashville: AME Sunday School Union Print, 1915), 94.

insisted that "There is a principle underlying this government . . . that liberty be
the corner-stone of the Republic . . . This is our country home; by birthright, and
by conquest." For members of the AME the promise of the American Revolution
had been far from fulfilled. Accordingly, they continuously reminded American
society in American terms that the republican form of government would not be
realized until racism was destroyed and African Americans participated fully in
the American political process.[21]

Ironically, women in the AME often turned the tables on men and
demanded greater and equal participation in denomination affairs. For instance, an
1886 contributor to the *Recorder* asserted that if the church only collected money
from male members, then the treasury would decrease by three fourths. She
maintained that church law "accepts men and women on an equal basis, and by so
doing implies an equal right to representation in that part of the Church that the
Dollar Money supports [the ministry]." The delegates at the First Woman's
Convention held in Nashville in 1895 placed "taxation without representation" as
number seven on their agenda and called for a greater role for women within the
church. One of the speakers at the convention maintained that one of the changes
the AME General Conference should make would be to "give the women an equal
footing with the rest of the laity." Not content to play a passive role within the
church, AME women actively sought greater equality in both the ministry and
laity and developed a political rhetoric partly based in American traditions.
Moreover, as illustrated by Josie Heard's letter to the Afro-American Council,
AME women, like AME men, sought a greater role in American politics and
fuller participation in American society.[22]

Many of the women and men of the AME considered the franchise as the
best means to secure and protect liberty and achieve equal participation in
American politics and society. They believed that through the vote African

---

[21] *Journal of Proceedings of the 19th Session of the Illinois Annual Conference of the AME
Church, August 6-12, 1890,* (Cairo, IL: Telegram Publishing, Co., 1890); *Minutes of the 25th
Session of the Illinois Annual Conference of the AME Church, September 17-22, 1897,*
(Metropolis, IL: Journal-Republican Power Print, 1897), 33: *Journal of Proceedings of the 40th
Session of the Illinois Annual Conference of the AME Church, September 30-May 4, 1911,*
(Nashville: AME Sunday School Union, 1911), 55.

[22] Alice Fells, *Christian Recorder*, 18 February 1886; Winfield Henry Mixon, *Christian Recorder*,
21 March 1895, 4; Jennie Higgins, "The Changes General Conference May Make," speech
presented at *1899 Womans' Day*, 38-40.

Americans would attain the autonomy that insured both full American citizenship and control over their own social institutions in a pluralistic American society. Throughout the era, AME members consistently opposed efforts to disfranchise African Americans and supported efforts to guarantee the right to vote. In 1890, Congress considered federal elections legislation, known as the Force Bill, that would authorize use of federal troops to protect African Americans voters. The bill received overwhelming support from many sectors of the denomination. Editorial writers for the *Recorder* considered the proposed law the best protection for the rights of African Americans. Reverdy Ransom, a rising star in the AME, supported the bill and denounced the "outrages and frauds committed against the ballot, especially in the South." Delegates at the 1890 Pittsburgh Conference favored the bill and voiced their "honest disapproval of attempts by the Mississippi Constitutional Convention to disfranchise" African Americans. The more radical Bishop Henry McNeal Turner, who often voiced opinions different from the mainstream of the church, also supported the bill, though reluctantly. Turner maintained that "weak as the bill is, it is a menace in our favor, at least. But it seems that the bill is to be defeated by Democrats, Negro-hating Republicans and a herd of Negro monstrosities." As predicted by Turner, Congress failed to pass the bill, which coupled with the introduction of the poll tax in Mississippi ushered in an era of disfranchisement for African Americans.[23]

Efforts to disfranchise African Americans and the effects of those efforts caused AME members to develop a political rhetoric of equality and liberty that expressed outrage and encouraged political activism. Members wrote articles in all the AME publications, denouncing Democrats for attempts to deny the vote to African Americans, chastising Republicans for remaining apathetic, and promoting government intervention to end racial disfranchisement. The delegates at the 1900 Ohio Conference declared that "we are now face to face with the question of our complete civil, social and political rights, and from this struggle we can not, we dare not retreat. We should stand firmly for equality of opportunity, the equality of right, and the equality of privilege." Two years later,

---

[23] *Christian Recorder*, 31 July 1890, 4; Reverdy C. Ransom, "The Federal Election Laws," *Christian Recorder*, 14 August 1890, 3; *Minutes of the 23rd Session of Pittsburgh Annual Conference of the AME Church, October 8-15, 1890*, (Pittsburgh: East End Journal Print, 1890), 39-40; Quoted in Edward L. Wheeler, *Uplifting the Race: The Black Minister in the New South, 1865-1902*, Lanham, MD: University Press of America, 1986), 77.

the Ohioans urged African Americans not to yield the "powerful weapon" of the ballot. Although a few AME members approved of the equal disfranchisement for all illiterate citizens, black and white, most AME leaders and members seemed to agree with the delegates of the 1901 North Ohio Conference who condemned North Carolina, South Carolina, Louisiana, and Mississippi for disfranchisement and called for the president to instruct the attorney general to institute proceedings against the four states. Delegates at the 1902 Pittsburgh Conference chastised the largely Republican Congress because it "failed to do for the negro that which is necessary to be done, relative to the protection of the rights of franchise in the South." Thus, combining the political rhetoric of liberty and equality with demands for constitutional enforcement, AME members sought to gain self-determination through the franchise.[24]

The separatist origins and organizational structure of the AME created a representative form of governance and a democratic atmosphere within the denomination that allowed members to actively participate in the political process within the church. Nearly every position in the church required some type of election, and the ministry and lay officials all served on the various church boards, councils, and conferences, making collective decisions. Moreover, the men and women of congregations voted on issues that directly affected their individual churches and for people who would represent them on the various boards, councils, and conferences. In addition, in a time of increasing political alienation of African Americans, the church provided an arena for the growth of political leadership and a platform from which that leadership spoke and acted. From that

---

[24] "How Negro Disfranchisement Has Worked," *AME Church Review*, 18 (October, 1901), 174; *1900 North Ohio Conference*, 37; *Minutes of the 72nd Session of the Ohio Annual Conference of the AME Church, October 1-5, 1902*, (Hamilton, OH: Brown and Whitaker, 1902), 58-59; *Minutes of the 70th Session of the Ohio Annual Conference of the AME Church, September 26-30, 1900*, (Hamilton, OH: Brown and Whitaker, 1900), 43; *Journal of Proceedings of the 35th Session of the Pittsburgh Annual Conference of the AME Church, October 15-19, 1902*, (Altoona, PA: H & W. H. Slep Printers, 1902), 36.

platform, AME members helped to develop a political rhetoric and ideology that demanded the promise of the American Revolution and the self-determination necessary for plural nationalism. Indeed, as the nation and the European and Asian "great powers" raced toward imperialism, AME members grappled with questions of self-determination on an international scale and searched for their place within a global community. The relationship between the AME church and the Republican party gravely affected the answers to those questions.

CHAPTER VIII

BREAKING THE GENDER BARRIER: AFRICAN-AMERICAN WOMEN AND LEADERSHIP
IN BLACK HOLINESS-PENTECOSTAL CHURCHES 1890-PRESENT

FELTON O. BEST

CENTRAL CONNECTICUT STATE UNIVERSITY

The Second Great Awakening (1790-1830) was responsible for the
conversions of a number of slaves in the ante-bellum south who found
membership in methodist and baptist evangelical churches. Several factors
enhanced this conversion. The fact that such churches embraced remnants of
"ecstatic behavior" in the forms of rhythematic handclapping, dancing, and
fainting led such enslaved Africans to feel that this revival embraced forms of
worship that resembled the African religious culture of "spirit possession"
practiced by their ancestors and passed on to them by cultural retention.
Eventually African-Americans would find ministerial and pastoral opportunities
in evangelical baptist and methodist churches as a result the growing population
of black members, the independent black church movement, the absence of a
formal education as a prerequisite for the ministry, and the ability of the laity-
including women to become extemporaneous preachers. By the end of the
nineteenth century many African-Americans determined that most black baptist
and methodist churches were endeavoring to assimilate from the Africanist rituals
of dancing, call and response singing, and fainting—thus now adopting European
church practices such as singing from hymnals and "rendering one self quiet in the
house of the Lord." In fact Richard Allen, the founder of the African Methodist
Episcopal church informed his congregates that most forms of ecstatic worship
such as dancing and excessive clapping were motivated by "satanic" influences
and rendered one to appear ignorant. Likewise such churches became rigid in
adopting European patriarchy. Many black baptist churches adopted policies
clearly excluding black women from leadership positions and while the black
methodist church had a few examples of preaching women practically none of
them pastored congregations.

By the late nineteenth and early twentieth centuries the pentecostal church,
which had black origins, emerged. Blacks who embraced pentecostalism did so as

an endeavor to preserve African religious culture while simultaneously resisting white dominant European Christianity. The issue however was much more complex for black women. In addition to endeavoring to maintain black culture African-American pentecostal women also were endeavoring to carve out positions of power for themselves—especially in a society that rendered them extremists because of their religion, lower class because they were black, and subservient because they were female. Thus, the focus of this paper is to examine the multiple means whereby black pentecostal women would endeavor to "break the gender barrier" and likewise to determine why such women have historically experienced greater successes in acquiring leadership roles in comparison to their sisters in other denominations.

Though African-American women in the holiness/ pentecostal church endeavored to increase the accessibility of leadership roles for themselves, they generally remained unsuccessful in their efforts to obtain "chief" positions. The positions which continued to elude women included appointments as bishops, general overseers, and in some cases, national church administrators.

For the most part, African American women were confined to such ministerial roles as presiding over a congregation in the absence of a pastor, serving as a missionary or "teacher" in the local assembly, or directing a women's department. Most Pentecostal denominations disallowed the ordination of women as pastors, and prior to 1924 no Pentecostal church in America would ordain a woman as a bishop.[1]

The Church of God in Christ (COGIC), headquartered in Memphis, is the oldest and largest black Pentecostal denomination in America. This church has historically limited women's mobility in the ministry. Women are denied the right to pastor churches, serve as Superintendents of church districts, receive ordination as bishops, and serve as Chairpersons of the General Assembly or as Chief Apostle of the denomination.[2] This mostly African-American group was founded

---

[1] See Charles Edwin Jones., *A Guide to the Study of the* Pentecostal Movement Vol I, 1983 p.168. Also see the *Church of God in Christ Official Manual* (Memphis, Tenn.: Church of God in Christ Publishing House p.158) regarding COGIC's perception of women's role in the ministry. David W. Faupel's *The American Pentecostal Movement* (1972) p.211 list the Mount Sinai Church as the first Pentecostal church in America where a woman was ordained as a Bishop. This woman was Ida Robinson in 1924.

[2] Church of God in Christ, *Official Manual with the* Doctrines and Discipline of the Church of God in Christ (Memphis, Tenn.: Church of God in Christ Publishing House, 1973) p.159 Cheryl

in Mississippi in 1897 by Charles Harrison Mason and Charles Prince Jones. COGIC rejected the ordination of females as bishops from its origin. The policy of refusing to ordain females as bishops probably arose as a result of Bishop Mason's earlier affiliation in the Baptist Church which enforced the same policy regarding female ministers. Women in the Church of God in Christ did establish churches, but they did not receive ordination to pastor them. In most cases such persons were licensed missionaries, "teachers," or church mothers.[3] COGIC women who have aspirations of ministering have historically been appointed as missionaries—a category given exclusively to them.[4] In 1918 Mother Arenia C. Mallory was employed as a teacher for Saints Academy, the COGIC college, in Lexington, Mississippi. Mallory's promotion to head of this school made her the first African-American female college president during the early twentieth century.[5]

The United Holy Church of America, the second largest African-American Pentecostal denomination in the United States, allowed women to pastor but also took a sexist attitude regarding their ordination as bishops. Although women in the United Holy Churches of America experienced more freedom in the ministry than the Churches of God in Christ, some African-American women determined

Townsend Gilkes, "Together and in Harness: Women's Traditions in the Sanctified Church" *Signs: Journal of Women and Culture in Society* Vol 10, No.4 Summer 1985 p.679. Gilkes explains that the Sanctified Church represents black religious institutions which emerged in response to postbellum changes in the worship traditions within the black community. Also see Bonnie Thornton Dill, "The Dialectics of Black Womanhood", *Signs: Journal of* Women in Culture and Society 4. No.3 (Spring 1979): 543-55.

[3] Women's Department, *COGIC Women's Handbook* (Memphis Tenn.: COGIC Publishing House. 1980) p.7-9

[4] Charles Edwin Jones, *A Guide to the Study of the Pentecostal Movement* Vol 1,1983 p.28

[5] COGIC women were great leaders. Mother Lillian Coffey used state and district supervisors of the Women's Department to collect money prior to and during the Convention. Cheryl Gilkes indicates that she presented Bishop Crouch of California with "thousands of dollars" in a paper bag. See Cheryl Townsend Gilkes, "Together and in Harness: Women's Traditions in the Sanctified Church" *Signs: Journal of Women in Culture and Society* (Vol 10 No.4 Summer, 1985 p.691) Gilkes stresses the significance and economic importance of African-American women in the Sanctified Church. In one such church that she visited the Women's day contribution was one third of the budget for the year (p.690). Oral tradition and interviews set the amount at a minimum of *10,000.00. See Lucille Cornelius, *The Pioneer History of the Church of God in Christ* (Memphis Tenn.: COGIC Publishing House 1975 p.24) Also see *Church of the Living God, Christian Workers for Fellowship, Glorious Heritage: The Golden Book Documentary and History* (n.p.: Church of the Living God, Christian Workers for Fellowship, 1976). Regarding the work of Mother Arenia C. Mallory see Lucille Cornelius, *The Pioneer History of the Church of God in Christ p.38-41* (Memphis Tenn.: COGIC Publishing House 1975)

they should be free from all types of religious oppression including not being allowed to pursue the office of bishop. Black women in this context established Pentecostal organizations which placed no restrictions on leadership roles.

Despite the sexist position of the Church of God in Christ regarding the role of women, the largest and most powerful Women's Department of any black denomination did emerge. Prominent women such as Ida B. Wells Barnett, Mary McLeod Bethune, Nannie Helen Burroughs, and Mary Church Terrell prompted Bishop Charles Harrison Mason, the founder of COGIC, to recruit Mother Lizzie Woods Robinson to become the first overseer of the Women's Department in 1910. Mother Robinson, a former Baptist teacher and academy matron, traveled the nation to recruit and enlist women workers while conducting revivals.

Religious Studies scholars such as Dr. Cheryl Townshend Gilkes in their research on black women in the "sanctified" church informs that while attempts were made to keep such church mothers from key leadership positions they were still able to exercise autonomy in some aspects of decision making. Additional historians of African-American religion such as Elizabeth Brooks-Higginsbotham, C. Eric Lincoln, and Albert J. Raboteau have confirmed that the pentecostal church was unique in that it placed fewer barriers on women regarding leadership positions. However no historian has examined the cultural, political, economic, and intellectual factors which encouraged African-American women to create their own pentecostal organizations. The churches that followed this trend include the Mount Sinai Church founded by Bishop Ida Robinson (156 churches in the U.S), The Church of the Living God founded by Bishop Lillian Tate (268 churches in the U.S), and the House of God founded by Bishop Mary Daniels, (412 churches in the U.S)

Bishop Ida Robinson and Mother Tate were examples of leadership among black women who responded to attempts to limit their ministerial roles by establishing their own pentecostal organizations. Ida Robinson would establish The Mount Sinai Holy Church, and Mother Tate would found The Church of the Living God, Pillar and Ground of the Truth, Without Controversy.

Bishop Ida Robinson, founder of the Mount Sinai Holy Church, responded to the restrictions placed on women in the church in a manner that many women of all walks of life and in a variety of endeavors would. She took an important stand against sexism by founding a Pentecostal organization in which the majority of its church hierarchy was female. What was most unusual about Mount Sinai Holy Church, however, is that it did not remain an all female denomination and yet it remains, even today, a female led denomination.

Bishop Ida Robinson began her ministry in Pensocola, Florida. She migrated to Philadelphia in 1917 where she was active in the Church of God denomination. Robinson continued her ministry at 17th and South Streets at a church pastored by the Rev. Benjamin Smith.[6] Among her responsibilities was assisting Brother Smith at this location by ministering to the church in his absence. In 1919 she left Smith's church and became the pastor of "Mount Olive" located at 505 South 11th Street. Mount Olive eventually became a part of the Northern District of the United Holy Church of America. Henry Lee Fisher, an official of the United Holy Church, publicly ordained her to the Gospel ministry. Fisher and G. J. Branch, the two leaders of this denomination, on occasion invited Sister Robinson to share the pulpit with them in evangelistic campaigns. In 1924 Fisher and Branch were consecrated as the first two bishops of the United Holy Church. Fisher later became the first president of the denomination and was succeeded after his death by Branch.

The year 1924 was also a pivotal point in Sister Robinson's ministry. Her church membership was growing and many spectators came to hear her preach, teach, and sing. The demand for her ministry spread from New York to North Carolina. Elder Minera Bell, church historian for Mount Sinai, indicated that during this year on some occasions Robinson's church was packed to capacity with adult men and women.[7] Many spectators came just to hear Robinson sing "What A Beautiful City" and "Oh I Want to See Him."

Despite Robinson's success, problems began to emerge in her denomination. The initial problem was that the ordination of women was challenged. Bishop Amy Stevens, the current president of this organization, indicated that Ida Robinson had been so influential in the United Holy Church that

---

[6] *Church Manual of the Mount Sinai Holy Church*, p.1. Most of the information in this manual was complied by Bishop Mary Jackson. Bishop Jackson completed a brief history of Mount Sinai which is included in this manual it is entitled, "Mount Sinai Holy Church is Born."

[7] *Ibid* p.2 Also see Minerva Bell's "Confirming our Earthly Heritage: Mount Sinai History and Roots" This paper was delivered by the church historian Elder Minerva Bell at the 60th Annual Convocation of the Mount Sinai Holy Church of America, Inc. September, 1984 in Philadelphia, Pennsylvania.

many women decided they would pursue the ministry as well. Since women outnumbered men in the United Holy Church by a ratio of two to one, the male leaders became very uneasy and inappropriately reactionary.[8] The critical point occurred when Pastor Robinson was informed that the United Holy Church would no longer publicly ordain women.[9]

Robinson embarked on what would be a ten day period of praying and fasting and determined that God had spoken to her saying, "Come out on Mount Sinai."[10] Robinson was convinced that African-American female ministers had been oppressed long enough by male religious leaders, and she sought and obtained legal advice in drawing up a charter for a new church. This new Pentecostal organization was known as "Mount Sinai Holy Church of America, Inc."[11] Elders G.J. Branch and J.P. Diggs from the United Holy Church, well aware of Robinson's leadership potential and importance to the United Holy Church, attempted to convince her to stay within their organization. Sister Robinson replied, "God commanded me to come out and loose the women." Frustrated by the retrogressive position regarding the public ordination of women she added, "If Mary the mother of Jesus could carry the Word of God in her womb, why can't holy women carry the word of God in their mouth?"[12]

Ida Robinson, founder of this denomination, also served as the organization's first bishop and president. The organizational hierarchy that Robinson developed also attests to her commitment to female leadership. Six of

---

[8] I interviewed Bishop Amy Stevens on February 12, 1989 at a District Convention of Mount Sinai held at Mount Sinai Holy Temple in Columbus, Ohio pastored by Elder Harry Bellinger. Bishop Stevens; who traveled and was taught by Bishop Robinson, tells the story of how Robinson's ministry influenced hundreds of female ministers. She also mentions that in many of the United Holy Churches that she visited men were rare commodities. In many such churches, according to Stevens, the only adult male was the pastor. Stevens estimates that women in the United Holy Church outnumbered men by a ratio of two to one. See also Clyde S. Bailey Pioneer Marvels of Faith: Wonderful 46 Years Experience Morristown Tenn.: the author, 1958. p.132 Apparently Stevens estimated is true for most American Pentecostal Churches. Bailey estimated that women constituted approximately 75% of the Pentecostal Church in America.

[9] *Manual of the Mount Sinai Holy Church of America, Incorporated* p.26 Also see the manuscript collections of the Mount Sinai Holy Churches of America. These manuscripts have been preserved by Elder Minera Bell, Church Historian for Mount Sinai. See Manuscript entitled, *The Fifteenth Annual Convocation Bulletin: Mount Sinai Holy Church of America. Inc.*

[10] *The Fifteenth Annual Convocation Bulletin: Mount Sinai Holy Church of America D.13*

[11] *Sixtieth Annual Convocation Bulletin of the Mount Sinai Holy Church of America. Inc.* p. 33

[12] Ibid p. 37

the nine elders on her church board were women. In June of 1924 Robinson held an ordination service for ministers at Mount Olive. Most of those ordained at this service were women.[13]

Bishop Robinson's leadership skills were quickly apparent. Her first convocation which was held in September 1925 witnessed seventeen churches, including several congregations from the United Holy Church, in attendance. Prior to the convention Bishop Robinson purchased a new church building from the Assemblies of God which had a seating capacity of 2,000. She established Monday night as "Women Preachers' Night", and allowed various "loosed" women to minister the gospel. Wednesday nights was also a "preachers' night" during which male ministers were featured.[14] Bishop Robinson, who was concerned about equal ministerial opportunities of men and women within her denomination, established these preachers' night services to ensure that neither gender was excluded from ministerial opportunities, although her primary aim was that the "loosed women"could exercise their gifts.

Between the years of 1924-1946 Robinson built a organization of eighty-four churches which extended from New England to Florida.[15] By 1946 she had ordained 163 Elders of which 125 were women. Additionally, she built an accredited elementary and high school, established missions in Cuba and Guyana, purchased a 140 acre farm which housed and employed people in New Jersey, and simultaneously pastored Mount Olive Church in Philadelphia and Bethel Holy Church in New York.[16] Elder Minerva Bell, church historian of the Mount Sinai Holy Churches of America, estimated that between 1924 and 1932 Bishop Robinson assisted in establishing every new church in the organization by conducting revivals in various regions of the United States and placing female

---

[13] Harold Dean Trulear, "Reshaping Black Pastoral Theology The Vision of Bishop Ida B. Robinson" p.8 (Unpublished Paper) Trulear interviewed several pioneers of Mount Sinai which was made possible from research grants from Drew University, the Association of Theological Schools of the United States and Canada, and the New Jersey State Historical Commission

[14] Minerva Bell, "Bishop Ida Robinson" Manuscript Collections Mount Sinai Papers. Bishop Robinson used the term "loosed" women to refer to liberated female ministers who could experience the same ministerial rights as men within her organization.

[15] Richard Crayne, *Early Twentieth Century Pentecost* (Morristown Tenn.: the author n.d.), p.25

[16] *The Fiftieth Annual Convocation Bulletin Mount Sinai Holy Church of America, Inc.* p.12

Elders over the new converts.[17] Robinson died after twenty two years of service as the Chief Apostle of the Mount Sinai Holy Churches of America, Inc.

Mount Sinai continued to grow and develop. In September 1946 at the Annual Convocation, Elder Emira Jeffries was made the Senior Bishop and President of Mount Sinai. In addition, Mary E. Jackson and Peter F. Jones were ordained as Bishops. Jackson became the Vice President and Peter Jones became the 2nd Vice President. By 1952 Mount Sinai established a nursing home under the administration of Bishop Emira Jeffries.[18] Bishop Peter Jones died in 1961 and was followed in death by Bishop Jeffries in 1964. Bishop Mary Jackson became the president of the organization after Jeffries' death. The current president of the organization is Bishop Amy Stevens.

A study of the Mount Sinai Holy Church Yearbooks from 1946-1988 reveals some interesting facts regarding the leadership roles of women, and the growth of male pastors. The statistics indicate that at the time of the founder's death women occupied a majority of the pastorate and the Board of Bishops. By 1972 the financial status of the organization improved and women continued to represent a majority of the pastorate positions and Board of Bishops.[19]

	1946	1972	1988	1996
Number of Churches	84	100	154	156
Number of Women Pastors	56	60	76	78
Number of Male Pastors	28	40	78	78
Percent of Women Pastors	69%	60%	49%	50%
Percent of Male Pastors	31%	40%	51%	50%

The Mount Sinai church women were doers. Unlike their religious sisters in the Church of God in Christ, they refused to stay within an organization which denied them ministerial opportunities at all levels. While the United Holy Church of America allowed some women to pastor, they simultaneously denied the office

---

[17] Minerva Bell, *"Bishop Ida Robinson" Manuscript Collections Mount Sinai Papers.*

[18] Mount Sinai Holy Church Yearbooks 1946-1972 In 1925   one year after the church was organized men accounted for 6% of the pastorate, 1934-10%, 1946-31%, 1972-40%, 1998-51%, 1996-50%.

[19] *Mount Sinai Holy Church Yearbooks 1946-1996.*

of the bishop to women and discontinued public ordination for women ministers-a policy that would not change until the late 1960's. Ida Robinson responded by creating an independent organization which "loosed" women from the bondage of religious male domination. Each new president of Mount Sinai has selected a five member Board of Bishops. Such bishops are the chief administrators of the church. Thoughout their seventy-one year history every Senior Bishop of Mount Sinai has been female even when three members of the Board of Bishops have been male. Such African American women have continued to obtain a majority of the chief positions in the church hierarchy. This organization has grown into the largest African-American Pentecostal church founded by a woman. And perhaps, more important, even as the number of male pastors grew—becoming the majority in 1988, the men have historically supported their religious church mothers as the chief administrators of the organization. This trend of church mothers as the chief leaders of the church continued until 1996 although the percentage of male to female pastors were even.[20]

Mount Sinai has never witnessed a male competitor for the presidency of the church. Conflict has not emerged nor is there any record of a group or individual expressing resentment toward female leadership. Mount Sinai men view their church mothers as pure leaders. The late Bishop Ronald Brown, former jurisdictional bishop of Mount Sinai's Southern District, regarded Bishop Amy Stevens as a great leader.[21] Brown, who was the husband of Olive Brown, the founder's daughter, attests to the excellent leadership from Mount Sinai women.

---

[20] Felton Best, interview with Bishop Amy Stevens on February 12, 1989, at a District Convention held at Mount Sinai Holy Temple, Columbus Ohio. Stevens indicated that Mount Sinai men have historically supported their church mothers for the Board of Bishops which is the chief administrative unit within the organization. The Board of Bishops establishes church policy, assists the Senior Bishop in the selection of pastors for local congregations, and is regarded as the executive cabinet of the church. Stevens further indicates that such men have seen the administrators as competent leaders.

[21] February 12, 1989 District Convention of Mount Sinai held at Mount Sinai Holy Temple Columbus, Ohio pastored by Elder Harry Bellinger. During this convention Bishop Brown expressed his admiration for Amy Stevens. Brown regarded Stevens as a great leader, and a committed saint who is worthy of the church's financial and spiritual support. I met Bishop Brown in a conference at the Quail Roust Retreat Center near Durham, North Carolina. Bishop Brown who was lecturing on, "The Position of Mount Sinai Regarding Marriage, Divorce, and Remarriage as It Relates to Church Membership: A Theological Perspective" made numerous comments in his introduction regarding the excellent leadership skills of its current president, Bishop Amy Stevens.

His wife, Elder Olive Brown, is the pastor of Jerusalem Holy Temple which is one of the largest African-American churches in Richmond, Virginia. Bishop Emanuel Hollands of North Carolina maintained that the growth and strength of Mount Sinai is, "a direct reflection of Bishop Robinson and the church presidents thereafter."[22]

It is clear that the male leadership in Mount Sinai accepts female leadership. At church conventions they demonstrate respect and reverence toward Bishop Amy Stevens and additional church mothers. Such male pastors have not subjected themselves to biased theology regarding the limited roles of women in the ministry. Doctors Kenneth Coward and Ray McKenzie, who are the leading theologians in Mount Sinai, have determined that gender is an insignificant factor regarding the roles that women can assume. These men who are also pastors continue to express satisfaction in the female leadership of the church.[23] Elder Harry Bellinger, pastor of Mount Sinai Holy Temple in Columbus, Ohio, has referred to Bishop Amy Stevens as, "a beautiful personality, competent leader and administrator who has led Mount Sinai to new heights."[24]

An additional case study of an organization established by a black pentecostal women for the purpose of providing leadership roles for females is the Church of the Living God, Pillar and Ground of the Truth, Without Controversy founded by Bishop L. Tate. Bishop Tate, an educated woman herself, founded the Church of the Living God in Hartford Connecticut. The organization, like the Mount Sinai Church spread along the east coast with churches located from New England to Florida and the Midwestern states. "Mother Tate" as she was often called, established an elementary through secondary school in Orlanda, Florida.[25] Elder Ozzie Davis, who attended this school, indicated that Mother Tate served as the administrator by day and an overseer of churches in Florida by night. Mother Tate, Davis explained, was a gifted orator and theologian and was regarded as the

---

[22] Felton O. Best, interview with Bishop Emanuel Hollands, Greensboro Street, Asheboro, North Carolina July 1989.

[23] Felton O. Best, interview with Dr. Kenneth Coward and Dr. Ray Mckenzie on February 12, 1989 at the District Convention of Mount Sinai held at Mount Sinai Holy Temple Columbus, Ohio.

[24] Elder Harry Bellinger, host pastor of the February 12, 1989 District Convention held at Columbus, Ohio made these remarks to the convention delegates prior to Bishop Stevens address.

[25] Official Manual of the Church of the Living God, (House of God) Pillar and Ground of the Truth, Without Controversy, 1993 edition.

most prominent black minister in Orlando despite the fact that she was a woman.[26] Like the Mount Sinai organization the church recognized the ordination of women as bishops. Unlike the Mount Sinai church however female bishops would not control the majority of the seats on the Board of Bishops a fact that remains true even until this day—although out of the 268 such churches in the United States approximately 40% are pastored by women and 30% of the positions on the Board of bishops are held by women.

The lower representation of women in the Church of the Living God in comparison to their counterparts in the Mount Sinai Church can be attributed to the early representation of male leadership in the organization. Bishop Archibald White of Philadelphia became the second president of this organization. Like Bishop Charles Harrison Mason, the founder of the Church of God in Christ, Bishop White's initial ordination occurred in the Baptist church which took a conservative position on the ordination of women for the ministry and clearly did not approve of women as bishops. Bishop Jesse White, Sr. of Hartford, Connecticut who is the nephew of the late Bishop Archibald White, and the current President of the Church of the Living God, as well as the former pastor of the Church of the Living God in Hartford, Connecticut indicated that, "while my uncle recognized the importance of women in the ministry he did not think too strongly of their roles as bishops especially if too many of them were on the Board of Bishops...perceiving that they would cause too many problems." [27]

Despite this sexist attitude by Bishop A.H. White, strong women in the church insisted that additional clergy women be named to the Board of Bishops. At the 1981 General Assembly of the Church of the Living God in Orlando Florida Elders L.C. Williams of Newark and L. Ward of Camden, New Jersey refused to accept males as their Bishops. In fact these church women insisted that they be consecrated to the office of Bishop-thus allowing them to oversee their "church and the additional churches preached out by them... including any female or male pastor that desired to join their diocese." These female elders were protesting a trend in the church which allowed men with fewer years in the

---

[26] Felton O. Best interview with Elder Ozzie Davis, 1992 Annual General Assembly Convention Orlando, Florida.

[27] Felton O. Best interview with Bishop Jesse White, Presiding Bishop, Church of the Living God, 70 Whitney Street, Hartford, Connecticut, 1992.

ministry and in many cases a lower educational attainment to be consecrated bishop prior to women with more experience. After threatening to leave the church and possibly take several female pastors with them Bishop A.H. White decided to ordain both of them to the office of bishop.

Some black pentecostal bodies are notorious for supporting a subordinate role for African-American women in the church whereas others have placed no restrictions upon them. Organizations that promote a subordinate role for women include the Church of God in Christ, the largest pentecostal denomination in the United States. Additional groups who support subordination are mostly Apostolic or "oneness" pentecostal churches. Whereas some of them recognize women as preachers, none of them can find scriptural justification to sanction their roles as pastors or bishops. Such organizations include the Church of Our Lord Jesus Christ, founded in 1919 by Bishop R.C. Lawson, the Pentecostal Assemblies of the World, and the Bible Way Church of Our Lord Jesus Christ, World Wide founded in 1957 by Bishop Smallwood E. Williams.

The manual of the Church of God in Christ initially appears to be liberal regarding the leadership roles of women however its conservative perceptions of women's ministry roles erupts quickly. While the church acknowledges that God uses women it simultaneously states that no women are "called to preach" or to perform most clerical functions. The manual states:

> The Church of God in Christ recognizes that there are thousands of talented, spirit-filled, and dedicated and well informed devout women capable of conducting the affairs of the church both administratively and spiritually... It is evident in the New Testament and in the writings of the New Testament and in the writings of the Apostolic Fathers that women, through the agency of two ecclesiastical orders, were assigned official duties in the conduct and ministration of the early church. The Church of God in Christ recognizes the scriptural importance of women in the Christian ministry...but nowhere can we find a mandate to ordain women to be an Elder, Bishop, or Pastor. Women may teach the gospel to others, have charge of a church in the absence of its pastor, if the pastor so wishes, without adopting the title of Elder, Reverend, Bishop or Pastors. Therefore, the Church of God in Christ cannot accept the following scriptures as a mandate to ordain women preachers; Joel 2:28, Gal. 3:28-29, Matt 28:9-11.

The qualifications for an Elder, Bishop, or Pastor are found in I. Timm. 3:2-7 and Titus 1:7-9. We exhort all to take heed.[28]

Like the Church of God in Christ, the Bible Way Church of Our Lord Jesus Christ and the Pentecostal Assemblies of the World provide their theological positions in their manuals justifying the subordinate roles of women. The Bible Way Church argues that, "We have no record of Jesus calling a woman to preach and minister in the way that he authorized the disciples", whereas the Pentecostal Assemblies of the World state that they do not, "endorse any woman leaving her husband and going into the work of the ministry without her husband's consent" and added that women evangelist were only allowed to officiate at a wedding, baptismal service, funeral, and communion service in cases of emergencies when permission is granted by the bishop or district elder.[29]

The aforementioned theological positions of such church bodies has been met with opposition from activist church women within their organizations. In some cases COGIC men who had wives that acknowledged a calling to the gospel ministry established team ministries and purchased churches in their own names to prevent church leaders from taking such property from the spouse at their husband's death. Some examples include Mother Mable Smith who actually pastored Rescue Temple Church of God in Christ in Greensboro North Carolina under the covering of her husband. Mother Smith was known throughout the state of North Carolina and the South as a noted evangelist, songster, and administrator. She actually preached out seven churches during her revival campaigns. Likewise Mother Smith preached from the pulpit at Rescue Temple COGIC and always acknowledged that she was called of God to "preach the gospel." She served as a District Missionary for the Sanford, N.C. district and as a State Supervisor of Women's Works in the 2nd Jurisdiction of the Church of God in Christ in Charlotte, North Carolina. By her own example, however; she demonstrated that women did not have to be confined to the male prescribed roles of missionaries and evangelists. In a sermon that she gave in a state COGIC convention in Washington, N.C. she indicated:

---

28 Women's Department, *COGIC Women's Handbook* (Memphis, Tenn.: COGIC Publishing House, 1980) p.7-9

29 Pearl Williams Jones, "A Minority Report: Black Pentecostal Women" *Spirit: A Journal of Issues Incident to Black Pentecostalism*, Vol I, 1977, Number 2, pp 38-39.

I was not called to be a missionary. God told me that I was a
prophetess. Yes a prophetess! As a prophetess I was not called to
fry fish and chicken, roles that have been designated for
missionaries. God sent me forth to establish churches. In fact he
has used me to establish seven of them. I don't have the title of a
pastor but I'm doing the work. I don't have the title of a district
superintendent but I assist my husband who is a district
superintendent in supervising the Churches in the district that I
personally hewed out. My ministry has not been certified by man
but it has been sanctioned by God. God has used me to pray for the
sick and see them recover, and I have conducted numerous revivals
in convention halls with hundreds of people in attendance. After all
God places no restrictions on women, only men do. After God has
removed the yokes from our necks men have tried to put them back
on us. Which is better, to be appointed by a man to do a work or to
be anointed by God to do it. After all the scriptures clearly tells us
that there is neither Jew nor Greek, bond nor free, male nor
female.[30]

Recognizing that the battle for becoming the official pastor of Rescue
Temple COGIC might be too severe for Mother Smith, Elder Smith asked his wife
while severely ill not to endeavor to pastor the church after his death. While she
followed her husband's request at his death she brought in her brother to pastor the
church in order that she could continue to assume her same role however under
her brother's covering. This action clearly demonstrates that COGIC women were
not powerless victims of a sexist religious order.

Several additional COGIC women followed the trend of Mother Mable
Smith. In Philadelphia, Mother Irene Oakley, the widow of the late Bishop B.M.
Oakley, pastored the church under the title of "shepherdess." Likewise in
Paterson, N.J. Mother Alleyne Gilmore, widow of a bishop and pastor, assumed
the local pastorate under the title of "shepherdess." In Columbus Ohio Jordon
Memorial Church of God in Christ in Columbus, Ohio, is pastored by
Shepherdess Ruth Jordon whose husband was the original founder and pastor.[31]

---

[30] First Jurisdiction, Greater North Carolina Church of God in Christ, State Convention, August
1981, Washington, North Carolina, COGIC State Temple.

[31] *Ameritech Pages Plus Columbus and Vicinity Yellow Pages* 1989-1990. Ohio Bell an
Ameritech Company (Ameritech Publishing, Inc. 1986) p.427 This directory lists Jordon's
Memorial Temple as a local church in the Church of God in Christ. It is listed with additional
Churches of God in Christ who all have their headquarters in Memphis Tennessee (COGIC)

African-American women allied themselves with the Pentecostal Church because they perceived that they would benefit in a number of ways. It was regarded as an agent of cultural retention which allowed for Africanist forms of worship through dance, singing preachers, call and response singing, and the usage of tambourines, drums, guitars, organs, and pianos during religious services. It allowed black women to gain community power through the autonomous institution of black the church, an extremely important benefit, especially considering that they were excluded from white male dominated organizations. It granted them economic power as pastors, district missionaries, evangelists, district elders, state supervisors of women's department and bishops. It also granted them political power. The pulpit became an avenue to promote issues that benefited women as Mother Mable Smith had done in a state convention. Even in situations when they could not obtain chief positions in the church they able to influence policy formation since they constituted a collective majority in the church and simultaneously the majority of the funds. In short, the black pentecostal church embodied African rituals, leadership roles for women—a custom that existed in some African societies, maintained in large slave communities, later finding its way into the pentecostal church. The pentecostal church also had black roots thus making it attractive to blacks in general and women in particular since by definition it endeavored to purge itself from European customs which included sexist while male overtones. Most importantly, it was through the pentecostal church that African-American women could perceive leadership roles in the church as "neither male nor female." Afterall, Bishop Tate had once stated:

> God has already told us in his word that there are no distinctions made on sex regarding leading a church. His word states that there is neither male nor female, Jew nor Greek, bond nor free... but we are all one in Christ. If Christ can move the sex and race barrier why cant we? In reality God does not see sex... he sees a spirit. All Christians receive the same Spirit. There is not a separate Spirit for men and women. A woman receives the same Spirit as a man therefore she can do any work in the church that a man can.[32]

---

founded by Bishop Charles Harrison Mason. The directory lists the pastor as "Shepherdess" Ruth Jordan. The address is 1971 Payne Avenue, Columbus, Ohio.

[32] *Official Manual of the Church of the Living God, (House of God) Pillar and Ground of the Truth, Without Controversy*, 1993 edition.

This theological perception of Bishop Tate clearly defines the position of the majority of African-American women in the pentecostal church throughout history. Black pentecostal women refused to accept the patriarchal beliefs of white theologians as their African-American church brethren had done. In fact these women developed their own Africanist theological perspective which assumed that women were natural spiritual leaders. This study also reveals that African-American female pentecostal church leaders also "covertly" and "overtly" socialized their sons and grandsons in a matriarchal manner. For example, Dr. Kenneth Coward, the grandson of a prominent female Mount Sinai female bishop, never questioned the theological justification of women embarking upon chief leadership positions. He was covertly socialized as a youngster by recognizing that his grandmother was a pastor and a bishop. In addition he was simultaneously overtly socialized from childhood to adulthood by her occasional sermons justifying that God had "broken the gender barrier" placed on them by a sexist patriarchal society which endeavored to exclude black church women from chief leadership roles. African-American pentecostal women thus became the pioneers of leadership roles for black women in Baptist, Methodist, Episcopal, and additional protestant churches in the late twentieth century.

CHAPTER IX

FOR STRANGERS, UNBORN BABES, UNCREATED WORLDS:
THE MISSION OF MALCOLM X

STEPHEN R. MORRIS
CENTRAL CONNECTICUT STATE UNIVERSITY

As Martin Luther King, Jr. triumphed on the dais beneath the Lincoln
Memorial in the culminating moment of the March on Washington, Malcolm X
stood by fulminating, frozen in the minds of many that day in an image of
impotent resentment.[1] James H. Cone's account of the same event—a crux in his
tale of conflict, contrast, and convergence between King and Malcolm X—offers
instructive perspective on this image.[2] For Cone, the March was occasion for
some of Malcolm's most trenchant rhetoric—memorable not just for its inspired
truculence,[3] but more importantly for its acuity in highlighting contradictions
inherent in the projects of the civil rights movement. The March, Cone suggests,
ended up a celebration of fellowship and shared hope by whites and middle-class
blacks; but meanwhile, as Malcolm put it, "the black masses are still unemployed,
still starving, and still living in slums...and, I might add, getting angrier and more
explosive every day. "[4]

There was another member of the pantheon of 20th century black
American leaders who was absent yet present on the Mall on 28 August 1963, and

---

[1] But not to all, to be sure, even among those on the dais. As Taylor Branch notes in *Parting the Waters: America in the King Years, 1954-63* (New York: Simon and Schuster, 1988), 874-5, John Lewis had been seeking a photo-op with Malcolm just hours before his speech.

[2] James H. Cone *Martin & Malcolm & America: A Dream or a Nightmare* (New York: Orbis, 1991), 112-119.

[3] See especially the "Message to the Grass Roots," in George Breitman, ed. *Malcolm X Speaks* (New York: Grove Weidenfeld, 1990), 14-15, where Malcolm evokes Kennedy's skillful appropriation of the March as a confrontation between the Administration and the "Big Six"—the National Negro leaders" (King, A. Philip Randolph, Roy Wilkins, James Farmer, John Lewis, and Whitney Young). In Malcolm's telling, Kennedy orders them to "Call it off." The Big Six, here gathered up in the persona of "Old Tom," respond pathetically: "Boss, I can't stop it, because I didn't start it."

[4] From "God's Judgment of White America," in Malcolm X, *The End of White Supremacy*, Benjamin Goodman, ed. (New York: Merlin House, 1971), 146.

whose marginality that day takes on in retrospect an ironic resonance.[5] It was, of course, the day of W.E.B. DuBois' death in Accra, Ghana, where he had sought refuge two years before from the "cruel, receding mirage" which Martin King's "Promised Land" had become for him.[6] A year before his departure, DuBois had addressed himself to contradictions in the Civil Rights movement from his own perspective. Civil and social equality were "in sight" he told a conference of the Association of Black Social Science Teachers on 2 April 1960. But even the realization of these coveted goals would not bring an "end to the so-called Negro problems, but a beginning of even more difficult problems of race and culture." Because, he continued,

> what we must now ask ourselves is when we become equal American citizens what will be our aims and ideals. Are we to assume that we will simply adopt the ideals of Americans and become what they are or want to be and that we will have in this process no ideals of our own?[7]

I call attention to the seemingly fortuitous intersection of DuBois and Malcolm X at the March on Washington in order to propose the heuristic framework of this essay. I want to consider Malcolm X within contexts of inquiry and reflection derived from DuBois. More specifically, I shall argue that DuBois realizes in his life and his theorizing (and especially, in his several theorized lives, his autobiographies[8]) a paradigm of black leadership of which Malcolm X can be seen as an idiosyncratic, but nevertheless representative instance. In broad terms, I contend that the dilemmas, contradictions, and tensions which conditioned Malcolm X's evolving articulation of his political and cultural missions, had

---

[5] Roy Wilkins' announcement of DuBois' death at the March is the setting for the opening pages of David Levering Lewis' *W.E.B. DuBois: Biography of a Race, 1868-1919* (New York: Henry Holt, 1993), 1-4.

[6] Lewis, *op. cit.*, 3. See too Herbert Aptheker "On DuBois' Move to Africa," *Monthly Review* 45:7 (December 1993), 36-40.

[7] From "Whither Now and Why?" in W.E.B. DuBois *The Education of Black People: Ten Critiques*, 1906-1960, Herbert Aptheker ed. (New York: Monthly Review Press, 1973), 149.

[8] William L. Andrews lists no fewer than 60 autobiographical works by DuBois in his "Checklist of DuBois's Autobiographical Writings" collected in *Critical Essays on W.E.B. DuBois* William L. Andrews ed. (Boston: Hall, 1985), 226-30.

already been identified and delineated with precision by DuBois.[9] In this essay, I shall focus on three such loci—three structures of argument and concept which DuBois elaborated in his life and thought, which in turn Malcolm X expressed in his own distinctive idiom.

First, for DuBois race was something which the black leader is not just born into. It is something, in addition, which he or she must choose by an act of will and reason, must take on as a fundamental spiritual commitment. To overstate the point, but only slightly, the DuBoisian black leader must become a sort of cynosure, in whose life the destiny of all African Americans becomes more fully actualized.[10] I shall show how Malcolm X instantiates this characteristic by an analysis of his rhetorical distinction between being "black," and being "Negro."

A second and closely related condition on black leadership emerges from DuBois' reflection on the intimate connection in a leader's vocation between composing his life and organizing his people. For DuBois, a black leader must harmonize and unify his own self, before he can do the same for his people, and in both cases he must commit himself to tasks that are vexed and paradoxical. He must become a person who lives such contradictions, but with style—in such a way that just by living he makes the case that contradictions can be lived (that they need not simply be surrendered to). After indicating how I see this theme at work in DuBois' career, I shall draw it out of Malcolm's, focusing in particular on his conversion in prison, the first great caesura of his life. I shall read this crucial moment as a double conversion, one impulse of which ends up suppressed until the second great caesura, the break with Elijah Muhammad—an example then precisely of the DuBoisian leader's commitment to living contradictions with style.

Finally, I shall turn to DuBois' recurrent reflection on the problem of authority and democracy—the deep conflict with which he believed any leader must grapple between the tactical imperative to organize his people, and the moral

---

[9] Robert Franklin, in *Liberating Visions: Human Fulfillment and Social Justice in African-American Thought* (Minneapolis: Augsburg, 1990), also considers Malcolm X in light, partly, of prior reflection on DuBois.

[10] My debt to Lewis here will be obvious to his readers, and is indicated in its very title (which in turn alludes to the subtitle of DuBois' second autobiography, *Dusk of Dawn: An Essay toward an Autobiography of a Race Concept*). For Lewis, a biography of DuBois must also be a biography of a race—the story of how "the life and destiny of Africans in America merged inseparably with his own." (Lewis, *on. cit.*, 81; cf. 132)

imperative to promote their power and autonomy. For DuBois, this conflict served as the dialectical matrix for a life-time of theorizing on what it is to be a black leader. I shall argue that the problem plays a catalytic role in Malcolm X's career as well.

Beyond the particular claims and arguments I shall be making, my aim in this essay is simple: to start a conversation about Malcolm X that takes its point of departure from the fecund contexts provided by W.E.B. DuBois. It is one of the more sharpedged ironies of Malcolm's life that he was so unaware of DuBois as a contemporary[11]—an irony embedded in structural distortions imposed by Cold War parochialism on American culture and politics in the 1950's and 60's.[12]The luxury of synchronic perspective affords us, looking back, the chance to adjust some of those distortions, and to examine the connections and continuities that emerge from behind them.

I. RACE AS VOCATION: THE DIALECTIC OF RACIALIZED INDIVIDUALITY

Looking back on his years at Fisk from the perspective of his tenth decade, DuBois emphasizes, on two different occasions, the voluntary dimension of the racial identity he was so assiduously cultivating throughout that period. In an interview recorded shortly before his final departure for Ghana, DuBois remarks that by the time of his graduation, he had become "quite willing to be a Negro and to work with the Negro group."[13] A few years before, he had expressed the same thought in his *Autobiography*, writing of Fisk that it was "a microcosm of a world and a civilization in potentiality." Reflecting on his place in this cosmos, he continues: "A new loyalty and allegiance replaced my Americanism:

---

[11] Of course Malcolm X knew of DuBois, but his allusions to him are surprisingly terse. *The Souls of Black Folk* was part of his reading in prison, interestingly recalled for the glimpse it provided "into black people's history before they came to this country." And during his visit to Ghana in May of 1964 he was feted in the Ghanaian press as "the first Afro-American leader of national standing to make an independent trip to Africa since Dr. DuBois came to Ghana. See Malcolm X, with the assistance of Alex Haley, *The Autobiography of Malcolm X* (New York: Grove Press, 1965), 175 and 352-60.

[12] Gerald Horne offers a searing and cogent delineation of these distortions in *Black and Red: W.E.B. DuBois and the Afro-American Response to the Cold War, 1944-1963* (Albany: SUNY Press, 1986).

[13] Lewis, *on. cit.*, 73. The quote is from "W.E.B. Dubois/A Recorded Autobiography" (interviewed by Moses Asch), Folkways Records (FH 5511, 1961), cited by Lewis on page 597, note 42.

henceforward I was a Negro."[14] Lewis' gloss on the significance of DuBois' "racial identity" claim is illuminating. He characterizes DuBois' "racial shape" as "an alloy, never entirely pure." DuBois' ambivalence, Lewis contends,

> endowed him with a resilient superiority complex, and that...complex convinced Willie...that his lifelong espousal of the 'Darker World' was an optional commitment based above all upon principles and reason, rather than a dazzling advocacy he was born into.[15]

Ambivalence, or double consciousness, is the most well-known motif of DuBois' thinking on race. But what we find in the exuberant juncture to which Lewis draws our attention strikes a very different note from the agonized reflections in "Of Our Spiritual Strivings".[16] It may be ambivalence, but it is ambivalence resolved for a moment in an attitude of deliberate affirmation.

In DuBois, this attitude was an achievement, and this achievement in turn sets a standard by which to judge Malcolm X's striving in the same arena. I shall briefly describe the contours of this arena as I understand them, and then indicate how Malcolm and DuBois both can be situated within it.

In Aristotle's theory of individuation, individuality emerges as a point of intersection between a universal principle (that is, a principle of form, such as a

---

[14] W.E.B. DuBois, *The Autobiography of W.E.B. DuBois: A Soliloquy on Viewing MVP Life from the Last Decade of its First Century* (New York: International Publishers, 1968), 108.

[15] Lewis attributes this observation in part to E. Franklin Frazier. See Lewis, *on. cit.*, 73 and 597, note 44.

[16] As in this justly famous passage: "It is a peculiar sensation, this double-consciousness, this sense of always looking at one's self through the eyes of others, of measuring one's soul by the tape of a world that looks on in amused contempt and pity. One ever feels his twoness—an American, a Negro; two souls, two thoughts, two unreconciled strivings; two warring ideals in one dark body, whose dogged strength alone keeps it from being torn asunder " (*The Souls of Black Folk* (Harmondsworth: Penguin, 1989), 5). Compare the image in *Dusk of Dawn*, in which the "full psychological meaning of caste segregation" is analogized to the condition of prisoners held behind a "thick sheet of invisible but horribly tangible plate glass." DuBois remarks: "It is hard under such circumstances to be philosophical and calm, and to think through a method of approach and accommodation between castes. The entombed find themselves not simply trying to make the outer world understand their essential and common humanity but even more, as they become inured to their experience, they have to keep reminding themselves that the great and oppressive world outside is also real and human and in its essence honest. All my life I have had continually to haul my soul back and say, 'All white folk are not scoundrels nor murderers. They are, even as I am, painfully human." *Dusk of Dawn* (New York: Harcourt Brace, 1940), 130-132.
The parade of white people through Malcolm X's memory as he reflects on his brothers dictum that The white man is the devil," provides an instructive contrast (see the *Autobiography*, 159-60).

genus or species), and a principle of particularity (for Aristotle, matter). The fruitful problem with this theory is that the notion of form deployed within it is ambiguous. For form is both what transcends individuality (by being something which many individuals share in), and something that shapes and determines individuality (by being that in virtue of which a particular individual is the sort of substance he or she happens to be). The upshot is a dialectical tension between form-determined and matter-determined conceptions of individuality. Within the former, what individuals have in common, what binds them together into collective unities is valorized; within the latter conception, uniqueness gets valorized—what sets individuals apart from each other falls more prominently into theoretical view.[17] The question that falls out of this dialectic that is most interesting for our purposes is simple: to what extent can one's individuality be fully realized within the forms that constitute and construct it?

Aristotle understood by "form," a natural kind. Thus his theoretical schema becomes problematized when the principles of form in question are political or social kinds. Indeed, I think DuBois' ruminations on race can be usefully seen as a politicizing of the old Aristotelian dialectic of individuality. For the principle of individuality-shaping form which most preoccupies DuBois is never, in his view, an unambiguously natural principle.[18] To be sure, DuBois understands that race acts like Aristotelian form in so far as it acts to determine

---

[17] The terms of this summation are mine, but they are conventional. See Mary Louise Gill *Aristotle on Substance: The Paradox of Unity* (Princeton: Princeton University Press, 1989) for a more detailed presentation of this schema.

[18] There are moments when DuBois didactically adopts the natural kind racial idiom that was so pervasive around the turn of the century. See, for example "The Conservation of Races," in *The W.E.B. DuBois Reader* Andrew Paschal ed. (New York: Macmillan, 1971), 19-31. Nancy Stepan and Sander Gilman (in "Reappropriating the Idioms of Science: The Rejection of Scientific Racism," in Sandra Harding, ed. *The Racial Economy of Science* (Bloomington: Indiana University Press, 1993), 176-193) argue that this essay can be read as a rhetorical appropriation of the dominant racialist idiom of the day, for the purposes of subtly undermining the racist presumptions which that idiom expresses (a reading for which Lewis, *on. cit.*, 170-74, provides some historical basis). Anthony Appiah seems unpersuaded in "The Uncompleted Argument: DuBois and the Illusion of Race," collected in Henry Louis Gates, Jr., ed. *Race: Writing and Difference* (Chicago: University of Chicago Press, 1985), 21-37 (an argument recapitulated in the second chapter of Appiah's *In My Father's House: Africa in the Philosophy of Culture* (Oxford: Oxford University Press, 1992)). Wilson Jeremiah Moses provides crucial historical perspective on the dispute between Appiah and Stepan and Gilman, in chapter 6 of *The Golden Age of Black Nationalism 1850-1925* (Oxford: Oxford University Press, 1978). See also Lucius T. Outlaw, Jr., *On Race and Philosophy* (New York: Routledge, 1996) for a vigorous defense of DuBois' standpoint in the "Conservation" essay.

and constrain individuality. But he understands too the political and cultural malleability of this constraining—understands race "as a symptom, not a cause; ..as a long historic development and not a transient occurrence."[19] Thus he understands the form of race as Aristotle never imagined form could be understood—namely, as something more than a structuring principle of the world, available to the scientific imagination for its delectation and edification, but otherwise immutable. For DuBois, race is a site of ambiguity and flux, to be approached "by way of philosophy and history rather than by physics and biology. "[20] That is, unlike Aristotelian form race is the kind of universal that is transformable precisely through being understood.

DuBois signals his awareness of the mutability of the race concept, and of the power he senses developing within himself to re-shape this concept, in his enthusiasm about "discovering" that he is a Negro. At this point, on my reading, he has made a crucial intervention in the dialectic of individuality. He has seized hold of a form—the American race principle—that threatens to crush his individuality, over-determining his life so oppressively that he, like all others born under its sway, risks becoming a cipher of suffering and futility under its weight— and he has made that form into the form of his own individuality. He has sensed that he might become the form, without being submerged by it.

DuBois' emergence into a racialized individuality crafted by his own will and reason marks the development of a "superiority complex" that remains the foundation of his psyche throughout his life. For all the torment racism undoubtedly caused him, it is hard not to feel of DuBois that he never needed the therapy Malcolm X strove to provide: "to revolutionize the American black man's thinking, opening his eyes until he would never again look in the same fearful, worshipful way at the white man."[21] Yet surely Malcolm did need it, and so too did uncounted black Americans—"so called Negroes" whom Malcolm summoned to a Blackness not made in the image of humiliation, depression, and degradation. The circumstances of Malcolm's emergence into racialized individuality differ

---

[19] *The Autobiography of W.E.B. DuBois*, 198-199.

[20] ibid, 149.

[21] Malcolm X, *Autobiography of Malcom X* , 289. Compare pages 312 ff. where he presents his qualifications for leadership as a function of his insight into the pathology of the "black man in North America...mentally sick in his cooperative, sheeplike acceptance of the white man's culture."

significantly from DuBois', of course. DuBois' ambivalence coursed between a serene, almost imperial sense of unassailable superiority, and his clear-sighted but nonetheless bitter understanding of the basic rule of racial standing in America— that he, as a Negro, would always have to work harder, and accomplish much more, for far less recognition and remuneration than his white contemporaries, no matter what the forum, and no matter where the truth and merit might lie.[22] Thus, DuBois knew very early in his life that he was ineluctably committed to a larger struggle than the quest for his own bread. But from the start he confronted this daunting fact as an opportunity to achieve and shine.

By contrast, Malcolm X comes to "some of the first serious thoughts" of his life[23] from the infernal depths of confinement in the Norfolk Prison Colony.[24] Strikingly, however, these thoughts lead him through a process similar in structure to patterns already articulated by DuBois. At the heart of this process is the insight that race is not an immutable determinant of individuality. In Malcolm X's experience this insight is the recurrent motif of the complex discovering that marks his prison conversion (the first caesura, as I have called it). Throughout the *Autobiography's* narrative of this experience, Malcolm distinguishes his "brain-washed" condition before the break, with his newly heightened consciousness after, a consciousness he summed up a few years later by proclaiming: "I'm not an American. I'm one of the 22 million black people who are the victims of Americanism."[25] For Malcolm X, the rhetorical flourish with which he claimed being black as against being Negro marked a fundamental shift in psychic orientation. In the following section, I shall explore this shift in detail, by way of arguing for a schema for understanding what precisely happened to Malcolm X in prison.

---

[22] Bitter though this understanding may have been, his reaction in one instance—the University of Pennsylvania's refusal to offer him even a temporary instructorship upon his completion of *The Philadelphia Negro* is typical: "...I did not mention this rebuff. I did not let myself think of it. But then, as now, I know an insult when I see it." *The Autobiography of W.E.B. DuBois*, 199 .

[23] Malcolm X, *Autobiography of Malcom X* , 161.

[24] Ibid, 150: "..the very bottom of the American white man's society...."

[25] From "The Ballot or the Bullet" in Breitman ed. *Malcolm X Speaks,* 26. Similar sentiments open the "Message to the Grass Roots," in the same volume. Minutes later in the former, Malcolm adds: "...you and I, 22 million African-Americans -that's what we are—Africans who are in America."

II. A THEORIZED LIFE: MALCOLM X'S DOUBLE CONVERSION

Malcolm prefaces the chapter of his *Autobiography* on his prison years with these remarks on the autobiographical construction of identity:[26]

> But people are always speculating—why am I as I am? To understand that of any person, his whole life, from birth, must be reviewed. All of our experiences fuse into our personality. Everything that ever happened to us is an ingredient.[27]

Here is a thought which, I submit, must be linked to the idea of realizing one's individuality through a claiming of and a merging with one's people, one's culture, one's race. Further, any process of self-realization will be a process of composition, like in nature to the process of making literature out of the chaos of affect and incident that is experience. Thus in undertaking to fashion oneself into "a race man", who manages at once not to lose himself in a universal, one is undertaking to fashion one's *self*. One is undertaking to bring form and style to "all sorts of illogical trends and irreconcilable tendencies...contradictory forces, facts."[28] This creative act is, it should be clear, a double act—it is the telling of the

---

[26] Commentary on African American autobiography as a genre is extensive. Joe Weixlmann's bibliographical essay in *Black American Literature Forum* 24:2 (Summer 1990), 375-415, provides essential guidance, to literature on the genre as well as on Malcolm X's contribution to it. See too Eric Michael Dyson's two review essays, "Probing a Divided Metaphor: Malcolm X and His Readers," in his collection *Reflecting Black: African-American Cultural Criticism* (Minneapolis: University of Minnesota Press, 1993), 115-128, and "X Marks the Plots: A Critical Reading of Malcolm's Readers," chapter 2 of his indispensable *Making Malcolm: The Myth and Meaning of Malcolm X* (Oxford: Oxford University Press, 1995), 21-76.

[27] Malcolm X *Autobiography of Malcom X*, 150. The formulation here recalls Alexander Nehamas' reading of Nietzsche's concepts of self and character: "Because organization is the most crucial feature of literary characters, the quality of their actions is secondary: the significance and nature of a character's action is inseparable from its place in that organization. Ideally, absolutely everything a character does is equally essential to it; characters are supposed to be constructed so that their every feature supports and is supported by every other." Nehamas, *Nietzsche: Life as Literature* (Cambridge: Harvard University Press, 1985), 193-4.

In what follows I shall continue to refer to the *Autobiography* as a product of Malcolm's creative imagination, rather than as a collaboration with Alex Haley. Albert E. Stone, in *Autobiographical Occasions and Original Acts: Versions of American Identity from Henry Adams to Nate Shaw* (Philadelphia: University of Pennsylvania Press, 1982), 282ff. makes the case for regarding the *Autobiography* as a case in which "Two Recreate One." But, as Stone also observes, a good part of the strength of the collaboration derives from Haley's deliberate subordination of himself beside Malcolm. That is, if Haley is Plato to Malcolm's Socrates, it is the Socrates of the *Apology* we should have in analogical view -since that Socrates is the one Plato would have taken the greatest pains to paint closest to the image preserved in memory.

[28] DuBois, *Dusk of Dawn*, 133.

story of a self that is at once "an attempt to write the black community into freedom."[29]

To be sure, autobiography conceived under such strictures lends itself readily to didacticism, in which the composition of racial selfhood becomes a constant retouching of the "details of life in order to produce the desired image of impregnable racial pride."[30] But didacticism fast becomes tedium when it is the sole, or even dominant principle of a work—usually a tincture suffices. Indeed, both Malcolm X and DuBois employ it as only one strategy among many—thus, the fascination they both continue to exert as exemplars of the theorized life. I begin with the hermeneutical presumption that only unities wrought from underlying complexity, ambiguity, tension, and contradiction end up exerting such fascination. In trying, as he professes, to synthesize all of his experiences and everything that ever happened to him into a coherent story, Malcolm X starts with chaotic recalcitrance—life and memory and the impulse to speak—and finishes, thanks to Haley, with a composed work. But this work continues to attract readers, in part, because the chaos did not fully submit to the composition.[31] I offer a reading of Malcolm's conversion in illustration of my claim.

The conversion scene in chapter 10 of Malcolm X's *Autobiography* does momentarily suggest Augustine's weeping beneath the fig tree in Book VIII of the *Confessions*.[32] Malcolm himself invokes, modestly to be sure, the Pauline exemplar.[33] And I think there is little question that religious conversion is the dominant theme of the transformation he underwent between 1946 and 1952. But to characterize that transformation solely in terms of the fierce devotion he conceived through it to Elijah Muhammad and the Nation of Islam is a two-fold mistake. It is a misreading of Malcolm X's own account of what actually happened. And, it hinders understanding of the second caesura of his life, the

---

[29] Craig Werner "On the Ends of Afro-American 'Modernist' Autobiography." *Black American Literature Forum* 24 (1990): 205.

[30] Lewis, op; cit, ,3

[31] Paul John Eakin in "Malcolm X and the Limits of Autobiography." *Criticism* 18(1976): 230-42 makes a similar point employing a different conceptual frame. See too David P. Demarest, Jr.'s "The Autobiography of Malcolm X: Beyond Didacticism." *CLA Journal* 16(1972): 179-87.

[32] This is one of Barrett John Mandel's contentions in "The Didactic Achievement of Malcolm X's Autobiography." *Afro-American Studies* 2 (1972): 269-74.

[33] Malcolm X, *Autobiography of Malcom X*, 163.

break with the Nation, and therefore of his life's second great transformative period, from March of 1964 to February of 1965.

In fact, Malcolm X underwent two conversions during his prison years, under the guidance of quite distinct mentors, to two radically different, indeed antipodally opposed, spiritual (and intellectual) orientations. One of these conversions was to Elijah Muhammad's idiosyncratic brand of American Islam, and the mentoring in this instance was initiated by his brothers, Wilfred, Reginald, and Philbert, and his sister Hilda (before being assumed by Elijah Muhammad himself). But how should we understand this conversion, still so intensely felt in the telling a decade later, even as the wild doctrines that were its putative vehicle are held at disdainful distance, and dismissed as "tales" uttered in a "vacuum into which any religious faker could step and mislead our people"?[34]

To understand it fully, we must assess it in light of the conversion prior to it, the conversion presided over by a fellow inmate, Bimbi.[35] This was not of course a religious conversion (Bimbi himself seems to have been an atheist). Malcolm X's first conversion in prison was to humanism.[36]

By this seemingly provocative claim I mean something simple: *before* Malcolm X found the Nation of Islam, he re-discovered his tenacious capacity for

---

[34] Malcolm X, *Autobiography of Malcom X*, 168.

[35] See Bruce Perry, *Malcolm: The Life of a Man Who Changed Black America* (Barrytown, N.Y.: Station Hill Press, 1991). Perry identifies Bimbi as John Elton Bembry (at 108). Louis A. DeCaro, Jr., *On this Side of My People: A Religious Life of Malcolm X* (New York: New York University Press, 1996), reads Bimbi as atheist foil to Malcolm (see DeCaro at 77-78). Thus, for DeCaro, Bimbi is significant as the cool, rationalist alter ego to Malcolm's angry, contemptuous, street-hardened rebel. DeCaro does emphasize Bimbi's "fundamental" influence on Malcolm (at 227), citing an interview with Malcolm by D.G. Bridson, on 2 December 1964. In the course of that interview, Malcolm stated:
"And he [Bimbi] started me reading myself; in fact, his influence turned me from reading what you might call cowboy books, which was my diet at that time, into a higher level of reading."
DeCaro's thesis about Malcolm's spiritiual transcendence of Bimbi's cyncial atheism is plausible. DeCaro insists, in fact, that without the NOI, Malcolm would have developed, like Bimbi, into a cynic.

[36] In employing this much-abused term I have in mind especially three general attitudes of Italian Humanism: first, the conception of education as the development of historical consciousness; second, the attitude of respect for (but not veneration of) texts as human artifacts; third, the emphasis on the comparative study of languages, and of texts in their original languages. I believe that Malcolm X, in assuming his humanist vocation, exemplified all three attitudes, to varying degrees. See Paul O. Kristeller *Renaissance Concerts of Man* (New York: Harper and Row, 1972), and Eugenio Garin *Italian Humanism* trans. Peter Munz (New York: Harper and Row, 1965). See also Norman Allen, *African-American Humanism: An Anthology* (Buffalo, N.Y.: Prometheus, 1991).

critical reasoning; and he re-discovered his love of learning for its own sake (and in particular, his love of reading). The significance of the priority of this conversion cannot be over-stated I believe, since it was in ground made fertile by it that Islam subsequently took root. Moreover, it was his yearning intellect (and concomitant humanist sensibilities) that would eventually provoke his banishment from Elijah Muhammad's Nation. Finally, it was the recrudescence of those sensibilities (so long suppressed in deference to the pervasive dogmatism of Nation ideology), and of the humanist vocation Malcolm had received from Bimbi, which proved such potent stimuli to his development during the final year of his life, as I shall argue below in detail.

First, I want to call attention to the salient features of Malcolm X's humanist turn as they emerge in his own account of it. Malcolm X initially recalls Bimbi as "the first man I met in prison who made any positive impression on me".[37] Malcolm was drawn to Bimbi's demeanor, an emanation of wisdom and dignity rare to encounter in that environment. Malcolm came to admire Bimbi's articulate erudition, the product of hours spent immersed in the prison's library (of which he was the "best customer"). What fascinated him most about Bimbi was that "he was the first man I had ever seen command total respect...with his words."[38]

Malcolm's insight about Bimbi recalls the lesson inferred from his run-in with the drunk "cracker soldier" who threatened him one night on the Yankee Clipper from New York to Boston. Malcolm had him stripped to his waist and the entire car laughing at him before a blow had landed. "I never would forget that," he concludes, "-that I couldn't have whipped that white man as badly with a club as I had with my mind."[39]

It is Bimbi who reminds Malcolm that he has a mind, and who stirs him to begin cultivating it—to begin acquiring "some kind of a homemade education."[40] This begins with a correspondence course in English, and then another one in

---

[37] Malcolm X, *Autobiography of Malcom X*, 153. Spike Lee's *Malcolm* X collapses Bimbi into a proselyte for the Nation of Islam—a serious distortion on my reading of the *Autobiography*, and not just another instance of cinematic composition of character to facilitate narration.
[38] Malcolm X, *Autobiography of Malcom X*, 154.
[39] *Ibid.*, 77. Compare his "confused Negro" ploy with Boston police-in which he exploits the fact 'that the white man is rare who will ever consider that a Negro can outsmart him" (*ibid.*, 144-45).
[40] Ibid., 171.

Latin. And then a crux. A letter arrives from Reginald, with news of the Nation, and exhortations to "pray to Allah." Malcolm's first inclination is to "consult with Bimbi." But "some instinct" restrains him.

And so, a second conversion unfolds. Malcolm acquires a new mentor, and a far more focused vocational goal. But throughout the process of his assimilation into the Nation, the humanist impulses awakened by Bimbi continue to make themselves felt as a formative influence. To be sure, his reading is mostly undertaken under impetus provided by his inculcation into the world-view of W.D. Fard and Elijah Muhammad. But unlike what one gathers about his brothers and sister, Malcolm insists on *reading* his way through this inculcation, creating a sort of textual elaboration of it that is uniquely his, and not part of the Nation's official program. Hilda may have been content with "Yacub's history" as it stood.[41] But Malcolm connects it with *Paradise Lost*, concluding that "Milton and Mr. Elijah Muhammad were actually saying the same thing"![42] The hermeneutics may be questionable; but my point is, the hermeneutics is alive. With Bimbi, and then with Elijah Muhammad, Malcolm X discovers vivid and spiritually galvanizing context for naming and analyzing his experience of racism in America. But in coming to that discovery, Malcolm X also comes to taste of the sheer emancipatory pleasure of the text.

Malcolm says, "You will never catch me with a free fifteen minutes in which I'm not studying something I feel might be able to help the black man."[43] But what we risk missing in judging this statement is how rich, in practice, Malcolm's conception was of what might end up "helping". That is, we risk not seeing how much Malcolm enjoyed learning for its own sake. "Books," he responded to an English writer's query about his "alma mater"—a quintessentially humanist thought.[44] Books, he meant, of history and social analysis, certainly, for weaving his textualist's appropriation of Fardian theology—but books too on the identity of Shakespeare, or on "Grimm's Law" in philology.[45] These latter he read

---

[41] Ibid., 164-168.

[42] Ibid., 185-186. Compare page 175, where Malcolm describes his reading of Mendel's *Findings in Genetics*, again in an effort to give argument and evidence in his own voice to Nation dogma.

[43] Ibid., 179.

[44] Ibid.

[45] Ibid., 185 and 393. Compare Haley's story of Malcolm's connecting a bit of research on the aardvark with his interest in philology, p. 416.

because reading, for him, was freedom—something, he says, "I could spend the rest of my life [doing], just satisfying curiosity—because you can hardly mention anything I'm not curious about."[46]

The schema of double conversion offers ready perspective on the deep tensions embedded within Malcolm X's ministry in the Nation of Islam, tensions which eventually burst into bitter rift between them. I have claimed that Malcolm, inspired by Bimbi's humanist vocation, and then by his gradual initiation into the art of reading, created a distinctive textual appropriation of the Nation's teachings. From the standpoint of Nation ideologues, this would have marked Malcolm from the start as a problematic acolyte—and even more, as a problematic missionary. Malcolm's theology, after all, was hermeneutically open, continually under "elenctic revision,"[47] and subject to reassessment in light of new "readings" of his experience. Inevitably, Malcolm's attitude would lead him to a critical view of the Nation's policy of "non-engagement" with political conflict.[48] This policy expressed the monological parochialism that was such a pronounced force within it and that made the Nation under Elijah Muhammad such a profoundly apolitical organization.[49] We can hear Malcolm X inveighing against that parochialism

---

[46] Ibid., 180, and compare the moving peroration of the final chapter of the *Autobiography of Malcom X* in which Malcolm speaks of his love of languages, and the cherished, forever-deferred wish to study: "I mean ranging study, because I have a wide-open mind. I'm interested in almost any subject you can mention." Ibid. , 380.

[47] This term derives from the Greek word *elenchus* (meaning refutation, examination, testing) which Socrates uses to characterize his method — that is, the Socratic method. See, for context, Plato's *Apology* 21c, 21e, 23b, 27ab, 29de, 36c, 38a. For an indication of the joy Malcolm X took in the give-and-take of Socratic debate, see the *Autobiography* 184 and 282 (and see Haley's vignette at 415). His mastery of this ancient genre can be observed in almost any of his encounters with such as Bayard Rustin, John Davis, and Kenneth Clark. See Cone, op cit., 102. Dyson notes the roots of Malcolm's rhetorical virtuosity in African American traditions for the cultivation of verbal prowess, in *Making Malcolm*, 85.

[48] Malcolm X, *Autobiography of Malcom X,* 289.

[49] The character of the organization has obviously changed under Farrakhan. Still, the untold story in the U.S. media coverage of the Nation of Islam is how marginal it is to Islam in the United States today. There are close to six million practicing Muslims in the U.S. (including close to a million African American Sunni Muslims, mostly followers of Wallace Muhammad's American Muslim Mission). The Nation of Islam numbers between 5,000 and 20,000 adherents. See J. Gordon Melton *The Encyclopedia of American Religions* 2nd ed. (Detroit: Gale Research, 1987), 683ff.

Lest my remarks about the Nation of Islam seem unduly hostile, I should confess that my view of it has been shaped by Harold Bloom's sententious comments in *The American Religion: The Emergence of the Post-Christian Nation* (New York: Simon and Schuster, 1992), 248-252. The Nation, on his reading, is a marginal sect of the "American religion" — and so, a minor (among other things) in his confrontation with the "super-sleuth" agent shadowing him in Africa:

> I said [to the super-sleuth] I was seeking for the truth, and I was trying to weigh—objectively -everything on its own merit. I said what I was against was straight-jacketed thinking, and straight-jacketed societies. I said I respected every man's right to believe whatever his intelligence tells him is intellectually sound, and I expect everyone else to respect my right to believe likewise.

Ironically, the super-sleuth hadn't heard of Malcolm's break with the Nation of Islam—more than two months after it had been front-page news. [50]

During his years in the Nation, Malcolm's spiritual and intellectual commitments—at once to a parochial and dogmatic caricature of Islam, and to humanism—struggled for his soul. Only with the break in 1964 could this struggle aspire to a higher harmony; and because it was so tragically foreshortened, all comment about the music that harmony might have become remains speculation. I venture this much. With the break and the trip to Mecca, Malcolm discovered "real Islam".[51] He also found himself suddenly thinking in more fluid, no longer straight-jacketed media and fore—free to connect and synthesize the humanist and orthodox religious, the nationalist and Pan-Africanist, the black capitalist and socialist voices that contended within him. The effect of this "second caesura" in his life, in short, was to allow the two trajectories defined in the moment of his double conversion in prison to combine in a newly integrated, and far more complex mission than he had yet undertaken.

III. AUTHORITY, DEMOCRACY, AND SOLIDARITY

I have argued thus far for two theses. First, I have argued that W.E.B. DuBois created in his life and work a paradigm of the African American leader as an "artist of himself"[52]—whose artistry consists in reconciling the imperative to

---

expression of a "dominant Gnosticism." That is, it is yet another American religious aspiring to a certain kind of knowledge, "by and of an uncreated self, or self-within-the-self, [which] knowledge leads to freedom, a dangerous and doom-eager freedom: from nature, time, history, community, other selves." (ibid., 49)

[50] Malcolm X, *Autobiography of Malcom X,* 371-2.

[51] Ibid., 168.

[52] The phrase is Hegel's, from a lecture collected in *The Philosophy of Fine Art,* Trans. F.P.B. Osmaston (London: G. Bell, 1920), vol. IV, 337.

represent and exemplify the race, with the arduous labor of retaining his individuality, and indeed, a unique and aesthetically stylized individuality. I suggested too that the artistry deployed in this sort of endeavor consists precisely in successfully harmonizing forces in conflict and tension—creating fields of coexistence not won at the price of repressive denial, or dogmatism.

I have argued, second, that Malcolm X exemplifies the DuBoisian paradigm in a particular way: over the course of his life, he creates a life in which deeply contradictory impulses are woven together into a mission neither acting by itself could have realized. I went on to identify those impulses by way of a reading of the *Autobiography* which reveals Malcolm X's conversion in prison as a double conversion, and which emphasizes the humanist dimension of Malcolm X's evolving sense of vocation.

If what I have said thus far holds together, then we should be able to return at this point to the DuBoisian paradigm for indications of potentialities left unactualized by the death of Malcolm X. I shall point to and briefly elaborate on two themes, united by a point of departure in chapter III of *The Souls of Black Folk*.

Addressing himself to the Tuskegee Machine's increasingly suffocating domination of the civil rights agenda in the turn-of-the-century United States,[53] DuBois writes:

> Honest and earnest criticism from those whose interests are most nearly touched...is the soul of democracy and the safeguard of modern society. If the best of the American Negroes receive by outer pressure a leader whom they had not recognized before, manifestly there is here a certain palpable gain. Yet there is also irreparable loss—a loss of that peculiarly valuable education which a group receives when by search and criticism it finds and commissions its own leaders. The way in which this is done is at once the most elementary and the nicest problem of social growth. History is but the record of such group-leadership; and yet how infinitely changeful is its type and character. And of all types and kinds, what can be more instructive than the leadership of a group within a group?—that curious double movement where real progress may be negative and actual advance be relative

---

[53] See Lewis' account of the complex relationship between DuBois and Washington, *on. cit.*, 255-385.

retrogression. All this is the social student's inspiration and despair.[54]

This is a complex and highly allusive passage, and I do not propose an exhaustive analysis of it. Instead, I want to pick up the thread of a problem it glances off of, a problem at the heart of Malcolm X's unrealized vocation. DuBois speaks of a "curious double movement" by which a "group within a group attains to unity and cohesion." Partly this attainment is a function of able leadership—the organizing influence of effective authority. But effective authority in turn can subvert democracy—the process by which a group "by search and criticism...finds and commissions its own leaders." By the same token, a group tends to languish and become vulnerable to outer pressure in the absence of effective authority. Thus the "nicest problem" for leaders (such as Malcolm X) is how to promote democracy (power in the hands of black people to control their own lives) through the assertion of effective authority (authority that promotes group unity without undercutting group empowerment).

By 1964 Malcolm X had experienced definitively the way that excessive authority can extinguish democracy in a group. For some eleven months after leaving the Nation of Islam, he grappled with ideas, themes, and initiatives, in search of a point of equilibrium from which to re-engage the "curious double movement" of leadership. Two of those themes resonate nicely with DuBoisian motifs, and I take them up in turn.

Years later, and from an avowedly socialist internationalist perspective, DuBois would look back in his *Autobiography* on his "becoming" a Negro as the rejection of another, antithetical allegiance: Americanism.[55] This may not have been how DuBois saw it at the time ("I was [then] blithely European and imperialist in outlook"[56]), but in this case hindsight is illuminating. Within little more than a decade of leaving Fisk, DuBois was announcing to the 1900 Pan-African Congress that the "problem of the twentieth century is the problem of the color line."[57] As Crummell, Delany, and Blyden had seen before him, to discover that one is black in America is not just to discover the debilitating paradox of

---

[54] DuBois, *The Souls of Black Folk*, 40.
[55] DuBois, *Autobiography*, 108.
[56] *Ibid.*, 126.
[57] See Lewis' account of the Congress, *on. cit.*, 248-52.

one's Americanness. It is also, and more stirringly, to discover one's solidarity with an African world beyond America's shores.[58] When Malcolm X declares that to be black is precisely not to be American (or, as he puts it in the same speech, to be "African-American"[59]), and then connects that thought to the idea of internationalizing the civil rights movement (by petitioning the UN Human Rights Commission[60]), he places himself squarely within a tradition of thinking and strategizing to which DuBois had devoted himself for over six decades.

We find a second strain of thematic resonance between DuBois' and Malcolm's thinking on education, and in particular on how to reform the university (and especially, the "Negro university"). Both DuBois and Malcolm X delighted in stirring up university audiences; indeed, Malcolm X raised what DuBois engaged in as pastime to high rhetorical art, routinely flaying accomplished and articulate Ph.D. interlocutors in debate.[61] But Malcolm X had only vague inklings of what he would have done were he "president of one of these black colleges."[62] DuBois had done the fundamental work limning the structure and content of an Afrocentric humanist curriculum for the Negro university, and in 1960, as I have noted, he issued a plaintive warning that desegregation should not mean the abandonment of that still unrealized goal. In 1964 Malcolm X, ready, he says, "to go back into any New York City public school and start where I left off at the ninth grade, and go on through a degree,"[63] is uniquely positioned to hear and act on DuBois' warning. DuBois had created,

---

[58] Paul Gilroy's *The Black Atlantic: Modernity and Double Consciousness* (Cambridge: Harvard University Press, 1993) is a virtuoso reading of the world culture which an American's consciousness so stirred would connect to today. Much has changed since the days in the early 1960's when Nkrumah's latest revolutionary tract could quicken the blood (as they clearly did both DuBois' and Malcolm X's).

[59] See Breitman, ed. *Malcolm X Speaks*, 26 and 36.

[60] *Ibid.*, 34-35. Malcolm X appears unaware (as of 3 April 1964) that DuBois had already done this, in 1947. See DuBois' *Autobiography*, 332-3, and Horne, *op cit.*, 100-1.

[61] For DuBois see the introductory and "envoy" remarks that frame the first seven talks in *The Education of Black People*. For Malcolm X, see the *Autobiography*, 282-5, where he says, *inter alia*: "Except for all-black audiences, I liked the college audiences best. The college sessions sometimes ran two to four hours—they often ran overtime. Challenges, queries, and criticisms were fired at me by the usually objective and always alive and searching minds of undergraduate and graduate students, and their faculties. The college sessions never failed to be exhilarating.

[62] Ibid.. 181.

[63] Ibid., 380.

after all, the degree program Malcolm craved[64]; meanwhile, Malcolm looked poised to lead a political movement that would not stand by indifferent while DuBois' dream of a revolutionary university was forsaken.

Such a symbiosis was not to be—at least, was not to be crafted by Malcolm X. But the idea of it, I think, sheds light on what lies at the heart of the unfinished mission Malcolm X bequeathed. It is an idea to which DuBois gave succinct expression one June afternoon at Howard University, a month or so after Malcolm Little's fifth birthday—in words which serve as a fitting epigram on the bond I have tried in this essay to forge between the two:

> It is silly to tell intelligent human beings: be good and you will be happy. The truth is today, be good, be decent, be honorable and self-sacrificing and you will not always be happy. You will often be desperately unhappy. You may even be crucified, dead and buried; and the third day you will be just as dead as the first. But with the death of your happiness may easily come increased happiness and satisfaction and fulfillment for other people—strangers, unborn babes, uncreated worlds. If this is not sufficient incentive, never try it—remain hogs.[65]

---

[64] Think of *The Negro* (1915) and *The World and Africa* (1947) as the bookends of a research agenda for such a program, the administrative ideal for which is articulated in a 1933 speech at Fisk, "The Field and Function of the Negro College" (collected in *The Education of Black People*—see especially page 95).

[65] *Ibid.*, 80.

CHAPTER X

NATIONAL NEWS MAGAZINES PORTRAYAL OF THE REVEREND JESSE JACKSON AS A
MYTHICAL HERO DURING THE 1988 U.S. PRESIDENTIAL CAMPAIGN

NANNETTA DURNELL
FLORIDA ATLANTIC UNIVERSITY

INTRODUCTION

A myth is a special kind of story that deals with the gods or the forces of
creation, and the relationship of those forces to human beings[1] Vogler describes
myth as a comparison that helps us to understand by analogy some aspect of our
mysterious selves. Therefore, a myth is not an untruth, but a way of reaching
profound truth.[2]

The word hero is Greek, from a root that means "to protect and to serve."[3]
Heroes may be described as individuals who slay dragons, rescue damsels or other
victims in distress, and find and bring back treasures.[4] However combined,
"mythical heroes" are individuals who achieve or accomplish a deed beyond what
is viewed as the normal range of achievement or experience, and give their lives
to something bigger.[5]

This study is an analysis of the portrayal of the Reverend Jesse Louis
Jackson as a "mythical hero." In order to investigate the portrayal of Jackson,
news stories from *Newsweek, Time,* and *U.S. News and World Report*'s coverage
of the 1988 presidential campaign were analyzed for their mythical content. (This
particular time period was selected because it was a year when Jackson received
heavy coverage by the national news media.) The question then was asked: "Did
national news magazines portray Jesse Jackson's 1988 presidential campaign as a

---

[1] David Feinstein and Stanley Krippner, *Personal Mythology: The Psychology of Your Evolving
Self* Los Angeles: Jeremy Tarcher, Inc., 1988).
[2] Christopher Vogler, The Writer's Journey: Mythic Structure for *Storytellers and Screenwriters*
(Michigan: Braun-Brumfield, Inc., 1992).
[3] Carol Pearson, *Awakeninq the Heroes Within* (San Francisco: Harper Collins Publishers, 1991).
[4] Ibid.
[5] Joseph Campbell, *The Hero With A Thousand Faces* (Princeton: Princeton University Press,
1973).

mythical motif?" In asking this question, others arose: Was Jackson portrayed as a mythical hero? If Jackson was portrayed as a mythical hero, which heroic qualities did he possess? Did mythical themes structure much of the content in national news magazines coverage of Jackson's presidential campaign?

DEFINING THE MYTHICAL HERO

In the book entitled *Mythology*, Leeming describes the mythical hero as a universal phenomenon occurring in every culture—different in detail, but fundamentally the same.[6] During the hero's lifetime the hero is repeatedly tested in a series of adventures, which Leeming explains, also serve to establish the hero's identity. These adventures may be national, religious, cultural, or ideological— that is, they are consciously searching for the meaning of life. In this search, heroes break through the barriers erected by their particular culture, and in doing so become universal human figures.

Joseph Campbell, one of the world's leading scholars of mythology, describes in *The Power of Myth* that in all cultures there are two types of deeds performed by mythical heroes.[7] First, there are "physical deeds" where heroes perform a "war act" or "physical act" (i.e., saving a life or sacrificing themselves for another). The second type are described as "spiritual deeds" where heroes find and experience some supernormal range of spiritual life, and come back to the world to communicate about it. This spiritual journey involves heroes finding their center—a place of rest inside themselves. Campbell states that by holding on to their center, heroes can act (carry out their duties) and not be compelled to action by desire, fear, or social commitment.

In addition to the heroic deeds, Campbell explains in *The Hero With A Thousand Faces* that the mythical hero must also partake in an adventure.[8] This heroic adventure begins with the departure where the hero sets forth from his/her hut or castle (the world of the familiarity) and is lured, carried away, or voluntarily proceeds to the threshold (unfamiliarity) of the adventure. At the

---

[6] David Leeming, *Mythology* (New York: Newsweek Books, 1976).

[7] Joseph Campbell, *The Power of Myth* Princeton: Princeton University Press, 1988.

[8] Joseph Campbell, *The Hero With A Thousand Faces* (Princeton: Princeton University Press, 1973).

threshold the hero encounters a shadowy presence (power) that guards the passage to the threshold. At this point the hero must either win the trust of this power and go alive into the kingdom of the dread, or the hero will be slain by this power and descend into death.[9]

If the hero wins the presence's trust, the hero now moves on to the next stage of the adventure; described as the initiation process.[10] At this point the hero enters the threshold and is met by a dragon. This encounter between the hero and the dragon will end in one of two ways: (1) the hero will be cut into pieces and descend into the belly of the monster; eventually to be resurrected, or (2) the hero may kill the dragon, taste its blood, and receive its powers. If the dragon is defeated, the hero transcends humanity and is reassociated with the powers of nature—the powers of life.[11]

Next, the hero moves beyond the threshold and journeys to the nadir (the treasure), traveling through a world of unfamiliar and strange forces; some which threaten and test the hero, others which offer magical aid. Upon reaching the nadir, the hero either obtains the treasure (i.e., reward, blessing or knowledge) or is met by doom. [12]

The last stage of the hero's adventure is the return—the journey back to the world of the familiar. In this phase of the adventure, the hero returns to the threshold either under protective powers or the hero is constantly pursued. Once reaching the threshold the hero re-emerges and returns from the kingdom of the dread to the land of familiarity. Consequently, if the hero was victorious in this quest, the nadir that the hero brings will restore the world.[13]

Houston notes that this image of the hero's adventure is universal phenomenon—young heroes seeking magic swords, maidens risking death to save loved ones, knights riding off to fight evil dragons deep in caves, etc.—and act as symbols of universal life experiences.[14] In fact, Houston adds, these universal

---

[9] Ibid.

[10] Ibid., and Christopher Vogler, *The Writer's Journey: Mythic Structure for Storytellers and Screenwriters* (Michigan: Braun-Brumfield, Inc., 1992).

[11] Ibid.

[12] Ibid.

[13] Ibid.

[14] Jean Houston, "The Search for The Beloved: Journeys" in *Mythology* Los Angeles: Jeremy P. Tarcher, Inc., 1990).

symbols are constantly changing to fit the needs of a society or culture.[15] For example, modern heroes may not be going into caves and labyrinths to fight mythical beast, but they do enter a "special world" and an "inmost cave" by venturing into space, to the bottom of the sea, into the depths of a modern city, or into their own hearts.

In addition to the deeds and adventures of the mythical hero, there are certain "archetypes" or personality traits that characterize this phenomenon. According to Campbell, the most frequently occurring archetypes of the mythical hero are: "the Warrior," "the Lover," "the Savior" and "the Ruler."[16] According to Pearson, these archetypes are not rigid character roles, but are seen as flexible character functions performed temporarily by the hero to achieve certain affects during the adventure.

In this sense, a hero can manifest the qualities of more than one of the aforementioned archetypes. These archetypes can be thought of as masks, Volger explains, worn by the hero temporarily as they are needed to advance the adventure. For example, an individual might enter the story performing a function of the "Warrior" then switch masks to perform a function as a "Lover," "Ruler," or "Savior." In addition, each major or superordinal archetype is comprised of the following minor or subordinal constructs which characterize and describe the superordinal archetypes in detail:

Warrior	Lover	Savior	Ruler
Courageous	Compassionate	Rescuer	Proud
Strong	Commitment	Saint	Authoritative
Admirable	Skillful	Creates Hope	Tyrannical
Fighter	Magical	Sacrificing	Manipulative

Krippner and Houston note that heroic archetypes are similar throughout all times and cultures; in the dreams and personalities of individuals, as well as, in

---

[15] Ibid.

[16] Joseph Campbell, *The Hero With A Thousand Faces* (Princeton: Princeton University Press, 1973).

the mythic imagination of the entire world.[17] In fact, Vogler adds that heroic archetypes are part of the universal language of storytelling and therefore, recognizable to everyone. "You can't read stories without them. For the storyteller, certain character archetypes are indispensable tools of the trade."[18]

JESSE JACKSON'S RISE AS A NATIONAL BLACK LEADER

Jesse Jackson's rise in the media as America's most prominent black leader of the 1980s and 90s can first, be traced back to his "political base" in the black community, which grew out of his involvement in the Civil Rights Movement of the 1960s. As a student at North Carolina Agricultural and Technical State University in Greensboro, North Carolina, Jackson led demonstrations in the city that set forth the sit-ins movement.[19]

In 1963, Jackson became a staff member of the Southern Christian Leadership Conference (SCLC), and in 1966, Jackson established his SCLC base of operations in Chicago, Illinois, after Dr. Martin Luther King, Jr. (SCLC president) directed a desegregation campaign in Chicago.[20] Jackson headed the SCLC's "operation Breadbasket" project in Chicago; which applied economic pressure on white-owned businesses to open up job opportunities for blacks.[21] Franklin and Moss point out, that Jackson launched a number of protest campaigns in Chicago against discriminatory employment practices—which were met with varying degrees of success.[22]

Reynolds describes in *Jesse Jackson: the Man, the Movement, and the Myth,* that within a short period following King's death in 1968, Jackson became a national figure in America. In 1971, Jackson resigned from the SCLC and formed

[17] Jean Houston, "The Search for The Beloved: Journeys" in *Mythology* Los Angeles: Jeremy P. Tarcher, Inc., 1990), and Stanley Krippner, *Dreamtime and Dreamwork: Decoding the Language of the Night* (Los Angeles: Jeremy P. Tarcher, Inc., 1990).

[18] Ibid., and Christopher Vogler, *The Writer's Journey: Mythic Structure for Storytellers and Screenwriters* (Michigan: Braun-Brumfield, Inc., 1992).

[19] John White, *Black Leadership in America: From Booker T. Washington to Jesse Jackson* (New York: The Longman Group, 1990).

[20] John Hope Franklin and Alfred Moss, *From Slavery To Freedom: A History of Negro Americans* (New York: McGraw-Hill Publishing Company, 1988).

[21] Thomas Landess and Richard Quinn, *Jesse Jackson and the Politics of Race* (Ottawa, Illinois: James Books, 1985).

[22] John Hope Franklin and Alfred Moss, *From Slavery To Freedom: A History of Negro Americans* (New York: McGraw-Hill Publishing Company, 1988).

a new Chicago-based organization to carry on the work he started with the SCLC—Operation Push (People United to Save Humanity); which emphasized black economic self-help.[23] From his base of operations at PUSH, Jackson initiated boycotts, held voter registration drives, furnished campaign workers, and conducted weekly radio broadcast which publicized the concerns of the black community. By linking "protest" with "electoral politics," and mobilizing local communities to shape national agendas, Jackson carried on the tradition of the Civil Rights Movement.[24]

The second factor attributing to Jackson's rise as America's black spokesman is his "personality." No matter what the accomplishments or failures of Jesse Jackson, most people continue to be fascinated by him. Both Reed and Barker report, that admirers and critics of Jackson view him as a "charismatic leader."[25]

Reynolds writes, that Jackson rose to national prominence as successor to King (another "charismatic leader"), and won the mantle of black leadership through his own personal talents and the intensive support of various segments of the media—which projected him as King's successor.[26] In fact, Colton adds, in *The Jackson Phenomenon*, Jackson understood the media and learned to use it well. He possessed everything that the media wanted—he preached nonviolence, was photogenic, articulate, charismatic, and said controversial things. In the black community, Reynolds describes how Jackson possessed tremendous "charisma" and was often referred to as the "Black Jesus," "Black Messiah," or "Black Moses."[27]

According to Franklin and Moss, Jackson's leadership encompassed a bold, broad and all inclusive agenda; which extended from the goals and

---

[23] Barbara Reynolds, *Jesse Jackson: the Man, the Movement, and the Myth*. Chicago: Nelson-Hall, 1975).

[24] Ernest House, *Jesse Jackson and the Politics of Charisma: The Rise and Fall of the PUSH/Excel Program* (Boulder: Westview Press, 1988).

[25] Lucius Barker, *Our Time Has Come: A Delegate's Diary of Jesse Jackson's 1984 Presidential Campaign* (Chicago: University of Illinois Press, 1988), and Adolph Reed, *The Jesse Jackson Phenomenon: The Crisis of Purpose in Afro-American Politics* (New Haven: Yale University Press, 1986).

[26] Barbara Reynolds, *Jesse Jackson: the Man, the Movement and the Myth*. Chicago: Nelson-Hall, 1975).

[27] Ibid.

objectives of King and the Civil Rights Movement. In Barker's 1984 study of the United States presidential campaign, he describes in *Our Time Has Come*, how black Americans supported Jackson because (a) they understood him, (b) he was one of them, and (c) he supported their interest.[28]

In *Black Leadership in America*, White notes how Jackson, as did King and the Civil Rights Movement, called for a rebirth of America by appealing to the basic goodness and morality of all Americans.[29] Barker adds, that Jackson presented himself as a reasonable, caring, knowledgeable, experienced, and professional leader; demonstrating a strong commitment to civil rights, poverty, hunger, unemployment, apartheid, and peace and justice for all Americans.[30]

The third reason why Jackson maintains the reign as black America's leader stems from his "philosophy." Faw and Skelton describe in *Thunder in America*, how Jackson argues for creating a new America that is concerned about jobs, peace, and justice. For example, "Invest in America" was Jackson's 1984 presidential campaign theme.[31] Barker points out that this theme not only recognized the various issues and groups of people in America, but also stressed the importance of hope and vision in regard to public policy issues.[32]

Hatch assesses in *Beyond Opportunity*, that Jackson's view on domestic political issues focuses primarily on black economic development, educational reform, and poverty and hunger.[33] According to Hatch, Jackson's position is that it is better and cheaper in the long run to avoid and/or solve social problems in advance, by "developing America" and its people, rather than, trying to pick up the pieces when they fall apart.[34]

---

[28] Lucius Barker, *Our Time Has Come: A Delegate's Diary of Jesse Jackson's 1984 Presidential Campaign* (Chicago: University of Illinois Press, 1988).

[29] John White, *Black Leadership in America: From Booker T. Washington to Jesse Jackson* (New York: The Longman Group, 1990).

[30] Lucius Barker, *Our Time Has Come: A Delegate's Diary of Jesse Jackson's 1984 Presidential Campaign* (Chicago: University of Illinois Press, 1988).

[31] Bob Faw and Nancy Skelton, *Thunder,* John Hope Franklin and Alfred Moss, *From Slavery To Freedom: A History of Negro Americans* (New York: McGraw-Hill Publishing Company, 1988).*America* (Austin, Texas: Monthly Press, Inc., 1986).

[32] Lucius Barker, *Our Time Has Come: A Delegate's Diary of Jesse Jackson's 1984 Presidential Campaign* (Chicago: University of Illinois Press, 1988).

[33] Roger Hatch, *Beyond Opportunity: Jesse* Jackson's *Vision for America* Philadelphia: Fortress Press, 1988).

[34] Ibid.

Elizabeth Colton, who served as Jackson's press secretary for the 1988 presidential campaign, posits that Jackson is rapidly becoming the most famous American in the world. At home in America, she writes, Jackson is building his machine and creating his "myth."[35]

He has spent his entire lifetime as a leader, organizer and advocate for justice and peace and economic development in American and the world. He has achieved a well-deserved reputation as an activist for social and economic change, a successful negotiator, a master mediator, a defender of the poor and disadvantaged, a consummate organizer and manager of nationwide organizations. Jesse Jackson's name is known around the world because of the leadership role he has taken at home and abroad.[36] (p.4)

Yet, despite Jackson's rise as national black leader in America, Broh points out in *A Horse of A Different Color*, that the overriding barrier facing Jackson's vision for America in the 1990s is the same obstacle faced by Jackson in the 1960s—"racism." However, despite the roadblocks and obstacles, Jackson remains forever the optimist and tells his followers: "Never surrender and go forward...America will get better and better."[37] (p.278)

PURPOSE OF THE RESEARCH

In many ways the media have the most fundamental power of all in the United States because they have the power of appraisal—that is, they have the power to determine priorities and establish who or what is important. Today, the news media have become the primary transmitters of information, norms, and cultural values. The media (magazines, newspapers, television, radio, movies, etc.) have replaced the religious institution, the home, and the school as the essential educator of our day.[38] In fact, the media have been known to either contribute to the success or the downfall of an individual.

---

[35] Elizabeth Colton, *The Jackson Phenomenon: The Man. The Power The Message* (New York: Doubleday, 1989).

[36] Ibid.

[37] Ibid.

[38] Christopher F. Arterton, *Media Politics: The New Strategies of Presidential Campaigns*. Lexington: D.C. Health and Company, 1984, and Thomas Patterson, *The Mass Election*. New York: Praeger, 1980.

For example, both admirers and critics of Jackson agree that Jackson's success as spokesperson for Black America is attributed to the support from the mass media.[39] In national polls Jackson is one of the most admired figures in America; respected by both blacks and whites alike, one of the few blacks so honored. John White describes in *Black Leadership In America* that from Booker T. Washington through Dr. Martin Luther King, Jr. the media traditionally accepts only one primary black spokesperson/leader at a time. So when the media personnel want to know what blacks think about a particular issue, these individuals always turn to that one charismatic individual who presumably represents the black viewpoint.[40]

After King's death, media personnel chose Jesse Jackson as the spokesperson for black America. Jackson was a popular choice because he was a capitalist, had moral authority, and possessed tremendous charisma in the black community. He was also highly articulate, photogenic, nonviolent—yet said controversial things—all of which attracted audiences.[41] In other words, Jackson won the mantle of black leadership through his own personal talents and the intensive support of the mass media.

Reed, a well-known critic of Jackson, argues in *The Jesse Jackson Phenomenon*, that Jackson is too much the creation of the media. Reed asserts that Jackson, in his rise to national prominence as America's black leader, did not address the real concerns of poor black people, and that the media did not always concentrate on the content of his message, but focused instead on his performance.[42] However, House and Reynolds point out that regardless of what critics had to say about Jackson, his rise to power was and remains strongly supported by segments of the popular media; who label Jackson as a spellbinding

---

[39] Lucius Barker, *Our Time Has Come: A Delegate's Diary of Jesse Jackson's 1984 Presidential Campaign* (Chicago: University of Illinois Press, 1988), Adolph Reed, *The Jesse Jackson Phenomenon: The Crisis of Purpose in Afro-American Politics* (New Haven: Yale University Press, 1986), and Barbara Reynolds, *Jesse Jackson: the Man the Movement and the Myth.* Chicago: Nelson-Hall, 1975).

[40] John White, *Black Leadership in America: From Booker T. Washington to Jesse Jackson* (New York: The Longman Group, 1990).

[41] Henry Young, *Major Black Religious Leaders Since 1940* (Nashville: The Parthenon Press, 1979), and Barbara Reynolds, *Jesse Jackson: the Man the Movement and the Myth.* Chicago: Nelson-Hall, 1975).

[42] Adolph Reed, *The Jesse Jackson Phenomenon: The Crisis of Purpose in Afro-American Politics* (New Haven: Yale University Press, 1986).

orator with mesmerizing power—a "Black Jesus," "Black Moses," or a "Black Messiah."[43]

In this context, House describes how Jackson is viewed as an individual who possesses superhuman, supernatural, and extraordinary powers which sets him apart from ordinary people—Jackson is considered divinely inspired.[44] Hamilton explains how this messiah complex is characterized as the emergence of an articulate, black, male leader during a time of crisis, who builds a strong protest organization around himself and leads a fight to advance the interest of the poor, the working class, and the oppressed.

Today, as in the past, the political style and discourse of black America is heavily identified with the church. In fact, most black political leaders in the United States have been Christian ministers or religious figures. However, the purpose of this research was to look beyond the religious stature, political-base, personality, and philosophies of Jackson; which have been identified as contributors to Jackson's rise as a black national leader. Instead this study examines the portrayal of Jackson as a mythical hero in contemporary society.

To review, the mythical hero is a universal phenomenon occurring in every culture. This universal hero represents the shared values already established in a culture.[45] Upon entering the world of the mythical hero, one becomes aware of recurring archetypes or personality traits: "the Warrior," "the Lover," "the Savior," and "the Ruler." These archetypes can be thought of as masks worn by the hero temporarily as they are needed throughout the hero's adventure and depending on the particular task at hand.

RESEARCH QUESTION

Did *Time, Newsweek,* and *U.S. News and World Report* magazines portray the Reverend Jesse Jackson as a mythical hero in their coverage of the 1988 United States presidential campaign?

---

[43] Ernest House, *Jesse Jackson and the Politics of Charisma: The Rise and Fall of the PUSH/Excel Program* (Boulder: Westview Press, 1988), and Barbara Reynolds, *Jesse Jackson: the Man, the Movement and the Myth.* Chicago: Nelson-Hall, 1975).

[44] Ernest House, *Jesse Jackson and the Politics of Charisma: The Rise and Fall of the PUSH/Excel Program* (Boulder: Westview Press, 1988).

[45] David Leeming, *Mythology* (New York: Newsweek Books, 1976).

ASSUMPTIONS

The following assumptions are made concerning the study of a mythical hero: (1) the mythical hero is perceived by his/her followers as being somewhat superhuman; (2) followers blindly believe the mythical hero's statements; (3) followers comply with the mythical hero's directives; and (4) followers give the mythical hero emotional commitment.[46]

METHODOLOGY

A textural analysis was conducted of national news magazines to ascertain whether *Time*, *Newsweek*, and *U.S. News and World Report*'s coverage of Jesse Jackson's 1988 presidential campaign consisted of mythical motifs. The application of a textual approach allows for the study of content of any magazine, book, newspaper, movie, news broadcast, photograph, cartoon, comic strip, or a combination of any one of these items.[47] Instead of observing the behavior of people directly or interviewing them, textual analysis allows the investigator to observe communication messages at times and places of the investigator's own choosing, without fear that the attention will bias the communicator.[48]

Wimmer and Dominick report that another important reason for using a textual analysis approach is that it is often identified with image analysis.[49] An increasing number of textural analysis studies have focused on exploring the images of women, minorities, the elderly, and children in the media. According to Wimmer and Dominick, with the information provided from a textual analysis the investigator can give a detailed account of a communication situation and make predictions about the process and effects of communication.[50]

---

[46] Ann Willner, *The Spellbinders: Charismatic Political Leadership* (New Haven: Yale University Press, 1984).

[47] Roger D. Wimmer and Joseph R. Dominick, *Mass Media Research: An Introduction.* Belmont, California: Wadsworth Publishing Company, 1991.

[48] Richard W. Budd, Robert K. Thorp, and Lewis Donohew, *Content Analysis of Communication.* New York: Macmillan Company, 1967.

[49] Roger D. Wimmer and Joseph R. Dominick, *Mass Media Research: An Introduction.* Belmont, California: Wadsworth Publishing Company, 1991.

[50] Ibid.

A useful coding method for a textual analysis, Berelson suggests, is a thematic approach.[51] A thematic investigation allows the researcher to identify major heroic themes in their various statement forms and provides a systematic method for placing assertions under their proper categories.[52] According to Berelson these categories act as compartments into which content is grouped for analysis. These categories are chosen according to the research problem, the research goals, and the hypothesis to be tested.[53] In this study four major heroic themes or categories emerged from the content: "the Warrior," "the Lover," "the Savior," and "the Ruler."

A census of news articles mentioning Jackson and/or his presidential campaign were taken from *Time, Newsweek,* and *U.S. News and World Report* from January 1 through December 31, 1988. Assertions mentioning Jackson or the Jackson campaign were classified according to their appropriate heroic archetype. Assertions were identified as an article, paragraph, sentence, part of a sentence, or even a single word.[54] For example, the statement "Jackson is courageous" represents a single assertion. The statement "Jackson is a courageous, a fighter and proud" demonstrates three separate assertions: (1) Jackson the courageous, (2) Jackson the fighter, and (3) Jackson the proud.

In order to code the data, subcategories or subordinal constructs were used as descriptors for the four major categories or superordinal archetypes: Jackson the Warrior—courageous, strong, admirable, a fighter; Jackson the Lover— committed, passionate, skillful and magical; Jackson the Savior—rescuer, saintly, creator of hope, and sacrificing; and Jackson the Ruler—proud, authoritative, tyrannical, and manipulative.

A total of 184 articles consisting of 2,100 assertions were identified and analyzed for their mythical content. In instances where investigators encountered an assertion that could not be classified as heroic, that assertion was placed in a miscellaneous category and was coded as (a) favorable towards Jackson, (b) unfavorable towards Jackson, or (c) neutral towards Jackson.

---

[51] Bernard Berelson, *Content Analysis in Communication Research.* New York: Hafner Publishing Company, 1971.

[52] Ibid.

[53] Ibid.

[54] Richard W. Budd, Robert K. Thorp, and Lewis Donohew, *Content Analysis of Communication.* New York: Macmillan Company, 1967.

Once the articles mentioning Jackson or his campaign had been selected the next step was to identify and place each assertion into their proper heroic category. Overall, *Time* carried 51 articles consisting of 793 heroic assertions, *Newsweek* printed 76 articles consisting of 812 heroic assertions, and *U.S. News and World Report* (henceforth written as *U.S. News*) carried 57 stories with 495 heroic assertions.

RESULTS

THE PORTRAYAL OF THE WARRIOR

The Warrior is viewed as a courageous individual who possesses tremendous strength, has the admiration of others, and has the ability to fight when necessary for the sake of others. According to Pearson and Campbell, Warrioring is about claiming one's power in the world, and making the world a better place.[55] Pearson adds it is about being "tough enough to have things one's own sweet way."[56]

Above all else, the well-developed warrior protects the citizens boundaries. Without courageous, disciplined, and well-trained warriors, the kingdom is always in danger of being overrun by the barbarians. And without a strong warrior one has no defense against the demands and the intrusions of others.

Examples of assertions listed in national news magazines, from January 1 to December 31, 1988, describing "Jackson the Warrior" were:

Courageous:	He is a man of *courage*.
Strong:	True, Jackson will have a *strong hold*, if he *outpolls* Dukakis.
Admiration:	Young explained that *he admired Jackson*, but wanted a winner.
Fighter:	*He fought* for the right to unionize plants in New Hampshire.

---

[55] Joseph Campbell, *The Hero With A Thousand Faces* (Princeton: Princeton University Press, 1973), and Carol Pearson, *Awakening the Heroes Within* (San Francisco: Harper Collins Publishers, 1991).

[56] Carol Pearson, *Awakening the Heroes Within* (San Francisco: Harper Collins Publishers, 1991).

As Table 2 illustrates, of the 1,406 heroic assertions mentioning Jackson or his campaign from January 1 through December 31, 1988, 37% or 518 assertions portrayed Jackson as a Warrior. From this number, *Time* magazine's coverage consisted of 205 Warrior assertions, *Newsweek* carried 199, and *U.S. News* had 114.

In all three magazines the Warrior quality of the fighter was reported the most often: *Time* carried 145 assertions portraying Jackson as a fighter, *Newsweek* reported 139, and *U.S. News* coverage consisted of 74. The Warrior trait of strength was ranked second by all three magazines. *Newsweek* carried 47 assertions pertaining to the strength of Jackson and his campaign, *Time* carried 45, and *U.S. News* carried 31.

The Warrior quality of admiration was ranked third by all three magazines. *Time* reported 14 assertions which admired Jackson and his campaign, *Newsweek* mentioned 11 assertions and *U.S. News* carried 9. The Warrior trait of courage was reported the least often by all three magazines. *Newsweek* carried 2 courageous assertions pertaining to Jackson, *Time* reported 1, and *U.S. News* did not carry any assertions in this subcategory.

THE PORTRAYAL OF THE LOVER

The Lover demonstrates compassion, commitment, skill, and is magical. The love that is emoted from the hero is viewed as a passionate connection to a cause, particular landscape, to his/her work, to an activity, a religion, or a way of life. Most important, it is this passion, attachment, desire, and lust that really makes the hero come alive.[57]

The hero's love for humankind means working for the betterment of others. When love captures the hero this person is no longer free to attend to their own desires and wishes. Instead the hero will make choices based on the good of what and whom he/she loves.[58] In that the hero is inspired by love and vision, this individual is committed to the people, work, or set of values that he/she loves.[59] Some examples of assertions describing "Jackson as the Lover" were:

---

[57] Ibid.
[58] Ibid.
[59] Ibid.

Compassion:	The field house in Steubenville, Ohio, was still ringing with Jesse Jackson's *passionate* cadences
Commitment:	In the jargon of modern *romance*, Dukakis and Jackson are *trying to make their relationship work.*
Skillful:	He's one of the most *skillful* politicians to come along in decades.
Magical:	Tom Peneski saw *Jackson's magic* at 10:30 last Thursday morning in Sheboygan, Wisconsin.

Findings from the data reveal that of the 1,406 heroic assertions mentioning Jackson or his campaign, 20% or 287 assertions described "Jackson as a Lover." Table 2 shows that *Time's* coverage consisted of 123 Lover assertions, *Newsweek* carried 100, and *U.S. News* had 64.

Time and *U.S. News* magazines reported the compassion trait with more frequency than the commitment, skillful, or magical traits. *Time* carried 42 assertions pertaining to Jackson a man of compassion, and *U.S. News* carried 21. However, *Newsweek* reported the most assertions in the magical subcategory with 41.

The skillful trait was reported the second most often by both *Time* and *Newsweek* magazines with 38 and 24 assertions respectively. The compassion trait also tied for second place in *Newsweek's* coverage with 24 assertions. However, ranked as second for *U.S. News* was the magical trait with 17 assertions. *Time's* coverage of the magical trait came in third with 30 assertions. Coming in third for *U.S. News* was the commitment trait with 16 assertions. Jackson's commitment was reported the least often in *Time* with 13 assertions and *Newsweek* with 11. The subcategory mentioned with the least amount of frequency in *U.S. News* was the skillful trait consisting of 10 assertions.

THE PORTRAYAL OF THE SAVIOR

The Savior is seen as an individual who creates hope, is saintly, a rescuer, and makes sacrifices for others or for the good of humanity. The Savior maintains an atmosphere and an environment in which people feel safe and at home. The Savior creates community by helping people feel that they belong, that they are valued and cared for, and encourages nurturing relationships between and among individuals and constituencies.[60]

The Savior is an individual who knows oneself and what he/she wants, but this individual's giving is even strong than their self-interest. The caring within this person is even stronger than the instinct for self-preservation. In this sense, the Savior is viewed as an individual who would give his/her life for another; either by their willingness to be martyred or by daily sacrifices in the service or cause of a mission. Examples of assertions describing "Jackson as a Savior" were:

Rescuer:	"*Jesse Jackson saved the whole convention* in Atlanta," said Turkish Reporter Turan Yavuz.
Saint:	*His presence* is really *symbolic.*
Creates Hope:	No other candidate comes close to the reaction Jackson gets when he calls "Down with dope. *Up with hope.*"
Sacrificing:	*Jackson has taken great pains to support difficult strikes-*—for instance at Patrick Cudahy meat packing plant in Milwaukee in April, 1987.

Table 2 reveals that of the 1,406 heroic assertions mentioning Jackson or his campaign 11% or 149 assertions described him as a Savior. *Newsweek's* coverage consisted of 66 Savior assertions, *Time* carried 54, and *U.S. News* had 29.

In the creates hope subcategory, *Newsweek* carried 28, *Time* reported 26, and *U.S. News* carried 16. The saint trait closely followed where *Newsweek* reported 24 assertions, *Time* carried 23, and *U.S. News* coverage consisted of 12. The sacrificing trait appeared third in *Newsweek* with 10 assertions and 4 were identified in *Time* magazine. Coming in third in *U.S. News'* Savior category was the rescuer trait which had only 1 assertion. The rescuer trait appeared the least often in *Newsweek* with 4 assertions and in *Time* with 1. *U.S. News* ranking of the sacrificing trait came in last with 0 assertions.

---

[60] Ibid.

THE PORTRAYAL OF THE RULER

The Ruler is seen as proud, authoritative, tyrannical, and manipulative. The Ruler is considered a rigid and controlling individual concerned with order. The Ruler's kingdom cannot be fully productive unless some harmony reigns and conflict is handled in a productive way.[61]

It is the task of the ruler to promote order, peace, prosperity, and abundance. The ruler does not so much create a life, as much as, maintain and govern it. This individual is concerned with the good of society and/or the planet; which entails helping different people to understand and appreciate the gifts of people different from themselves.[62]

Another interesting quality of the Ruler is the ability to demonstrate tyrannical behavior. In this case, the Ruler wants to force others to do things their way and will have tantrums if unsuccessful. This behavior is viewed as selfish, narrow-minded, and vindictive. Some examples of "Jackson as the Ruler" were:

Proud:	*Jesse Jackson can take pride* in knowing that he finally has a place at the table.
Authoritative:	A key question is *whether Jesse Jackson would approve* of Nunn's selection.
Tyrannical:	either aide had checked with Jackson first and *he was furious.*
Manipulative:	He knows instinctively *how to bluff and bargain, when to hold 'em, when to fold 'em.*

The results in the Ruler category revealed that of the 1,406 heroic assertions mentioning Jackson or his campaign, 32% or 452 assertions described "Jackson as a Ruler." Table 2 shows *Time's* coverage consisted of 183 Ruler assertions, *Newsweek* carried 164, and *U.S. News* had 105.

The majority of the assertions in all three magazines focused heavily on both the authoritative and tyrannical traits. *Newsweek* reported 61 assertions describing Jackson as an authoritative figure who likes to be in control of people

---

[61] Ibid.
[62] Ibid.

and situations. *Time's* coverage consisted of 66 assertions and *U.S. News* carried 47. Out of all of the magazines, *Time* reported the most assertions in the tyrannical subcategory. The tyrant trait also scored high on the list for *Newsweek* magazine which carried 60 assertions and *U.S. News* reporting of 32. Placing third in all three magazines was the manipulative trait with 27 assertions in *Newsweek*, 24 in *Time* and 14 in *U.S. News*. The proud subcategory was reported the least often by all three magazines. *Time* carried 17 assertions portraying Jackson as a proud man, *Newsweek* reported 16, and *U.S. News* coverage consisted of 12.

	Newsweek	Time	U.S. News	Total
Warrior				
Courage	2	1	0	3
Strong	47	45	31	123
Admirable	11	14	9	34
Fighter	139	145	74	358
Subtotal	199	205	114	518=37%
Lover				
Commitment	11	13	16	40
Compassion	24	42	21	87
Skillful	24	38	10	72
Magical	41	30	17	88
Subtotal	100	123	64	287=20%
Savior				
Rescuer	4	1	1	6
Saint	24	23	12	59
Creates Hope	28	26	16	70
Sacrificing	10	4	0	14
Subtotal	66	54	29	149=11%
Ruler				
Proud	16	17	12	45
Authoritative	61	66	47	175
Tyrannical	60	76	32	168
Manipulative	27	24	14	65

| Subtotal | 164 | 183 | 105 | 452=32% |
| Total | 529 | 565 | 312 | 1,406=100% |

Table 1 :Frequency of Heroic Themes in National News Magazines Coverage of Jackson's 1988 Presidential Campaign

Table 1 represents the *frequency* and *type* of heroic assertions that occurred from January 1 through December 31, 1988.

MISCELLANEOUS CATEGORY

Not every assertion reported from January 1 through December 31, 1988, could be classified under the heroic category, therefore, a miscellaneous category was included for the study. These assertions were identified and placed in the following subordinal categories: (a) favorable assertions mentioning Jackson or his campaign; (b) unfavorable assertions mentioning Jackson or his campaign; and (c) neutral assertions mentioning Jackson or his campaign. Examples of such assertions were:

Favorable:	Jackson's *support among Jews has risen* to 10 percent.
Unfavorable:	*Jackson on the ticket would hurt a lot.*
Neutral:	The story came from Gerald Austin, *Jackson's campaign manager.*

Table 2 reveals that of the 694 assertions in the miscellaneous category, 38% or 261 were neutral, 37% or 256 were favorable, and 25% or 177 were unfavorable.

	Newsweek	*Time*	*U.S. News*	*Total*
Neutral	104	89	68	261 = 38%
Favorable	118	75	63	256 = 37%
Unfavorable	61	64	52	177 = 25%
Total	283	228	183	694 = 100%

Table 2 Frequency of Assertions in the Miscellaneous Category

DISCUSSION

In order to examine the portrayal of Jesse Jackson as a mythical hero during the 1988 presidential campaign, three national news magazines were analyzed for their mythical content: *Time, Newsweek,* and *U.S. News.* Overall, 184 news articles, from January 1 through December 31, 1988, mentioning Jackson or his campaign were studied. Based on the content, 2,100 assertions were coded; 1,406 as heroic assertions and 694 were placed in a miscellaneous category. The data revealed that when *Time, Newsweek,* and *U.S.News* reported on Jackson and/or his presidential campaign, almost 70% of the time Jackson was portrayed as a mythical hero. In fact the overall "frequency of appearance" or ranking of the heroic categories by *Time, Newsweek,* and *U.S. News* were similar. (See Table 3) It is also interesting to note, that during those instances when Jackson was not described as a mythical hero, coverage by these national news magazines, for the most part, portrayed him in a favorable manner. (See Table 2)

Rank	Newsweek	Time	U.S. News
#1-Warrior	199 or 38%	205 or 36%	114 or 37%
#2-Ruler	164 or 31%	183 or 32%	105 or 34%
#3-Lover	100 or 19%	123 or 22%	64 or 20%
#4-Savior	66 or 12%	54 or 10%	29 or 9%
Total	529 or 100%	565 or 100%	312 or 100%

Table 3 Frequency of Appearance of Heroic Themes in National News Magazines Coverage of Jackson's 1988 Campaign

Myths explain the world, guide individual development, provide social direction, and address spiritual longings. In fact, a well-articulated, carefully examined mythology is one of the most effective devices available for understanding and encountering a world in constant turmoil. Realizing the power of mythical motifs, campaign organizations seek to communicate unique mythical themes or messages to the media.

For example, in most instances audiences develop images of candidates from news coverage where melodramatic images of victims, villains, and heroes are common.[63] In fact, the themes used to outline many news stories are constant: triumph of the individual over adversity, justice winning over evil, redemption of the individual through reform, and rewarding valor or heroism.[64] This message is simultaneously intended to attract political support and differentiate the candidate from his/her opponent.[65]

Explanations regarding the success of Jackson's campaign has been attributed by numerous authors to (1) his political base in the black community, (2) his philosophies, and (3) his shift from a civil rights leader to a political leader. In fact, many would argue that Jackson's success stems from his dynamic personality—his photogenic appeals, magnetic charisma, and his electrifying oratory. However, the findings in this study reveal that in addition to the variables mentioned above, the mythical motif that embodies Jackson's is another significant contributor to what is commonly referred to as the "Jackson Phenomenon."

This mythical component has significant implications for African American leaders. For while this study not only demonstrates the power of the media as an image-maker, but the importance of the media's role as storytellers to the masses. This study also reveals that to be regarded as a mythical hero means power—something Jackson has demonstrated during the past decades. This research reveals that to be identified as a Black leader in America, one needs to be more than articulate, charismatic, and religious oriented, this individual should possess the constructs of a mythical hero.

Mythical heroes dwell within each and every one of us. This study reveals that by understanding the principles that govern a society, culture, or community's underlying mythology, individuals can learn to influence patterns in their lives that once seemed predetermined or unattainable.

---

[63] Ruth Brennan and Dan Hahn, *Listening for a President: A Citizen's Campaign Methodology* (New York: Praeger Publishers, 1990).
[64] Ibid.
[65] Ibid.

CHAPTER XI

HOW SHOULD BLACK LEADERSHIP RESPOND TO FARRAKHAN'S ATTEMPT TO LEGITIMIZE HIS LEADERSHIP IN BLACK AMERICA?

CLARENCE TAYLOR

FLORIDA INTERNATIONAL UNIVERSITY

Black Nationalism is not monolithic. Its range includes reformists and revolutionaries, black capitalists and cultural nationalists. All black nationalist ideologies are in opposition to cultural assimilation, and the political and economic hegemony of the dominant society. However, as many scholars note, one dominant trend in black nationalism advances a broad-minded program. Proponents of this form of identity politics stress cultural pride and connect the predicament of African Americans to the problems of Africans throughout the world. These *radical* black nationalists advocate building institutions in the black community for social, political and economic empowerment and they consistently challenge the dominant's society's attempt to dehumanize people of African origins. They advocate racial consciousness not by denigrating other groups but by stressing the accomplishments of African people. Radical nationalists attempt to build coalitions across race and gender lines in the struggle against the forces that promote capitalist exploitation, imperialism, sexism and racism.[1]

Another form of nationalism is much more conservative. Advocates of this form of nationalism embrace pan-Africanism in name only, and attempt to isolate the black community by attempting to stop African Americans from building alliances with progressive people and other victims of oppression. The proponents of this narrow form of nationalism espouse racial chauvinism, sexism, homophobia, and leave unchallenged the harmful effects of capitalism and imperialism. This latter form of nationalism is the brand advocated by Louis Farrakhan and the leadership of the Nation of Islam (NOI) and even more apparently extreme members like Khalid Abdul Muhammad of the NOI.

---

[1] William L. Van DeBurg, *New Day in Babylon* (Chicago: University of Chicago Press, 1993), pp. 297-298; Manning Marable, "On Malcolm X: His Message & Meaning" Open Magazine Pamphlet Series # 22 (Westfield, New Jersey, 1992) pp.5-6.

The Congressional Black Caucus's chairperson, Kweisi Mfume's declaration that his organization had formed a covenant with the NOI and Farrakhan's participation at the Black Leadership Summit sponsored by the NAACP are clear examples of his success at influencing broader and more mainstream African-American groups far beyond his own limited organization. [2] Hence, a major question for black leadership is how should it react to Farrakhan's overtures? This is not an insignificant question. A *Time* magazine and CNN poll claimed that Farrakhan is one of the most popular leaders among blacks.[3] Mainstream leaders are impressed by the kind of crowds that Farrakhan has drawn. Consequently, some argue, that a rejection of the NOI leader's undertaking to reach out may indicate to his numerous supporters that they are being rebuffed by these mainstream leaders.

Supporters of the NOI not only note its popularity but point to its history of work with criminals, drug addicts, and prostitutes. They like to point out its emphasis on black pride, the family, and an anti-drug message. But there are other aspects of NOI that are not simply peripheral, that need to be open for comment and criticism.

A major objective of the Nation of Islam has been to whip up hatred of other groups that also have a long history of being victims of discrimination—Jews, gays, Catholics, and women. The demagogic words of Khalid Abdul Muhammad, a leading spokesperson for this group clearly demonstrates this point. He refers to Jews as bloodsuckers who deserved to experience the Holocaust. He calls homosexuals "faggots" and refers to the Pope as a "no good...cracker." In a speech at Kean College in New Jersey, this provocateur of hate advocated killing white South Africans indiscriminately. "We kill the women. We kill the children. We kill the babies. We kill the blind. We kill the cripples. We kill'em all. We kill the faggot. We kill the lesbian. We kill'em all." [4]

Although Minister Louis Farrakhan, the head of NOI, denounced the statements of Muhammad as mean spirited and repugnant, his words immediately

---

[2] Some even claim that Farrakhan is moderating his views. Sylvester Monroe, "Is Khalid Muhammad Hurting The Nation of Islam"? *Emerge*, Volume 5, Number 11, September, 1994, pp. 42-46.

[3] *Time*, 2/28/94, p.22

[4] *New York Times*, 1/16/94

proved meaningless when he directly followed them by declaring that he still supports the "truths" of the Kean speech. Farrakhan himself has also uttered similar words of hate and intolerance. Jews have been a favorite target of the minister. Farrakhan disseminates the old racist myth that Jews are naturally evil. Who can ever forget his claim that Judaism is "a gutter religion"? In 1985, he declared that he has a "controversy with the Jews." He compared himself to Jesus arguing that he like Jesus was hated by the Jews because he "exposed their wicked hypocrisy." He expounded that the Jews use their "stranglehold over the government" to smear him and they have no respect for the truth.[5]

Farrakhan continuously defends the NOI's anonymously published book, *The Secret Relationship between Blacks and Jews*, a book that falsely claims that Jews were the major backers of the international slave trade, as he rants and raves about a Jewish conspiracy aimed to stop him. At a rally in Harlem in January, 1994, Farrakhan asserted that "They [the Jews] don't want Farrakhan to do what he does. *They are plotting now as we speak.*"[6] In an interview with Wilbert Tatum of the *Amsterdam News*, Farrakhan declared that "The difference with us is we're not looking to the Jew for a damned dime. They've been working since nine years to stop me from eating. But I eat and I live as good as any man...because they can't get a ladder to go up to heaven to cut my blessings off. And that's why when I sit down with them (I can say) I don't owe you nothing. I don't need your money. I'm a man, damn it! My leader didn't make me a punk. He made me a man!"[7]

Farrakhan adroitly fabricates enemies of black men in order to present himself as the number one defender of black manhood. His declaration of independence from Jewish financial support, implies that Jews are a threat to black manhood because, he argues, they attempt to control black men through money, causing black leaders to simply acquiesce to their demands. Any black who works with Jews is tautologically tainted.

Positioning himself as the defender of "black manhood," Farrakhan has also taken aim at women. At the Harlem rally in January, Farrakhan excluded

---

[5] October 7, 1985 speech at Madison Square Garden, New York City, aired on "Like It Is" WABC.

[6] *Amsterdam News*, 1/29/94

[7], *New York Times*, 2/4/94; *Amsterdam News*, 1/8/94.

women under the pretense that the gathering was a "talk among brothers."[8] This action sends a clear message that the way to address vital issues in the black community is to practice gender discrimination. Farrakhan and the NOI clearly do not view gender oppression as a significant problem in the black community. In fact, feminism is presented as a direct menace to black manhood, and thus blacks in general. He has often said that the duty of women is to be subordinate to their husbands. In late July, Farrakhan told a group of women in Boston that they should put their families before their careers, stop wearing sexually provocative skirts and oppose abortion. He contended that women should not abandon cooking, cleaning and other homemaking skills for careers. And not surprisingly, he blames rape victims for their own victimization, saying they are manipulators of men who say no but really mean yes. [9] Farrakhan's reactionary views on gender explicitly state that black men must stand up to black women and relegate them to their "proper role," not as active agents working to improve the conditions of African-Americans, but as passive creatures who should be led by men. Khalid Abdul Muhammad's anti-Semitic and sexist remarks demonstrate that he has learned well from his "spiritual" leader.

The Nation of Islam's anti-Semitism, sexism, and gay-bashing and its campaign to promote a narrow nationalism, is not without other purposes. Most basically it legitimizes its own leadership in black communities by discrediting all others who don't take similar stands, "demonstrating" to millions of African Americans that it will do what other black leaders and organizations dare not, stand up to Jews, "male controlling women", and gays and lesbians who attempt to destroy the black family. It might be argued as I will later, that poverty and a collapsing economy are the real threats we face.

The attempt by some journalists, politicians and civic organizations to get black leaders to denounce the NOI is skillfully used by Farrakhan to show to the masses of blacks how defiant and independent he is, and how other blacks are manipulated by whites. Any African American who stands up and criticizes Farrakhan is accused by the NOI and its supporters of being a mouthpiece for

---

[8] *Amsterdam News*, 1/29/94.

[9] *New York Times*, 8/31/94. The theme that women should be homemakers is repeated in his book, *A Torchlight For America*. "Fallen Champ: The Untold Story of Mike Tyson," produced by Barbara Kopple for NBC.

Jews, working against the interest of African-Americans (Farrakhan has called them "silly Toms").[10] Thus, the NOI attempts to paint itself as the only organization dauntless enough to defend the interest of African Americans.[11]

The campaign is working. The NOI and Farrakhan's profile and popularity has risen in the black communities. Farrakhan speaks to large audiences. He spoke to twenty-five to thirty thousand people in December of 1993, at the Jacob Javitts Center in New York. Ten thousand heard him speak at the 369th Armory in Harlem in January while thousands remained outside unable to find seating. Khalid Muhammad is hot on the college lecture circuit receiving $2,650 a lecture. Young African Americans speak about the courage of Farrakhan, Khalid Muhammad, and other NOI speakers and refer to them as freedom fighters and role models.[12]

To many, the NOI seems to be a revolutionary organization willing to do battle with governmental authorities. Last winter's episode in New York City, where police and Muslims battled when the police entered a Mosque during services is a case in point. After the smoke cleared, eight police were injured and there were no immediate arrest of NOI members who were involved in the melee. The event left many with a sense of pride and proof that the NOI means business. The headline of the *Amsterdam News* reflected this sense of pride. It read: "Lesson #1, Muslims Don't Play." [13] The lesson was clear, NOI is the most militant black organization in the country.

However, there are deeper reasons for NOI's popularity in black communities. Historian Gerald Horne, and others, have convincingly argued that the destruction of indigenous black radicals and left-led CIO unions after 1948 led, in the vacuum, to the rise of narrow black nationalism in the black community. The government's persecution of black radicals, such as Ben Davis, Paul Robeson, W.E.B. Du Bois and later the Black Panthers, and the ousting of radicals from CIO unions, repressed a class and race critique of capitalism in black America. [14]

---

[10] Wilbert tatum's interview with Farrakhan, *Amsterdam News*, 1/8/94.

[11] Adolph Reed, "The Rise of Louis Farrakhan" *Nation*, 1/21/91, p.55.

[12] *Chronicle of Higher Education*, 1/19/94

[13]*Amsterdam News*, 1/15/94.

[14] Gerald Horne "'Myth' and the Making of Malcolm X" *American Historical Review*, Volume 98, Number 2, April 1993, pp. 441-447.

Black radicals and left-led unions attempted to build multiracial coalitions that toiled to make corporations and institutions hire African-Americans, improve the working conditions of workers, and challenged racism and class oppression. The Teacher's Union (TU) of the CIO local 555, United Public Workers is a good illustration. Between the late 1930s and 1950s, the TU conducted a campaign to push the New York City Board of Education to hire black teachers. It also attempted to force the Board of Education to remove textbooks that contained racist depictions of people of color. TU members also worked with parents in Harlem and Bedford-Stuyvesant, Brooklyn to force the Board of Education to furnish the same services it was providing to children attending schools in predominantly white neighborhoods. [15]

During the Cold War, left forces such as the TU were removed and in their absence innocuous voices to the United States government and corporate America, such as the NOI, were left to fill the vacuum. [16]

The growing popularity of the NOI is tied, as well, to the deteriorating economic and social conditions of the nation. The Recession, combined with the Reagan-Bush policies of the 1980s have led to climbing unemployment, an increasing number of people lacking adequate health insurance, an escalating infant mortality rate, a declining income for the poor, an increase in the number of the homeless, and a wider gap between the rich and the poor. Black communities were especially devastated by the Recession and the Reagan-Bush policies. The *Wall Street Journal* reported that blacks were the only racial group to "suffer a net job loss during the 1990-91 economic downturn at companies with 100 or more workers." At one large corporation, for instance, blacks absorbed 43.6% of the job cuts, even though they made up only about 26 % of the work force.[17]

---

[15] Employment of Negro Teachers in New York City Schools, 1951; Resolution on the Employment of Negro Teachers in the Schools of New York City, November 16, 1951; Teachers Union Report "Bias and Prejudice in Textbooks in Use in New York City Schools;" A report by the Harlem Committee on the campaign to hire black teachers, September 1951-June, 1952; "Better Schools Today" Annual Yearbook published by the School Council of Bedford-Stuyvesant-Williamsburg, 1946.

[16] Gerald Horne "'Myth" and the Making of "Malcolm X"' *American Historical Review*, Volume 98, Number 2, April 1993, pp.441-447; Gerald Horne, "Why NAACP Won't Disown Nation of Islam," *New York Times*, 1/19/94; David Caute, *The Great Fear*, (New York: Simon & Schuster, 1978), pp. 432-440.

[17] *The Wall Street Journal*, 9/14/93.

In 1992 the infant mortality rate for blacks was double that of whites. The problem of the growing disparity of infant mortality between blacks and whites is due, in part, to a lack of prenatal care and the rising number of low birth weights, especially among black infants. [18] During the Reagan years, the homeless rate in major cities in the United States doubled. For instance, in January 1983, the New York City provided shelter for 4,676 men and 638 women. By January 1987, the number had increased to 9,000 men and 1,100 women.[19] Moreover, Reagan and Bush helped create a racially charged atmosphere in the nation by undercutting civil rights enforcement, attacking affirmative action and other programs that benefit the poor, labeling them as handouts and characterizing their beneficiaries as undeserving. Poor people were simply blamed for their own poverty.

As the pie has shrunk, conservatives have encouraged the rest of us to fight for the crumbs, rather than joining in coalitions against these same conservatives. In a very important sense Reagan and Bush could find no finer champion of their politics of division and resentment than Louis Farrakhan.

Despite Bill Clinton's egalitarian lingo, he has not made room at the table for blacks. Instead, he has sent out an explicit message that his administration does not take black America's complaints seriously. Clinton's emphasis on "the plight of the middle class" is a lucid communique to Americans that blacks don't count. His abandonment of Lani Guinier, his pitiful plea to black ministers to be responsible and take care of their own, his rhetoric on welfare reform, and his backing of the "three strikes, you're out" crime proposal without serious preventive measures is proof that this president is more concerned about opinion polls than social and economic justice. His push for NAFTA, a trade agreement that will lead to the loss of more jobs, downward pressure on domestic wages, and the greater exploitation of workers outside of the United States by corporate capitalism, together with his focus on the fiscal deficit, and his corresponding lack of focus on the job deficit are all clear indications that Clinton does not have the interest of working class people at heart. His interest lies with corporate America. The lack of effective leadership to address the economic and social plight of

---

[18] *New York Times*, 9/16/93.

[19] Thomas Hirsch and Jamshid A. Momeni, "Homelessness in New York: A Demographic and Socioeconomic Analysis" in Jamshid Momeni ed. *Homelessness in the United States* (New York: Praeger Publishers, 1990), p.132.

millions of Americans has created a void, a feeling of despair and many are searching for answers. In this void NOI has prospered.

The political changes in big cities have also contributed to a feeling of hopelessness. The death of Harold Washington and the eventual takeover of Chicago by the machine politician, Richard Daley Jr; the election of Richard Riordan in Los Angeles, a millionaire, right wing ideologue with no political experience; and the defeat of David Dinkins in New York to Rudolph Giuliani, a law and order advocate also with no political experience, were clear signs of growing black disempowerment. Mayor Giuliani's plan to cut city expenses by firing 15,000 workers and drastically reducing social services will devastate working people.[20] Although Dinkins was a lackluster mayor who disappointed his progressive backers by not creating programs that would benefit the poor, Giuliani's merciless attempt to balance the city's budget off the backs of working people, indicates to blacks, Latinos and other working people that they have no voice in city government.

This political vacuum has allowed reactionary demagogues like Farrakhan to grab the spotlight. His insistent message that whites, especially Jews, are causing the social and economic ills of black America has endeared him to many in the absence of a viable, progressive alternative in this period of acute polarization.

But for all their posturing, the stark reality is that Farrakhan and the NOI have not addressed themselves to the deteriorating conditions of poor black Americans. They have not stood up to the forces that are responsible for the misery of the masses of blacks in this country. Farrakhan, like any other right wing demagogue never challenges the unequal distribution of wealth, the lack of jobs, the denial of adequate health care for millions of Americans, or the growing problem of homelessness. He never speaks out against Corporate America's decision to lay off workers while it makes enormous profits. He never speaks about the destruction of the environment by transnational corporations. Nor does he address the declining income and welfare benefits for the poor at a time when the rich continue to receive huge tax breaks.

---

[20] *New York Times*, 2/2/94.

NOI and Farrakhan oppose building a broad multiracial and progressive coalition that can effectively challenge racial, gender and class oppression in America and struggle for the redistribution of wealth. Instead Farrakhan advocates a watered down Booker T. Washington approach to black America's afflictions. He urges blacks to become members of the petty bourgeoisie by producing and selling toothpaste, sanitary napkins, mouthwash, toilet paper, and soap, and investing their profits in a black bank. The NOI leader may talk a tough game, but his solution for black America is as revolutionary as Thomas Sowell's. As political scientist Adolph Reed has aptly summarized, Farrakhan: "endorses moral repressiveness; he asserts racial essentialism; he affirms male authority; and he lauds bootstrap capitalism." [21] He espouses a culture of poverty thesis that blames blacks for being morally "sick" and devoid of an entrepreneurial spirit.

Farrakhan's conservativism was starkly exemplified recently when he told the publisher of the *Amsterdam News* that in order to solve the drug problem in black communities, a person need only change her "behavioral pattern." "You know, if you don't have an appetite for a thing it can be displayed in all the stores in which you go. You don't want it." [22] It seems that the minister's solution is just another version of Nancy Reagan's campaign to fight the influx of drugs in the black community by yelling "Just Say NO!" No call for treatment on demand. No call for jobs.

Similarly, Farrakhan's program for fighting crime in black communities is to "instill responsibility" in black men. Beneath the rhetoric of empowerment, this conservative notion argues that the burden for change must simply fall on the individual, the victim. Instead of working to build a movement to challenge the infiltration of drugs and guns in the black community and confront the social and economic conditions that have created desperation among so many young people, Farrakhan's revolutionary solution offers little more than "God helps those who help themselves."

The underlying mission of Farrakhan and the NOI is to legitimize their leadership and to hinder progress in building the type of effective coalition that could address the material realities of poverty. The scholar Henry Louis Gates has

---

[21] Adolph Reed, "False Prophet II" *Nation*, 1/28/91, pp.87-92.
[22] *Amsterdam News*, 1/8/94.

brilliantly argued that the strategy of Farrakhan and other black demagogues is to use anti-Semitism "as a weapon in the raging battle of who will speak for black America—those who have sought common cause with others or those who preach a barricaded withdrawal into racial authenticity. The strategy of these apostles of hate, I believe, is best understood as ethnic isolationism—they know that the more isolated black America becomes, the greater their power."[23]

WHAT MUST BE DONE?

In order to counter NOI's campaign of divide and conquer, progressive forces must be willing to expose NOI for what it is, a divisive force that is preventing the formation of a broad alliance of working people that can challenge our current ills. The task of exposing the NOI will not be easy because of the major influence Farrakhan and his organization have in the black communities and the growing nationalist sentiment in those communities. The risk is that those who stand up, especially blacks, will be stigmatized as enemies of the race, accused of doing the "white man's bidding."

Those who fear such a risk should look to the courage of Malcolm X as a guide. Despite great risk to himself —a much greater risk than most of us now face—he stood up and exposed NOI for what it really is, a narrow nationalistic organization. Malcolm attempted to move the NOI in a progressive direction by deemphasizing its spiritual nationalism while pushing it to become active in the civil rights movement, [24] and emphasizing a global analysis that was anti-imperialist, connecting the conditions of blacks in the United States to exploited people in the third world. He openly stated that he was willing to work with any progressive forces to build a movement that struggled for human rights and against the oppression of blacks. "It's true we are muslims and our religion is islam," Malcolm explained:

> But we don't mix our religion with our politics and our economics
> and our social and civic activities—not any more. After our

---

[23] Henry Louis Gates, "Black Demagogues and Pseudo-Scholars" *New York Times* Op-Ed, 7/20/92.

[24] Bruce Perry, *Malcolm* (Barrytown New York: Station Hill Press, 1991), pp.314-318, 322-324, 326; George Breitman, *The Last Year of Malcolm X* (New York: Pathfinder Press, 1967), pp.79, 113-118; Gerald Horne, "'Myth and the Making of 'Malcolm X'" in the *American Historical Review*, Volume 98, Number 2, April 1993, p.446

religious services are over, then as muslims we become involved in political action, economic action and social and civic action. *We become involved with anybody, anywhere, anytime,* and in any manner that's designed to eliminate the evils the political, economic and social evils that are afflicting the people in our community. [25]

Malcolm criticized capitalism for its exploitation of third world people and African Americans. He allied himself with the liberation forces struggling against western imperialism, arguing that these were the same forces black America must confront.   However, the extreme right wing of NOI, led by Elijah Muhammad, determining that it had too much to lose, reacted to Malcolm's crusade by ousting him and launching a drive to destroy him. Louis Farrakhan (then known as Louis X) was part of this effort to destroy Malcolm. In an article in NOI's newspaper, *Muhammad Speaks,* Farrakhan called Malcolm " a traitor who [was] worthy of death", [26] a statement he still defends (a surprise to many young people who simply view Farrakhan as a latter-day Malcolm).

Most importantly, black leadership and other progressive forces can also continue to work to build a strong coalition that will address the vital issues of working people. The suggestion that critics of NOI should contribute financially to surviving and emerging left-wing organizations seeking to organize across racial lines is a good one. It can further be encouraged that those who identify with the left but who are not active, become involved by educating and organizing people across race and gender lines to battle for adequate housing, education, health care for Americans and jobs and justice. They should be willing to build a national movement that will challenge the politics of greed and work for a just and humane society.

This paper is not an attempt to argue that dialogue between the NOI and black leadership should not take place. But the full nature of what the NOI represents has to be kept in mind and given the sought of criticism that is discussed in this work. We should be wary of anything that escalates from dialogue to endorsement.

---

[25] George Breitman, ed. *Malcolm X Speaks* (New York: Pathfinder Press, 1990), p.38.
[26] Bruce Perry, *Malcolm,* p.332; Adolph Reed, "The Rise of Louis Farrakhan," *The Nation,* 1/21/91, p. 56.

Because the Nation of Islam encourages black pride, works to reform drug addicts, and has some influence in black communities throughout America is no reason to excuse its campaign of racial, gender, and sexual orientation intolerance. Although the White Citizens Councils throughout the South had political influence in the 1960s, it was correct to condemn the language and activities of these groups because they were morally wrong. The hate crusade of the Nation of Islam is equally offensive and should be condemned.

CHAPTER XII

THE POLITICAL DILEMMA OF THE REVEREND AL SHARPTON

CLARENCE TAYLOR

FLORIDA INTERNATIONAL UNIVERSITY

Scholars and journalists who have written on the activities of the Reverend Al Sharpton have usually painted him as an opportunist, ambulance chaser, and media hound. However, the flamboyant minister from Brooklyn is an important cultural-political symbol, who remains a defiant voice for many working class African Americans. Moreover, with little doubt, Al Sharpton has become a significant political entity in New York City and New York State politics. He came in a respectable third in a four person race in the Democratic Senatorial Primary in 1992. He received over seventy-five percent of the black vote in that race. He has developed close ties with the Rev. Jesse Jackson and he has just published his autobiography, *Go and Tell Pharaoh*.

In spite of his notoriety and emergence as an important political force, a burning question that many still raise is who is Al Sharpton? Is he a progressive politician working to build a broad multiracial coalition, as he has claimed on many occasions, an opportunist or is he a black nationalist advocating that blacks turn inward to solve their problems? Defining his political position is clearly a dilemma for the minister from Brooklyn because making a choice between progressives and nationalists may determine whether he maintains his credibility with his long time supporters or whether he can build a broad base to help bring about significant political change.

In order to locate Sharpton on the political map, it is important to know where Sharpton came from. By exploring his past, it may provide us a better understanding of where he is and a greater appreciation of his dilemma.

Alfred Sharpton Jr. was born in Brownsville Brooklyn in 1954, the youngest child of Alfred and Ada Sharpton. Sharpton has an older half brother and sister and an older sister. His father was a landlord and contractor who owned several houses in both Brooklyn and Queens and provided a comfortable life for his family. In 1959, the Sharptons moved into a large private house in the middle class neighborhood of Hollis, Queens. [1]

Before moving to Queens, the Sharptons began attending Washington Temple COGIC regularly. At an early age, Sharpton was impressed with the charismatic preaching style of its founder and leader, Bishop Frederick D. Washington. Sharpton decided to become a minister and at the age of four gave his first sermon at the church entitled, "Let Not Your Heart be Troubled." By the time Sharpton had reached the age of ten, he was ordained as a COGIC minister by Bishop Washington. He became an itinerant preacher, giving guest sermons in various churches in New York. By the time he was thirteen, he started traveling with the famed gospel singers, Mahaila Jackson and Roberta. Because of his youth he became known and billed as the "wonder boy preacher." Sharpton was entrenched in a black Pentecostal church culture, where he saw and heard famed gospel singers, and ecstatic church services. Sharpton saw charismatic black preachers, black people controlling their church community and poor working class people moving into positions of control. In his autobiography Sharpton observes that he learned the art of preaching from Bishop Washington. Washington Temple became an important training ground where cultural practices of the black church were instilled in the young minister.[2]

Sharpton's political activism was probably sparked by the Reverend Adam Clayton Powell Jr. of Abyssinian Baptist Church in Harlem. The younger minister was attracted to Powell's outspokenness, political savvy, ability to handle the media and his defiance of Congress and those in power. Sharpton would tell the *New Times* years later, that he decided he wanted to be like the militant pastor from Harlem and become an activist preacher. [3]

---

[1] Al Sharpton, *Go and Tell Pharaoh: The Autobiography of the Reverend Al Sharpton* (New York: Doubleday, 1996), pp 9-19; *New York Post* , 4/11/71; Louise Mooney, ed., "Al Sharpton, *Newsmakers* , 1991, pp. 383-384; *New York Times* , 12/19/91.

[2] Clarence Taylor, *Black Churches of Brooklyn* (New York: Columbia University Press, 1994),p. 171; *New York Times* , 12/19/71; Louise Mooney, ed., "Al Sharpton," p.383. *Go and Tell Pharaoh*, pp. 31; pp.22-25. Sharpton's autobiography sheds some light on the black Pentecostal church culture, pp. 22-25.

[3] Sharpton, who met Powell for the first time at the age of twelve, recalled that he was amazed at how Powell handled the press during an interview the young Brooklyn attended. "It was the most amazing show I had ever seen in my life," Sharpton said. Shortly after the first encounter between the two ministers, they became friends. Powell took the young Sharpton to his first Broadway show and to the island of Bimini for a vocation. The Congressman even counseled the "wonder boy

Growing up in the 1960s, Sharpton was aware of many black clerical figures who were in the forefront of the civil rights movement. Their example probably helped shape his view on the relationship between the ministry and social issues. According to Sharpton, the minister must address and try to seek solutions for the social conditions of the economically disadvantaged and powerless. The role of the minister cannot be limited to the spiritual realm. Sharpton decided to become less active in Washington Temple because he claimed that the Bishop and the church were not in the vanguard of the struggle for economic and social justice.[4] By the time Sharpton was twelve, he developed a close connection with more activist ministers such as Reverend William Jones of Bethany Baptist Church. In the late 1960s, Jones had become the head of the New York branch of Operation Breadbasket. The National organization which struggled for economic justice for blacks, was headed by Reverend Jesse Jackson. Jones introduced Sharpton to Jackson. [5]

In 1969, when Sharpton was fifteen, Reverend Jesse Jackson appointed him youth director of the New York city chapter of Operation Breadbasket. The young activist minister participated in a number of campaigns including a boycott against the Atlantic and Pacific Tea Company (A&P) which operated a national chain of supermarkets. The boycott was launched by Jones and the New York chapter of Operation Breadbasket. It involved numerous ministers and won the support of several religious groups and a significant segment of the population. However, despite the fact that A&P reported a drop in its stock because of the boycott, the New York Chapter of Operation Breadbasket failed to win the support of the national organization for a nation wide boycott against the corporation. In the end, no agreement was reached between the opposing sides. [6]

---

preacher," *New York Times* , 1/13/91, 12/19/91; Sharpton, pp. 37-42; Clarence Taylor, p.211; Mike Sager, "The Sharpton Strategy" in *Esquire*, 1/91, pp.112-113.

[4] Taylor, pp. 211-212.

[5] Jim Sleeper, "A Man of too Many Parts," *The New Yorker* , 71/25/93, pp.58-60; William A. Jones, *God in the Ghetto* , (Elgin,Ill: Progressive Baptist Publishing House, 1979),pp.96-107 ; Clarence Taylor, *Black Churches* , pp.211-212.

[6] Jones, *God in the Ghetto* , pp. 98-100

Sharpton's involvement in the boycott radicalized him. He required a taste for street protests. In 1971, while still in high school, Sharpton told a *New York Post* reporter that he had been arrested four times in protest demonstrations. [7]

Throughout the 1970s and 1980s, Sharpton experimented with a variety of techniques—negotiation and threats, demonstrations and sit-ins—in order to accomplish his goals and also inspire media attention. Sharpton, along with his National Youth Movement, an organization he created while still in high School, held demonstrations at City Hall and other places demanding summer jobs for teens. In 1970, he held a sit-in at City Hall calling on city officials to provide jobs for African-American youths. He later held a sit-in at the New York City Board of Education office demanding the hiring of blacks for top positions. He was eventually ejected by security officers. On another occasion he and members of the NYM marched on Wall Street and painted X marks on office buildings where they claimed drug sales were taking place. [8]

Despite Sharpton's activism, he did not gain truly widespread prominence until 1986 with the Howard Beach case. In the winter of 1986, three young black men were beaten by a gang of white youths in the Howard Beach section of Queens, New York. One of the black men, twenty two year old Michael Griffith was beaten and chased by the gang onto a highway, struck by a car and killed. Although a group of white youths were arrested shortly after the incident, Sharpton, who became the spokesperson for Michael Griffith's family, and the family's attorneys, C. Vernon Mason and Alton Maddox, encouraged witnesses not to cooperate with the Queens District Attorney. Instead, they demanded that Governor Mario Cuomo appoint a special prosecutor to handle the investigation. The lawyers claimed that the Queens District Attorney's office and the police mishandled the investigation from the beginning by not arresting the driver of the car that killed Griffith. The driver had left the scene of the incident and washed

---

[7] Jack Robbins, "Daily Closeup," *New York Post*, 2/11/71. In an uncritical biography of Sharpton, National Alliance member Michael Klein asserts that Sharpton's first arrest was after he graduated Tilden High School and had formed the National Youth Movement. He and some members of the newly formed organization held a sit-in at the City's Department of Manpower demanding jobs for youths. In his autobiography, Sharpton points out that he was not arrested during the A&P boycott and protest Michael Klein, *The Man Behind the Sound Bite: The Real Story of the Rev. Al Sharpton* (New York: Castillo International, 1991), p. 96; Sharpton, pp. 55-58.

[8] Mooney, "Al Sharpton," *Newsmakers*, pp. 383-384.

the car before surrendering to authorities. The driver was never charged with any crime. [9]

In order to bring pressure on the Governor, Sharpton held highly publicized demonstrations in Howard Beach including one in which he went to the pizza shop the three black men had visited before they were attacked. In front of news cameras, Sharpton ordered a slice of pizza and said he and any other black person had a right to buy and eat pizza anywhere they wanted. When Mayor Koch met with other black leaders at City Hall to talk about ways of easing racial tension in the city, Sharpton held a press conference and called the Mayor's meeting a "coon show." Eventually, Governor Cuomo appointed attorney Charles Hynes as special prosecutor. Hynes won a conviction. [10]

Sharpton, Maddox, and Mason were revered by many as heroes. Their effective strategy won praise from the black press and radio and from New Yorkers who had witnessed a number of high publicity racial incidents, in which blacks were beaten or killed, resolved without a single conviction. Sharpton in particular gained media attention because of his outspokenness. They became the black bad men of New York, declaring that blacks were not going to take any garbage. They declared a new day in New York City politics championing a new black militancy. They warned not only white New Yorkers but the old black leadership that the days of uncle tomism were over. They were the new men in the hood.

In spite of his notoriety and prominence, questions about his integrity were raised. In January 1988, *New York Newsday* revealed that Sharpton had worked for the Federal Bureau of Investigation by supplying information on organized criminals, Don King, and black politicians. The minister admitted that he had supplied information to federal authorities on organized crime figures and crack dealers, but he emphatically denied spying on black leaders. According to federal authorities, Sharpton had a two hour interview with an undercover agent, Victor Quintana, posing as a rich South American. The undercover agent, asked Sharpton "if you can introduce me to somebody in drugs." According to Sharpton, he told the undercover agent that he does not deal with drugs nor does he deal with people

---

[9] Sharpton, pp. 97-119; *Newsday*, 1/20/88, 1/22/88; *Jet*, 2/8/88;
[10] Ibid.

who sell drugs. However, federal authorities stated that Sharpton agreed to assist.[11]

Sharpton claimed that two or three weeks after the meeting with Quintana, F.B.I. agents approached him and said they had a tape of him attempting to make a drug deal. He said that after he told the agents he was innocent, he agreed to work with them. He then claimed the agents asked him to provide information on Don King and Michael Franzese, a reputed Columbo Family crime person. Apparently Sharpton had come into contact with mob figures during his earlier involvement in the entertainment world. He agreed to provide information on the mob because "The problem I have with the entertainment world is that I represent a lot of blacks at the bottom, and these mobsters have used us. Sharpton claimed that because he threatened to boycott the Michael Jackson Concert in 1984, that Sal Posillo, an alleged crime figure connected with the tour, threatened to kill him. According to Sharpton this also explained his decision to work with the F.B.I.[12]

The most disturbing part of the interview with *Newsday* came when Sharpton asserted that unsolicited he went to the regional U.S. attorney's office in the Eastern District and gave them information "proving" that Major Owens and Al Vann were involved in election fraud. Sharpton said, I called for a meeting and said I had information on some election fraud-I had information on Al Vann and Major Owens being involved in a vote ring...." Although it is not clear why he decided to provide federal authorities information on Owens and Vann, he did admit that they were political enemies, which might prompt us to question both his motive and evidence. He also may have wished to get even with Owens whose previous challenges forced Sharpton off the ballot for State Senator in 1978. [13]

Despite his denial about making a drug deal, FBI officials claimed that they had a videotape of Sharpton inquiring about buying cocaine. They also said that the reason he was not indicted was because he agreed to cooperate. Wearing a hidden microphone he attended meetings between Don King and crime figures. Along with organized crime people, King, and Owens and Vann, the FBI also said

---

[11] *Newsday*, 1/20/88, 1/22/88; *Jet*, 2/8/88; *New York Times*, 12/19/91; In his autobiography, Sharpton denies ever being an informant, Sharpton p. 81-83.
[12] *Newsday*, 1/20/88; *New York Times*, 12/19/91.; Sharpton, pp. 81-83.
[13] Ibid.

he gave information on black activist Sonny Carson and a local African-American minister.[14]

But the impact of Sharpton's undercover work with federal authorities was relatively mild when compared to his actions in the Tawana Brawley case. On November 28,1987, fifteen year old Tawana Brawley was found near an apartment building in Wappingers Falls. She was wrapped in a plastic bag with "KKK," "bitch" and "nigger" scrawled on her chest in charcoal, and feces smeared over her body. The jeans she was wearing had been burnt in the crotch, thus suggesting that she might have been deliberately burned. She was taken to the emergency room of Saint Francis Hospital in Poughkeepsie New York. While in the hospital she indicated to a police officer that she had been kidnapped, taken to the woods and raped by white men. She said that one of the rapists was a "white cop." According to Brawley the men had made her perform oral sex.

Numerous law enforcement officials were assigned to investigate the alleged sexual assault and racially-motivated incident. Among the officials were African-Americans, women, and people with experience in sexual assault cases. In addition, the Dutchess County District Attorney contacted the F.B.I. informing it that civil rights violations may have occurred. The Bureau responded and assigned a female special agent who handles civil rights cases. [15]

Dutchess County law enforcement authorities attempted to interview Brawley on several occasions. Although she spoke to a deputy sheriff and detectives on November 28, two assistant district attorneys, an FBI agent, and two people specializing in child abuse cases, on November 30, by early December Brawley and her family refused to cooperate further with the investigation. [16]

But by early December the principle reason explaining their refusal to cooperate was the advice the family received from their legal counsel. On the second of December, the Brawley family announced that it had hired attorney Alton Maddox to represent Tawana because they claimed authorities were not properly handling the investigation. Maddox immediately advised the Brawleys

---

[14] Ibid.

[15] *Report of the Grand Jury and Related Documents Concerning the Tawana Brawley Investigation.* pp 7-8; Robert D, McFadden et al., *Outrage: The Story Behind the Tawana Brawley Hoax* (New York: Bantam, 1990),p. 11-48; *New York Times*, 2/3/88.

[16] *Grand Jury Report*, pp.68-69.

not to speak to local law enforcement officials. He claimed from his experience in the Howard Beach case, and other racially motivated incidents, that local law enforcement personnel could not be trusted. He cut off all access to Tawana and demanded that Governor Cuomo appoint a special prosecutor to handle the case. [17]

After the failed attempts of law enforcement authorities to make contact with both Maddox and Brawley on December 14, 15, and 17, the District Attorney wrote a letter to Mrs. Brawley and Maddox notifying them that a Grand Jury was "being impaneled and that he would like to prepare Tawana Brawley on January 5 for her Grand Jury appearance." They did not respond. When they failed to appear before the District Attorney he issued subpoenas for Tawana, her mother, and her aunt for their appearance before the Grand Jury on January 13. Again, they did not show up to the session.[18]

Al Sharpton decided to get involved in the Brawley case in early December. Sharpton, along with Maddox and Mason pressed Governor Cuomo to appoint a special prosecutor. The flamboyant Pentecostal minister's rhetoric was increasingly inflammatory. At a rally held in Newburgh, he said that blacks were being attacked and murdered daily in New York State and he referred to Governor Cuomo as a symbol of "urban racism." The Governor refused Sharpton's request, arguing that local officials were capable of handling the case. He contended that the system should be given a chance. The Governor did not want to undermine the authority of Dutchess County District Attorney William Grady who was handling the case. However, on December 18, Grady announced that his investigation had hit an impasse because Brawley refused to talk. Brawley's representatives said that she would not cooperate with any investigation handled by the Dutchess County office. They began to make claims that police officers were involved in the abduction and rape, including Harry Crist Jr. the part time police officer who had committed suicide on the first of December.[19]

---

[17] Ibid., pp.69-70; McFadden, *Outrage* , pp.80-84.

[18] *Grand Jury Report*, p.70; McFadden, *Outrage*, pp. 167-169.

[19] McFadden et al., *Outrage*, pp.137-138, 172-177; *Report of the Grand Jury*, pp.72-76, 77-84 73; "Abrams to Grievance Committee for the Second and Eleventh Judicial Districts" (October 6, 1988), in *Report of the Grand Jury* , pp.2-3.

On January 26, Governor Cuomo appointed state Attorney General Robert Abrams as a special prosecutor for the case. Despite the apparent victory of the Brawley representatives, they announced that Tawana would not cooperate because Abrams was not devoting his full time to the case. Abrams had appointed State assistant district attorney John Ryan to handle the day to day investigation. Alton Maddox claimed that Ryan had no experience prosecuting civil rights cases, therefore was not qualified to handle the Brawley case. Abrams acknowledged this but pointed out that Ryan, who headed the attorney's general prosecution bureau, was an experienced trial lawyer, while he was not. He had also assigned an eight member team of lawyers, three of whom were African-Americans, to assist in the investigation. Abrams pleaded with Brawley to cooperate with the investigation and provide information about her claims.[20]

Finally after months of impasse, Abrams directed assistant attorney general John M. Ryan to begin the investigation. In defiant language, Brawley's advisors denounced both Abrams and Ryan and insisted that the Wappingers Falls teenager would not cooperate in the investigation unless Abrams was removed as the special prosecutor. In the most divisive language, Sharpton compared Abrams, a man whose objectivity he had earlier praised, to Hitler. He said that asking Brawley to cooperate with the Grand Jury is "like *asking* someone who watched someone killed in the gas chamber to sit down with Mr. Hitler." To compound the hysteria, Maddox, furious over a television station that showed pictures taken of Tawana's partially clad body when she was at St. Francis, lashed out at Abrams and accused him of "masturbating" over the pictures of Brawley. Despite the growing criticism of their strategy, Sharpton and the lawyers continued to refuse Brawley to cooperate. In fact, they attempted to stall the investigation through a series of legal moves, making up new demands which included the Governor appointing a new special prosecutor, and seeking limits in inquiry into the case. When it became apparent that Brawley would not cooperate, Abrams impanelled a grand jury on February 28 to determine if any crimes had been committed against the Wappingers Falls teenager.[21]

---

[20] *New York Times*, February 3, 7, and 10, 1988.
[21] *Grand Jury Report*, Introduction; *New York Times*, 2/22/88, 2/25/88.

On October 6, after an eight month investigation, the Grand Jury released its report on the allegations made by Tawana Brawley. The Grand Jury relied on the testimony of one hundred and eighty witnesses, six thousand pages of testimony, two hundred and fifty exhibits brought into evidence, testimony from experts in forensic serology, chemistry, pathology, and psychiatry. Moreover, experts in fiber and hair analysis, and handwriting analysis testified and medical evidence was used. The Jury concluded that Brawley fabricated the abduction and rape. Between November 24 and 28, as the Grand Jury testimony reconstructed the event, Brawley hid in an apartment that she and her family had been evicted from months earlier, the Pavilion Apartments at 19A Carnaby Drive in Wappingers Falls.

On November 28, at 1 P.M., witnesses saw Brawley outside of her former apartment. They said they saw her take a large plastic bag, step into it and pull it up around her neck. She then hopped a few feet before lying in a fetal position. A witness also testified that she saw Glenda Brawley, Tawana's mother, sitting in a car during this time. Mrs. Brawley told police she had gone to the apartment to see if her daughter was there and to collect unforwarded mail. However, a mail carrier testified that no one had picked up the mail for days.[22]

A witness who lived in the apartment and had observed Brawley climb into the bag, called the police. At 1:44 p.m. Dutchess County Deputy Sheriff Eric Thurston had arrived at the Pavilion. He and the witnesses approached Brawley. They said that she appeared unconscious but they saw her open and close her eyes twice. After seeing her covered with feces, dirty, and in torn jeans, Thurston called for an ambulance.[23]

The ambulance arrived around 2 p.m. with two emergency medical technicians (emt). One emt who ripped opened the plastic bag found no injuries. During the emt's examination, Brawley grabbed, with both hands, the hand of one of the emt, a clear sign that she was conscious. Moreover, the emt found no signs of exposure, low body temperature, dehydration or undernourishment, in spite of the fact that the low temperature for the days she claimed to be in the woods were below freezing.[24] The ambulance crew took her to Saint Francis Hospital in

---

[22]*Grand Jury Report*, pp.27-29.
[23]*Grand Jury Report*, pp. 6-8.
[24] Ibid.

Poughkeepsie. In contradiction to her claims medical witnesses from Saint Francis who examined Brawley reported that she was never unconscious. A specialist in emergency medicine who examined the patient reported that Brawley had resisted opening her eyes indicating that she was conscious. Moreover, the physician administered a consciousness test by raising Ms. Brawley's arm directly above her face and letting it fall. If the patient is unconscious, the arm will strike his or her face; a conscious patient will be aware of the threat to his or her face and will alter the course of the arm's fall, according to the physician. In Mrs. Brawley's case, her arm did not strike her face." She also responded to vocal commands, including one that told her to sit up. The Grand Jury report also noted Brawley's physical condition:

> Her teeth were clean, and her mouth did not have a bad odor. In her testimony, the emergency room physician noted that a typical person who came into the emergency room having been out in the environment would not have brushed her teeth or have good hygiene of the mouth. This would result in a dab odor, even if the person was out only overnight. Ms. Brawley's good dental hygiene was inconsistent with not having brushed her teeth in three or four days.[25]

Furthermore, experts pointed out that the dog feces Tawana was covered with were the same feces found in the area where Tawana was found. The same feces was also found in the former Brawley/King apartment at Pavilion. In addition, an F.B.I. special agent who is an expert in forensic chemistry testified that he had cut off the tips of a pair of gloves that were also found under the plastic bag that Brawley was found in. The special agent found charred cotton fibers "inside the middle and pinky fingers of the right glove and bundles of such fibers in the thumb. He also found charred cotton fibers in the ring finger and in the thumb of the left glove. These same materials were found in the Pavilion apartment. The report concluded that Brawley's claim was fraudulent.[26]

In his autobiography, Sharpton maintains that Tawana Brawley was raped and attacks the Grand Jury Report. However, he does not bother touching on the overwhelming forensic evidence that disproves the young woman's accusations. In

---

[25]Ibid., pp. 34-35.
[26] *Grand Jury Report*, pp. 77-83.

a similar vein, Sharpton does not bother shedding any light on his connections with the New Alliance Party.[27]

By the late 1980s, Sharpton had developed a close relationship with the New Alliance Party. In fact, it was an important force behind the emergence of the "new" Al Sharpton. NAP was founded by Fred Newman, a therapist with a Ph.D in Philosophy, former ally of extremist Lyndon LaRouche, a self-styled Marxist. Newman runs a therapy group that argues that only a proletarian revolution can be successful in ending individual neuroses. Writer Bruce Shapiro contends:

> Newman and his original associates (all of them white and most of them women) were political hard-liners who argued that only a revolution of the working class could resolve the individual psychic crisis; at the same time, like practitioners of EST and other distinctly unMarxist products of the nascent human potential movement, they believed that the road to their revolutionary new age lay in an extreme version of confronting the oppressor within, stripping the ego of its bourgeois, individualistic detritus. ...[28]

In place of bourgeois patterns of thinking, came "new revolutionary patterns of consciousness." Sexual relationships, employment and other aspects of human existence were questioned. Disturbingly, Newman as part of a potentially abusive therapeutic process, required his "patients" to recruit, donate money and do political work. Out of this social therapy collective based in New York, Newman formed the International Workers Party in the mid-1970s, which formed an alliance with Lyndon LaRouche for a brief period in 1974, and by 1979, it had changed its name to the New Alliance Party.[29]

Sharpton acknowledged that NAP has attempted to reshape him to make him more appealing to the public. He has credited the chairperson of the party, Dr. Lenora Fulani, for toning down his inflammatory language.[30]

But the relationship between the Alliance and Sharpton went far beyond providing demonstrators, increasing the Pentecostal minister's income, and

---

[27]Sharpton, pp.121-142; Sharpton does not mention Lenora Fulani at all and only mentions the New Alliance Party once (p.181) in his autobiography.

[28] Bruce Shapiro, "Dr. Fulani's Snake-Oil Show," *The Nation* , May 4, 1992, pp. 585-92.

[29] Ibid.

[30] Mike Sager, "The Sharpton Strategy," *Esquire, January, 1991* p. 112; *New York Times,* 12/19/91.

rhetorical cosmetics. NAP was involved in molding Sharpton's political ideology. Although he contended that he had ideological disagreements with NAP, it was clear from his own speeches and writings, that he publicly adopted aspects of NAP's philosophy and jargon. He credits Newman for his view that Israel is a "military base for the United States."

NAP formed a strong alliance with Sharpton. The organization provided him with a standing army for his demonstrations. Newman estimated that NAP members account for fifty percent of the troops at Sharpton sponsored demonstrations. Newman has made Sharpton a partner in his nationwide teenage talent competition business. In 1988, the business brought Sharpton $12,000 in revenue. And *The New York Times* reported in February 1988 that NAP's lecture and media booking company arranged twenty speaking engagements for Sharpton which earned him an additional $20,000.[31]

Although Sharpton probably lost a great deal of support during and after the Brawley case, he managed to remain an important figure in the black community. This was due to the fact that he was able to present himself as radical black nationalist. He relied on the rhetoric of a black nationalist culture that many of his supporters supported. Sharpton was quite familiar with rhetoric and cultural politics of the period because he grew up during the height of the Black Power Movement. Part of that rhetoric was telling white people off in a masculine and defiant tone (which is usually equated with strength). He manipulated the language and style of Black Power culture by standing in front of microphones and television cameras and lambasting public figures, calling them racist, the enemies of the black nation and other derogatory names. He asserted his duty was to protect black women from white rapists who carried police badges. He safely led Glenda Brawley to "sanctuary," thus, standing up to the state. He expressed the feeling and became the voice of many street people. It did not matter that his charges were fantasy. Some interpreted his defiance as a political challenge to a white power structure that denied them any voice. Sharpton became their means at striking out at them. He presented a racialized image in the tradition of Marcus Garvey, Elijah Muhammad, Malcolm X and Louis Farrakhan. It did not matter that the news media charged that he was a clown. It had no control of Sharpton.

---

[31] *New York Times*, 2/14/88

He was able to take their image and use it to his advantage. The minister was able to manipulate the historical fact that the system destroyed strong black leaders by insisting what the media and politicians did to him, they did to other strong black leaders like King, Malcolm, Adam Clayton Powell, Marcus Garvey and W.E. B. Du Bois. He claimed to be part of a heritage of black freedom fighters who became targets of the white power structure. He was seen as the bad black man of African-American folklore.

WHERE IS AL SHARPTON TODAY?

There is little question that Sharpton has transformed since his first run for the senate. After 1992, and to his credit, Sharpton has severed ties with Lenora Fulani and the New Alliance Party. But his political significance is due not only to his political success, but in part, to cultural politics. Sharpton with the help of the media has presented to the public a "New Al Sharpton." Since his first run for the Senate in 1992, he has received a great deal of favorable press, noting the transformation of the activist minister. Both the *New York Times* and *New York Newsday* contended that Sharpton was the responsible candidate in the Democratic Senatorial primary in 1992. The newspapers asserted that the minister was the voice of reason, sticking to the issues and avoiding the personal attacks. He was endorsed by the largest black weekly in the nation, the New York *Amsterdam News*.[32]

His political success in 1992 has made him legitimate in the eyes of the major media. For the most part, he is no longer portrayed as a "rabble rouser" but a as an important political leader. In an issue of *New York Magazine,* titled "New York is Back" it listed the political moderation of Al Sharpton and how he has grown into a statesmen. In addition *Emerge,* the *New Yorker,* and others magazines have carried positive stories about Sharpton. During his last run for the Senate, author and Harvard University Professor Cornel West wrote a glowing endorsement of Sharpton which appeared in the *New York Daily News.* In 1993, Sharpton appeared on "Sixty Minutes" and the interviewer Mike Wallace spoke of the new Al Sharpton who was moderating his views. He has also appeared on

---

[32] *Newsday,* September 8, 1992; *New York Times*, 9/9/92; Catherine S. Manaegold, "The Reformation of a Street Preacher," *New York Times Magazine*, 1/24/93, pp. 18-26, 53.

shows like Gil Noble's "Like it Is," Black Entertainment Televisions' "Our Voices," and numerous public service programs.[33]

Thus, the public is bombarded with the image of Sharpton, the statesmen. Journalists have constructed a new public Al Sharpton that is more acceptable to the general public. In many ways he has become a symbol of the meaning of race and democracy in the post Cold War United States. It is what historian Ben Keppel so aptly labeled, the "deracialization of the Horatio Alger Myth." Any one can move from poor person, in this case from rabble rouser and an out of control opportunist to a almost gentile, dependable role model who espouses basic American values.[34]

Al Sharpton and those close to him have to be given the greatest credit for reshaping his image, a new image that has brought him significant political gains. I was told by a close ally of Sharpton that he is "a family man, a respected member of the community" and I had no right to raise questions about his past. There have been a number of pictures in the Amsterdam news of Sharpton with his wife and children. The black press also reported on a number of speeches the minister has given to civic and community groups, discussing individual responsibility.[35]

To help forge a new image of the responsible leader, Sharpton has changed religions, from Pentecostal to Baptist. This was not a trivial event. Although he claimed that he changed denominations because of spiritual reasons, he realized that if he wanted to extend his influence, he would have to travel in Baptist circles. Some of the most politically powerful ministers are Baptist and Sharpton has become part of their group. Since his conversion, Sharpton has moved closer to the Reverend Jesse Jackson. He now holds the position as national director of the ministers division of the Rainbow Coalition. He was the leading spokesperson for the group of New Jersey ministers challenging campaign strategist Ed Rollins's claim that he successfully bribed black ministers. Moreover, Sharpton is

---

[33] "Al's New Deal," *New York Magazine*, 12/19-26, 1994, p.95; Nick Charles, "The New Al Sharpton, *Emerge*, November, 1994, pp. 35-38; Richard Stengel, "Sharpton's March, *The New Yorker*, April 3, 1995, pp 30-34;

[34] Ben Keppel, *They Work for Democracy: Ralph Bunche, Kenneth B. Clarke, Lorraine Hansberry, and the Cultural Politics of Race* (Cambridge: Harvard University Press, 1995). p. 62.

[35] Tape, Clarence Taylor interview on the "Drive-In Morning Show" with Rev. Del Shields on Radio station, WWRL in New York, 11/16/94.

associated with ministers of the National Baptist Convention and the Progressive Convention, two of the largest black organizations in America. He has attended conferences sponsored by the Congressional Black Caucus. He is invited to forums that address various problems in the black community with such notables as Cornel West and Manning Marable. He attended the black leadership Conference and was interviewed on numerous occasions by the New York Times and other media. Hence, connected to Sharpton's new image is his growing political significance.[36]

Sharpton has built a powerful political machine based in New York, consisting of politicians, the clergy, journalists, and people associated with electronic media whose task is to help forge this new image and increase his political power. Adam Clayton Powell IV, son of the late Congressman from Harlem, Bob Laws, radio personality, Eric Adams, head of the Guardians, a New York City black policemen organization, Wilbert Tatum, publisher of the Amsterdam News, other radio personalities on stations WLIB and WWRL are part of the Sharpton machine. This machine has been used to carry on some dynamic campaigns. It launched a massive campaign to expose the racist radio talk host Bob Grant. It has been carrying on a campaign to oppose Giuliani's austere budget cuts, and it has criticized the Republican's "Contract with America. His machine raise the consciousness of New Yorkers and keeps them informed.[37]

Part of the new image package is the assertion that "the Rev" is left of center. In his recent run for the Senate, he claimed to be a progressive candidate working to build a broad base movement that would work for the poor. Despite his rhetoric, there is little evidence that he is working to build this coalition.[38]

Sharpton, with the support of his machine has led several demonstrations protesting police brutality and city budget cuts. But one must raise the question what have these demonstrations accomplished? No doubt they have given people an opportunity to vent their anger and raised people's consciousness. But they have not gone beyond that. They have increased the popularity of the Rev, but there is no grass-roots movement organizing people to take serious political

---

[36] Craig Horowitz, "The Sharpton Generation: How Al Sharpton and a Band of Young Insurgents are Making a Grab for Power in the Post-Dinkins Era," *New York*, April 4, 1994, pp.38-45.
[37] Ibid.
[38] Ibid.

action. Hence one must ask, are these demonstrations done to just bolster the image of Sharpton?

A yes answer is too simplistic. No doubt, a major aim is to bolster the image of the Sharpton. However, there is a deeper purpose. These demonstrations reassure many of his long term followers, who are nationalist, advocating that the blacks turn inward to solve their problems, that he has not changed. The demonstrations are done in order to assure them that he has not given up his defiant approach. He often tells them that he has not changed. He is the same old Al Sharpton. In 1994, he held a rally in Roy Wilkins Park, raising money to keep the park open. He used the rhetoric of self help, stating that blacks must rely on themselves in order save their community. The minister is doing a balancing act. At one moment he appears on colleges campuses and other places before large audiences, contending to be a progressive candidate working for a liberal alliance. At other times he asserts to many of his followers at the Slave Theater in Brooklyn or on black Talk radio station WLIB, that he has not changed and that he is still a nationalist, advocating blacks turn inward.

Sharpton realizes that his portrayal and the media's use of him, threatens the symbolic image of the militant black nationalist. Being portrayed as a moderate, works to undermine his legitimacy among the old guard. Consequently, the political cultural arena can be used to discredit his support among nationalists. On the other hand, if he falls back in the nationalist camp, he will probably erode what little support he has among progressives. It is a dangerous game.

One may raise the point that these two positions are not in opposition to one another. This is quite correct. However, in Sharpton's case, his strong support for the Nation of Islam; his close association with Alton Maddox, a man who has made it clear that whites and Latinos cannot be a part of any black movement; and his attack on those who are critical of these narrow nationalist elements, do not help his chances of gaining wider support among left of center forces. His identification with narrow nationalists raise questions on where he is on the political map. The fact that Sharpton has not built a multinational progressive grass-roots organization, despite his rhetoric, has cast some doubt about his new progressive image.

A fine example of Sharpton's balancing act is the Khalid Abdul Muhammad controversy. When Muhammad was being attacked for his Kean

College and other speeches, that were anti-Semitic, anti-Catholic, and homophobic, Sharpton appeared on T.V. (the Charlie Rose Show and said that the speech was offensive. But he quickly, pointed out the hypocrisy of the United States Senate for passing a resolution condemning the Nation of Islam and its leader Louis Farrakhan, but not saying a word about the racist remarks of one of its own, Senator Ernest Hollings from South Carolina who made a racist comment about Africans. This was smart politics. He played up to progressives and nationalists.[39]

Clearly, the Sharpton Machine has played to the old constituency. Besides being a voice for working class African Americans, it seems that the other agenda of the Sharpton Machine is to protect the minister by placing critics as anti-black or uncle toms, thus it relies on an old black nationalist rhetoric. It is not unusual to hear Sharpton, radio host, Bob Laws and others at a rally, calling black leaders "sellouts, "rent-a-toms," and "Driving Miss Daisy Negroes." Thus, Congressmen Major Owens of Brooklyn, a long time opponent of Sharpton, faced a barrage of these attacks because of his criticism of the Nation of Islam. In fact, the machine, selected Eric Adams, a close ally of Sharpton and New York City police officer, to challenge Owens in the 1994 congressional election. Owens, and others have been berated on by members of the machine. This was clearly divisive politics. But it played well to Sharpton's hardcore followers.[40]

One should raise the question what is the purpose of these attacks. What do they accomplish? They are done to bolster the image of Sharpton but they also are done to hold on to the image of a militant nationalist. However, they also limit his ability to become the politician with a far reach not only in the black community but in other working class communities.

The Giuliani Administration has presented a major challenge to progressive forces in New York. This administration has made it clear that it does not need the support of blacks. It is balancing the city's budget off the backs of poor people. Just last week it was reported that the Mayor is seeking the deepest cut in City Spending since the Depression. The services to the poor are the ones he has targeted including eliminating 1.3 billion dollars. It is estimated that he

---

[39] "The Charlie Rose Show," aired on PBS, 2/7/94.
[40] Craig Horowitz, "The Sharpton Generation: How Al Sharpton and a Band of Young Insugents are Making a Grab for Power in the Post-Dinkins Era." *New York* April, 4, 1994, pp37-45.

would have to close city hospitals, dramatically increase class size in schools, reduce medicaid and medicare benefits. His rationale is that the city has been "too generous" to the poor. His budget proposals will devastate the poor and working class in New York.

The political situation in New York offers Rev. Sharpton an opportunity to work for real change. He can join with progressive forces to build a movement that work for all people who are victims of those vicious policies. To be sure, he has the capability of becoming a major political force for change in New York. His recent attempt to register 200,000 new voters, if successful, can help defeat Giuliani in the next mayoral election.[41]

Unquestionably, Sharpton cannot throw off his past as an F.B.I. informant spying on black elected officials, a man involved with organized underworld figures, or as a member of the inner circle that attempted to perpetuate the Brawley hoax and play on the fears and angers of African-Americans without better explanation.

With little doubt, if Sharpton wants to broaden his support, he must be open about his past. If he intends to build a broad coalition and work for a progressive agenda, he must be candid about his involvement and admit it was detrimental to him and others. He will have to admit that he made mistakes no matter how painful. Although he will alienate some, he will gain the respect of others. This act will demonstrate that he has integrity and is serious about his transformation.

Sharpton must also be clear about which camp he belongs. There is little doubt that he has been successful in attracting both nationalists and to a lesser extent some progressive forces to his camp. However, if he is truly sincere about building a broad coalition to address the social ills of New York, he needs to reach out to others.

Moreover, he should run for a political office that he has a good chance of winning. This will give him political experience he needs and put him in a position to work for constructive change. After a long meeting with Sharpton, the

---

[41] *Amsterdam News*, 6/1/96.

philosopher Cornell West asserted that the ministers leadership is an open question. "He has the courage and the talent. Does he have the perseverance, the humility? Or will he fall back into opportunistic practices"[42]

---

[42] Cornel West is quoted in Jim Sleeper, "A Man of Too Many Parts," p. 58.

CHAPTER XIII

BLACK CHURCH POLITICS AND THE MILLION MAN MARCH

WILLIAM E. NELSON, JR.
RESEARCH PROFESSOR OF BLACK STUDIES
AND PROFESSOR OF POLITICAL SCIENCE
THE OHIO STATE UNIVERSITY

I.THE MILLION MAN MARCH: POLITICAL FOUNDATIONS.

October 16, 1995 will be recorded as one of the most important days in the political developmental history of African-Americans in the United States. This day witnessed the execution of the largest mass political demonstration in the history of America—the assemblage of more than 1.2 million African-American men in Washington, D.C. under the banner of the Million Man March.[1] Both the size and the overt political objectives of the March would set it firmly apart from the pallid, feeble demonstrations in Washington led by the NAACP in the 1980s; in its size and character, the march echoed the focus on power and system level change that emerged as the hallmark of the 1960s civil rights protest movement and the national mobilization against the war in Vietnam.

One key political objective of the March was to place the issue of Black suffering back on the national policy agenda.[2] Since the Republican triumph in the November 1994 elections and the publicizing of the party's Contract With America, the continuing and expanding social and economic crisis of the Black community had virtually disappeared as an arena of positive policy debate. Republican political rhetoric papered over the most vital dimensions of the crisis

---

[1] Within twenty-four hours after the conclusion of the March, the issue of the actual number of persons in attendance surfaced as a matter of major controversy. Initially, the National Park Service provided an official estimate of 400,000. After leaders of the march complained about an undercount the official estimate was raised to 850,000. The Million Man March Organizing Committee held to an estimate of well over 1 million. For those of us in attendance, there was, no doubt that the goal of million was easily surpassed. For the estimate of 1.2 million see Michael H. Cottman, *Million Man March* (New York: Crown Trade paperbacks, 1995), p. 9.

[2] Cornell West, "Historical Event," in Haki R. Madhubuti and Maulana Karenga, (eds.) *Million Man March/Day of Absence: A Commemorative Anthology* (Chicago: Third World Press, Los Angeles: University of Sankore Press, 1996), p. 98.

in international capitalism and blamed Black city victims for domestic economic woes that threatened to produce record deficits, massive unemployment, and uncontrolled inflation.[3] Absent from the analysis was a realistic appraisal of Black social and economic decline: a poverty rate of over 40 percent; unemployment rates that averaged two times that of whites; health and housing standards matching those of city dwellers in some of the world's poorest countries; median family incomes averaging 58 percent of white median family income, statistics regarding the social and economic status of Black men suggested that they were the special victims of American racial oppression. Environmental circumstances rendered the lives of young Black men extremely perilous. Homicide had become one of the leading causes of death among young Black men, with 72 Black men per 100,000 falling victim to homicide compared to 9.3 white men per 100,000.missing[4] Black male unemployment was scandalous: 11.1 percent of Black males were unemployed compared to 4.9 percent of white males. More tragically, in the age group 16-19, Black male unemployment topped 50 percent. In terms of median salary, the gap between the earnings of Black men and white men was over $8,000, $23,020 for Black men compared to 31,090 for white men.[5] Aggressive law enforcement and prison building policies had meant the incarceration of young Black men in unprecedented numbers, leaving a vacuum of political and family leadership that had a devastating impact on the sustained growth potential of the Black community.[6]

The Million Man March was, in part, Black America's response to these developments. Black men descended on Washington determined to bring the spiral of social and economic erosion in the Black community to a halt. Expressing extreme concern for increasing racism in America and the deterioration of the social cultual and moral fabric of the Black community, Black

---

[3] The adoption of this line of political argument was not an oversight development but the product of strategies crafted by both major political parties to use the issues of race, rights and taxes as mechanisms for producing electoral majorities in key political contests. For an exceptionally insightful analysis of Democratic and Republican racial strateties see Thomas Byrne Edsall and Mary D. Edsall, *Chain Reaction: The Impact of Race, Rights and Taxes on American Politics* (New York and London: W.W. Norton and Company, 1991).

[4] Lucius J. Baker and Mack H. Jones, *African Americans and the American Political System*, Third Edition (Englewood Cliffs, New Jersey: Prentice Hall, 1994), pp. 32-43.

[5] Smitherman, Ibid.

[6] Charshee McIntyre, "Why Focus on the Men?" in Madhubuti and Karenga, Op cit., pp. 114-115.

men came to Washington, in the words of the March's Mission Statement, "Committed to the ongoing struggle for a free and empowered community, a just society and a better world."[7] Defining ingredients of the march's political agenda included challenges to the government to stop the brutal assault against affirmative action, establish programs to provide affordable health care and housing, and pass legislation creating an economic bill of rights and a plan to rebuild America's declining cities.[8] One aspect of the march's political agenda also sought to repair the negative, stereotypical images of Black men manufactured by the American media. Worldwide publicity surrounding the lives of Black men like Willie Horton, Mike Tyson and O.J. Simpson stamped all Black men in America with a demonized personality, and placed Black men on a war-like footing with white America, especially the white media.

The emancipation of Black men has been abandoned. The communications with Black men have been cut off, which is what happens when you're on a war footing with the enemy. Talks break down and hostility begins. Their books are seldom used in college courses anymore. A variety of viewpoints from Black men are ignored by the white male run media who prefer athletes and criminals, and other dopey people and use Black and white feminists to blame all the social evils of society on Black men, while theirs go unchecked.[9]

To combat these negative stereotypes, and establish an enduring base of functional power for the entire Black community, the leaders of the march realized that the march must be well organized and coordinated, extraordinarily peaceful, and sufficiently inclusive to embrace the entire panoply of political interests in the Black community. In this regard it should be noted that the march was successful in drawing representation from virtually every sector of the Black community. One study conducted by a research team from Central State University found that occupations of the marchers ranged from business owners to a wide variety of unskilled workers, paraprofessionals, professionals and skilled

---

[7] *Mission Statement The Million Man March/Day of Absence* (Washington, D.C.: National Million Man March/Day of Absence Organizing Committee, 1995), p. 1.

[8] Mission Statement, Ibid, p. 12.

[9] Ishmael Reed, "Buck Passing: The Media, Black Men, O.J. and the Million Man March," in Madhubuti and Karenga, Op.cit., p. 133.

tradesmen.[10] The heavy representation of middle-class Black men at the march suggests that a broad reservoir of racial consciousness continues to exist among this important segment of the Black population. Apparently, class divisions in the Black community are decreasing as professional Black men realize that their high status positions cannot insulate them from the burdens and responsibilities of race in America.[11]

The policy goals of the march contained a pronounced political slant. Organizers of the March expressed the desire to see the mass mobilization in Washington result in highly successful voter education, registration, and turnout campaigns in cities, towns and hamlets across America. Relying heavily on the concepts of Black nationalism and self-determination, march leaders sought to establish grassroots networks in local communities capable of creating permanent bases of functional power for the Black community in local, state and national political and governmental arenas. Thus the Million Man March was viewed as more than a one day demonstration, but the pivotal foundation for a wider movement that would substantially transform the distribution of societal benefits and the workings of the governmental order.[12]

II. STRATEGIC MOBILIZATION

No project of the magnitude and ambition of the Million Man March could possibly succeed without strategic plans for broad scale mobilization. Formal planning for the march began to unfold with the recognition of Louis Farrakhan, head of the Nation of Islam, as the leader and guiding spirit of the march. Farrakhan's assumption of this role, while controversial, was a logical extension of a political/career that has seen him emerge as one of the best known and most popular political figures in Black America. Farrakhan was no newcomer to the American political scene. He first rose to prominence as a devout follower of Nation of Islam leader, Elijah Muhammed, who took the lead in denouncing

---

[10] Gerald S. Norde, "A Sociological Study of the Million Man March," (Xenix, Ohio: Unpublished Research Report, Department of Sociology, Central State University, 1996).

[11] See Ellis Cose, *The Rage of the Privileged Class* (New York: Harper-Collins publishers, 1993); Lawrence Otiose Graham, *Member of the Club: Reflections on Life in a Racially Polarized World* (New York: Harper-Collins publishers, 1995).

[12] Maulana Karenga, "The March, Day of Absence and the Movement," in Madhubuti and Karenga, Op. cit., pp. 5-7.

Malcolm X as a traitor "worthy of death" when Malcom broke from the ranks of the Nation of Islam to form a new organization, the Muslim Mosque, Inc.[13] Upon The death of Elijah Muhammed, Farrakhan emerged as a major victor in a battle waged with Elijah Mohammed's son, Wallace Deen Muhammed, over the resources and the political image of the Nation of Islam." Clinging tightly to the mantel of Elijah Muhammed, Farrakhan rose to the summit of leadership within the Nation of Islam and ultimately within Black America as a whole. A critical step in this journey was the highly visible role he played in the 1984 Jesse Jackson presidential campaign—Jewish leaders pressured Jackson to denounce Farrakhan and reject his support because of statements by Farrakhan which they claimed to be anti-semetic.[14]

Despite persistent attacks on Farrakhan by outside forces, including every segment of the white media, Farrakhan's popularity in the Black community has continued to rise. Farrakhan's genius has been to recognize leaders like Marcus Garvey, and the existence of an enduring commitment to Black nationalism among key sectors of the Black population, especially the Black poor. Farrakhan speaks of the hope for deliverance that rests in the souls of millions of Black people who possess a strong sense of racial pride and consciousness. In the 1990s Farrakhan has emerged as a popular and formidable force because he evokes in his speeches, symbols of defiance and liberation. Further, he evinces a fighting spirit that harkens back to the militant politics of Black leaders such as William Monroe Trotter, Marcus Garvey and Malcolm X. Clearly, masses of Blacks are looking for leaders who are willing to stand up and defend the interest of the race against the unvarnished attacks emanating out of Washington.[15] Farrakhan has demonstrated an uncommon willingness to talk in fighting terms—to tell it like it is. In doing so,he has appealed to a broad array of Black citizens across class lines.

The idea of a massive demonstration by Black men in Washington did not originate with Farrakhan but was first broached in a speech in Chicago by Reverend Hycel Taylor of Evanston, Illinois and later reinforced by conversations

---

[13] Arthur J. Magida, *Prophet of Rage: A Life of Louis Farrakhan and his Nation* (New York: Basic Books, 1996), pp. 80-83.

[14] They accused Farrakhan of calling Judiaism a dirty religion and referring to Hitler as a man who was "wickedly" great. See merged, Ibid, pp. 143-148.

[15] Ron Daniels, "The Meaning of the Million Man March and Day of Absence," in Madhubuti and Karenga, *Op cit.*, pp. 83-84.

between Farrakhan and James Bevel, a protégé of Martin Luther King during the heyday of SCLC. Eventually this idea crystallized into the concept of the Million Man March. Farrakhan teamed with Benjamin Chavis, former Executive Director of the NAACP and Director of the National African American Leadership Committee, to transform plans for the march into a program of action. A formal call for the march was made at a summit meeting of Black leaders in Washington, D.C. in November 1994. Under the guidance of Farrakhan, a massive mobilization campaign was launched by the Nation of Islam. Across the country Farrakhan began holding hug rallies for Black men only. The enthusiastic response to the meetings by a cross-section of the Black male population, convinced Farrakhan that a Million Man March in the nation's capital was very much within the realm of possibility.

Farrakhan's efforts alone would not, of course, be enough to assure the success of the march. The pivotal key to the march's success would be the generation of enthusiastic support for the march by masses of Black men across the country, many of whom would not be directly touched by Farrakhan's "men only" rallies. The process of grassroots mobilization was promoted at two levels. First, a National Million Man March Organizing Committee was formed, under the leadership of Benjamin Chavis, composed of representatives of a wide assortment of national organizations, as well as community activists, and scholars. Among the most prominent participants in this process were members of the African American Leadership Summit, members of the National Black United Front, members of the All African Revolutionary Party, members of the US Organization and individual scholars and activists such as Ron Daniels, Dr. Charshee McIntyre, Dr. Cornel West, Bob Law and Haki Madhubuti.[16] The heart of the grassroots mobilization effort was at the local level where local organizing committees were established in more than 400 cities.[17] In local communities the drum beat for the March was carried forth by a host of institutions including newspapers, radio stations, fraternities and sororities, professional organizations, colleges and universities, factories, bank, and hospitals.[18] Although displaying in

---

[16] Conrad W. Worrill, "Beyond the Million Man March", in Madhubuti and Karenga, Op. cit, p. 80.
[17] Worrill, Ibid., p. 81.
[18] Worrill, Ibid., p. 80.

its early stages signs of organizational disunity and ineffectiveness, the grassroots effort was eventually successful in transforming the campaign for the march into an emotional crusade. In this regard Reverend Willie F. Wilson, Pastor of the Union Temple Baptist Church of Washington, D.C. recalled:

> I personally felt that there was a need for less discussion and more doing. Therefore, I reorganized the men of Union Temple Baptist Church, along with a few men from other churches, to get out in the streets and sign up men for the March.
>
> To my utter amazement, there was an electrifying enthusiasm out in the streets. We didn't have to prompt, cajole or beg anybody to sign up. Wives signed up their husbands, mothers signed up their sons and men joyfully signed up on their own. We went into barber shops, went to street corners, and stood in malls. Everywhere we went the response was overwhelming. We signed up over 100,000 men in the Washington metropolitan area![19]

Two programmatic decisions made by the National Organizing Committee helped to stir enthusiasm for the march at the local level. First, the project would be billed not only as a March, but a "Holy Day of Atonement." This decision meant that the project would move beyond the articulation of Black grievances to embrace the concept of spiritual renewal and regeneration. Seeking to create higher levels of political consciousness in the Black community, project leaders would ask Black men to recognize past wrongs and to make amends by making a new vow of social responsibility and community uplift.[20] Second, the project would become not only a march, but a "Day of Absence". The objective of this stradegy was to formally incorporate Black women into the project at the grassroots level by asking them to support the March by staying away on the day of the march from a host of routine activities including work, school, and the patronizing of businesses and places of entertainment.[21]

Thus, the strategic plan anticipated the building of an inclusive united front in the Black community in support of the march. Given the array of diverse

---

[19] Willie F. Wilson, "The Miracle of the Million Man March," in Madhubuti and Karenga, Op. cit., pp. 57-58.

[20] Mission statement, Op. cit., pp. 5-6

[21] Mission statement , Ibid., pp. 15-17

political interests in the Black community, the call for a united front, while emotionally appealing, was probably unrealistic.

III.POLITICAL FALLOUT: DISSENSION AND DISUNITY

Cracks in the armor of the united front began to appear in the early phases of the national mobilization campaign. Several prominent Black women, including Angela Davis, Jewel Jackson McCabe and Michele Wallace, criticized the concept of the Million Man March as sexist and politically divisive. They believed that a March on Washington should be a collective enterprise involving the participation at every level of both Black men and women. This sentiment was shared by legendary Black writer Amiri Baraka. Commenting on the concept of the march Baraka asserted: "I wouldn't go to war and leave half the army at home."[22] Strong opposition to the march was voiced by Black Congressmen Gary Franks and John Lewis. While not objecting to the idea of the march, they expressed the view that they could not endorse or join a march lead by Farrakhan. Lewis suggested that it was impossible to separate the message from the messenger. He refused to lend his name to a march led by a man whom he believed to be a purveyor of racial hatred and an instigator of social conflicts.

A strong reiteration of this criticism of the March and Farrakhan appeared in a feature article published in the *Washington Post* a day after the march authored by A. Leon Higgenbothan Jr., a former federal district judge, and Professor in the Kennedy School at Harvard University. Higginbotham's article was entitled, "Why I Didn't March." It read in part:

> My decision not to participate came about because I believe that in its operational reality, the march basically was initiated, organized orchestrated overwhelmingly and almost exclusively controlled by the agenda established by Mr. Farrakhan and his major aides. This march was far different from the one in which I participated in August, 1963. I submit respectfully that Mr. Farrakhan and some of his purposed values are not those of the speakers in 1963: Martin Luther King, Jr., Roy Wilkins,Whitney Young, Walter Ruthers, Bayard Rustin, John Lewis and Rabbi Joachim Prinz.[23]

---

[22] Quoted in Herb Boyd, Claimed by Black People," in Madhubuti and Karenga, Op. cit., p. 89.

[23] A . Leon Higginbotheim Jr. "Why I Didn't March," *The Washington Post*, October 17, 1995, p. A 17.

Similar concerns about Farrakhan's role in the march motivated two of the Black community's most venerable civil rights organization, the NAACP and the Urban League, to issue statements that they would not officially endorse the march.

IV.RESPONSE OF THE BLACK CHURCH

The most potentially damaging Black resistance to the march took the form of decisions by leaders of important Black church organizations to express open, and unalterable opposition to the March. The specter of opposition to the march by the institutional Black church constituted a serious threat to the success of the national mobilization campaign. Historically, much of the organizational capacity of the Black community has resided in the influence and resources of the Black church. March leaders were compelled to confront and come to grips with the reality that "no successful movement for improving the conditions of life for the African-American people has been mounted without the support of the church."[24] The church's control over the emotions, behavior, preferences and resources of its members provides it with a formidable advantage over its political rivals in the Black community. Black churches have a long history of involvement in community service and social mobilization. In this regard, it should be noted that Black churches played central roles in the organization and implementation of programmatic objectives during the civil rights campaigns of the 1960s.[25] Black churches have engaged in a range of activities designed to strengthen the position of the Black community in the political process, including the organization of ministerial alliances, the publication and distribution of election documents, the selection and grooming of candidates for public office, the establishment of political action committees, the coordination and management of voter registration turnout campaigns, and public lobbying on a variety of social, economic and cultural issues.[26] Collectively Black churches represent an unrivaled structure of power in the Black community. Candidates for public office

---

[24] Andrew Billingsley, *Climbing Tacot's Ladder: The Enduring Legacy of African American Families* (New York: Simon and Schuster, 1992), p. 350.
[25] See William E. Nelson, Jr., *The Role of the Black Church in Politics,* Washington, D.C.: National Research Council Monograph, 1987), pp. 20-26.
[26] Nelson, *Ibid*

clearly recognize that any effort to mobilize mass support in the Black community must begin with the cultivation of strong support from individual Black ministers, and Black church institutions both separately and collectively.

The incorporation of Black churches and their leaders into the organizational and operational framework of the Million Man March mobilization efforts became, at an early stage, one of the central strategic objectives of organizing committees at both the national and local level. The response of the church to these efforts provides poignant insight into the complexity of Black church politics, and the volatile character of the political terrain of the Black community on a larger scale.

The call for the Million Man March resonated positively for a corps of progressive Black ministers with long histories of active, public political engagement. Prominent civil rights activists such as Reverend Al Sharpton of New York, Reverend Benjamin Chavis, Reverend Joseph Lowery of SCLC, and Archbishop George A. Stallings, founder of the Imani African-American Catholic Congregation, eagerly endorsed the march and agreed to play active roles in the national mobilization campaign. Other ministers of national prominence who became actively involved in the march's organizational efforts were Reverend Wyatt Tee Walker, Reverend Calvin Butts, Reverend Johnnie Ray Youngblood, Reverend Wendell Anthony, Reverend William Reverly, Jr., Reverend Frank M.Reid, Bishop H. Brookins, Reverend Jeremiah Wright, Reverend Kelvin Crosby and Reverend Willie Wilson. Notably absent from the list of early ministerial endorsement was the name of Jesse Jackson. For strategic reasons, Jackson maintained an arms length distance from the March until the later stages when it became clear that the March would be one of the most important gatherings in the history of Black America.

The religions foundations of the march were broad and deep, representing incredible support from the Muslim community, and strong support from a mosaic of Black Christian organizations. Opposition from within the ranks of the Black church was also very strong. Several nationally prominent Black ministers publicly refused to endorse the march, including Dr. B. W. Smith, Bishop Chandler Owens, and Dr. Henry Lyons. Local organizers reported stiff opposition from a rich variety of influential Black ministers. A number of factors impelled these ministers to oppose the march. Many ministers argued that they were compelled to oppose the march because of irreconcilable theological differences with Farrakhan. They believed that they could not, as Christian ministers, endorse a march led by a minister of the Islamic faith.[27]

> How can I maintain my credibility with my congregation if I support the leadership of a man who uses the Koran as his primary text, and then quotes passages from the Bible out of context. I do not believe in the Muslims. The Bible says thou shall have no other God before me. As a Christian I believe that all struggling groups should have common ground. We live more on our divisiveness than our togetherness.[28]

Many ministers also agreed with the statements of Black politicians who said they could not support Farrakhan because he preached a gospel of racial hatred and social conflict. They were especially disturbed by Farrakhan's support for Khallid Adul Muhammed, a Nation of Islam National spokesman, who persistently denounced Jews in strident terms, as well as by reports that Farrakhan had referred to Judaism as a dirty religion and Jews as bloodsuckers.

Some ministers opposed the march on political rather than theological grounds. Storm clouds have prevailed for more than a decade around the alleged invasion of Muslims into arenas formerly dominated and controlled exclusively by Black churches. Government contracts to Muslims to wage war on drugs or to provide security for housing projects have been met with resentment and protests from Black Christian ministers and their followers. Traditionally, Black churches have been the recipients of government largest as well as patronage from local political organizations.[29] The emergence of the Muslims as a strong political force threatened to weaken the stream of government benefits to Black churches and to shatter relations with external forces forged through years of strategic political interaction. Organizing activities around the Million Man March was viewed by some ministers as an extension of the Muslim program of invasion and political dilution. If the grassroots goals of the march were realized, control over

---

[27] See Michael H. Cottman, *Op. cit*, p. 43; also see Haki Madhubuti, "Took Back Our Tears, laughter and Love and Left A Big Dent in the Earth," in Haki Madhubuti and Maulana Karenga, *Op. cit.*, p. 3.

[28] Interview with Black Baptist Minister in Columbus, Ohio April, 1996.

[29] Nelson, *Op. cit* pp. 34-35.

community resources would become more decentralized, further undermining the effective control over such resources by Black churches.

Opposition by some Black ministers was spawned principally by their view that support for the march would be interpreted as support for a militant campaign antithetical to the interests of their white allies. This was the prevailing view among conservative Black ministers who took great pride in the roles they played as racial diplomats.

One respondent explained the opposition to the march by this element of Black ministerial leadership in the following manner:

> After 500 years of Negroness it is hard for them to stand on their own feet. They want to make Farrakhan a devil because the white man says he's a devil. If I start to upset the white man he is going to upset me. They did not want to upset Newt Gingrich and his boys. Too many are Negroes, they did what they believed their white benefactors wanted them to do. We must expose them for what they are. They are not representing the Black community. They are preaching their own form of self-hate. They practice a form of feel good religion. It is all about preaching and having a good time. They are afraid of white people so they won't tell their members that our liberation can't be from the top down but must come from the bottom up.[30]

Reverend Willie Wilson's efforts to garner cooperation from Black ministers in Washington, D.C. revealed in dramatic terms the political and emotional insecurity of Black ministers who consider themselves trapped in the racial divide.

> I made a request to the largest Christian ministers' conference in Washington, D.C. to allow Minister Louis Farrakhan to speak to the several hundred pastors affiliated with that body to share the vision of the Million Man March.

> Needless to say, the ministers were so impressed with Minister Farrakhan's grip on Christian scriptures that they over whelmingly voted to support the march. However two weeks later, the Conference President explained their backpedaling this way: "Y'all don't want to say it, but we are scared!! I'm from down deep South and I know what white people will do to you. White people will

---

[30] Interview with Black United Methodist Minister in Columbus, Ohio April, 1996.

kill you!! We are afraid of white folks! That's why we don't want to march."[31]

There is evidence to support the proposition that opposition to the march by some Black church forces emanated, in some measure, from the internal politics of national Black church organizations. The refusal on the part of Dr. Henry Lyons, President of the Nation Baptist Convention, USA, with 8.7 million members, to endorse the march was a product of the bruising battle we had to endure to win the presidency of this massive and powerful religious organization. Lyons came to power in 1994 on the heels of a major controversy surrounding the retirement from the presidency of Reverend T. J. Jemison. Jemison had threatened to run for another term despite provisions in the Convention Bylaws that limited the presidency to a maximum of 10 years—the number of years he had already served. Jemison reluctantly stepped aside, naming as his heir apparent F. W. Richardson of New York. The election for the presidency, held in New Orleans in 1993, was hotly contested. Lyons announced his opposition to Richardson along with William Shaw from Pennsylvania and C. A. Clark from Texas.

A major dispute emerged over whether or not voting would be by secret ballot. Additional wrangling surfaced over the issue of the supervision of the election by New Orleans election officials. When these issues were resolved the balloting was held; the final results showed Lyons winning by 1,000 votes. The Jemison and Richardson forces refused to accept the outcome, charging in a legal suit that the election was rigged. Although the suit was resolved in Lyons favor, the legal action delayed his formal installation as president by several months.

Lyons moved into the presidency in December 1993 determined to extricate himself from the shadow of controversy and to establish his position as a strong independent leader. It was in this context that he announced his position on a number of issues-including the Million Man March—and set forward a new operational agenda. One of his first actions at the 1994 Convention in Birmingham was to announce his opposition to the Million Man March. This decision was made principally on the basis of Lyon's need to demonstrate leadership and establish a functional power base within his organization.

---

[31] Willie F. Wilson, Op. cit., p. 58.

He was trying to give focus to the convention. He realized that a lot
of the membership would go to the March, but he was a new
president trying to get people to follow him. He could not afford to
be seen as a follower of someone else.[32]

In retrospect, some of Lyons' supporters believed that his failure to endorse
the march was a tactical blunder: "He probably should have said nothing. It is
difficult to become president of eight million people. He exercised poor judgment
on this issue and damaged his relations with the progressive wing of the
Convention."[33]

Lyons has sought to overcome the controversy surrounding his decision on
the march by moving aggressively to implement his own community action
agenda. As an answer to the Million Man March, he organized his own march in
Atlanta, Georgia. The march was held in November, 1995. Approximately 5,000
people are reported to have attended.[34]

Lyons' most important community outreach initiative has been the Trusted
Partners Program. This was an idea originally included in the campaign literature
of Cleo McConnell running for president of the National Laymen's Movement of
the National Baptist Convention USA. Essentially, Trusted Partners is a program
designed to get Black men involved in the process of bringing young Black boys
to manhood. Through a series of seminars, one on one counseling sessions, and
planed activities such as field trips, Baptist laymen are given an opportunity to
establish close personal relations with young Black men at a crucial turning point
in their lives. The central objective is to provide alternatives for young Black men
to the urban street culture, alternatives that will motivate them to stay in school
and build for themselves stable, productive patterns of development in the broader
society.[35] Although Lyons is aware that this program may overlap with some of
the youth programs in the Black community already in place such as Simba, he is
convinced that the Black church is in a better position to accomplish the goals of
Trusted Partners than any other community institution.

---

[32] Interview with Black Baptist Minister in Nebraska, May 1996.
[33] Ibid.
[34] Interview with Black Baptist Layman in Los Angeles, California, May 1996.
[35] Ibid.

V. CONCLUSION

The Million Man March, was, in many ways, a watershed event in the political history of African-Americans. Its crowning accomplishment was the bringing together of more than 1 million Black men in a spirit of peace, unity, reconciliation, atonement and renewal. The symbolism of One Million Black Men massed in Washington conveyed to the world a number of critical messages:

1. That in 1995 Black America would not allow white America to choose and certify its leaders.
2. That Black people had sufficient leadership skill and logistical capability to pull off a march of unprecedented size and complexity.
3. That millions of Black men were politically conscious and politically
4. That all Black men were not thugs, hoodlums and criminals.
5. That Black people were capable of financing their own liberation struggles.
6. That special bonds of fellowship existed between Black men across class and ideological lines.
7. That Black people were not prepared to accept the consequences of the Republican Revolution without a militant response.

The negative response of some elements of Black church leadership to the March sheds penetrating light on the continuing existence of fissiparous tendencies in the internal political environment of the Black community. These tendencies serve notice that much work remains to be done if the spirit of the Million Man March is to be transformed into an effective program of action in the service of African liberation.

INDEX

BLACK STUDIES

1. Joseph R. Washington, Jr., **The First Afro-American Honorary Degree Recipient**

2. E. Lama Wonkeryor, **On Afrocentricity, Intercultural Communication, and Racism**

3. Felton O. Best (ed.), **Black Religious Leadership From the Slave Community to the Million Man March: Flames of Fire**